A TRAILS BOOKS GUIDE

EXPLORE
Wisconsin
Rivers

DORIS GREEN with
MICHAEL H. KNIGHT

TRAILS BOOKS
Madison, Wisconsin

Library of Congress Control Number: 2008925080
ISBN: 978-1-934553-12-1

Editor: Mark Knickelbine
Book Design: Rebecca Finkel
All interior photos: Michael H. Knight
Cover photo: Bob Firth

Printed in the United States of America

13 12 11 10 09 08   6 5 4 3 2 1

TRAILS BOOKS
a division of Big Earth Publishing
923 Williamson Street • Madison, WI 53703
(800) 258-5830 • www.trailsbooks.com

Acknowledgments

This book would not have been possible or as historically rich or accurate without the support of my husband, Michael H. Knight. His father, Oliver H. Knight, a historian of the American West, once complimented Mike: "He'll do to ride the river with." This Old West tribute refers to the challenge of herding cattle over a dangerous river crossing. I've always agreed with Oliver, and on our journeys for this book, I trusted Mike to hold us on a steady course.

Friends also made this volume possible, especially Mary Lou and Rick Santovec, who completed their own Trails book while I simultaneously followed this dream. I'm grateful to other friends and colleagues who suggested paddling trips, or quietly overlooked delayed or unfinished projects while I tracked this adventurous obsession.

Much appreciation goes to many individuals who gladly answered questions and shared ideas, among them: Brett Altergott, Adam Alix, William Annis, Betty Bakken, Andrew Brodzeller, Marsha Burzynski, Denny Canneff, Bob Comargo, Melissa Cook, Scott Craven, Mark Cupp, Michael Edmonds, William Eldred, Janet Fugate, Bonnie Gruber, Jane Hedeen, Sandra Hudson, Randy King, Ed Kleckner, Jerry Leiterman, Angela Mack, Laura Maker, Lisa Marshall, Dave Martin, Phyllis McKenzie, Josie Minskey, Janean Mollet-Van Beckum, Angelique Peterson, Gail Gilson Pierce, Nathan Ruble, Helen Sarakinos, Emily Stanley, Bill Sturtevant, Lori Yahr, and David Zosel.

Finally, this volume has depended on the suggestions and rigorous editing of Mark Knickelbine, along with the publishing expertise of Eva Solcova and the assistance of Big Earth designers and other staff. Thank you all.

Table of Contents

Introduction

Dip a toe or a paddle or a line into a Wisconsin river and it's not only a fish that might get hooked.

When I was growing up, to me "the river" meant the Root in Racine County. My great, great grandfather established a farm on the Root, a farm where my mother was born and where first, second, and third cousins still live. The Root is where my mother once swam, where I skated in winter and fished with my father in summer. I suppose other states have rivers as intimate as the Root and as defining as the Wisconsin. But these are the waters I know and treasure, the ones that are kin to me and my people.

Today, anglers still fish the Root, and hikers now travel the Root River Pathway, which offers interpretive signage and extends along the river upstream from Racine's Main Street Bridge. The Root River Parkway preserves marshes, old beech trees, and prairies from northern Milwaukee County into Racine County. Upriver from Quarry Lake Park, the River Bend Nature Center, 3600 North Green Bay Road, Racine, offers hikes and canoe trips, and protects forest, field, and wetland habitats for varied plant and wildlife communities. These developments make the Root more accessible, and build awareness of the need to protect and preserve all Wisconsin rivers and their environs.

My present river home lies in the broad valley of the lower Wisconsin, where sandhill cranes and bald eagles fly, and coyotes sometimes howl on a summer's eve. My husband Mike and I bought land overlooking the river and the Lone Rock Bridge in 1983. Today we live on an adjacent parcel, where in winter we can glimpse the river through bare branches of oak, maple, and aspen.

Finding a river to play on, hike beside, or camp along is easy in the Badger State. Wisconsin has more than 12,600 rivers and streams with more than 40,000 stream miles, including more than 30,000 miles that flow year-round. Of these, almost 2,700 streams contain more than 10,370 miles of trout habitat. More than 500 river miles of whitewater attract experienced paddlers, and the state has recognized more than 1,500 river miles as Outstanding Water Resources. Wisconsin is home to the Namekagon and the St. Croix—among the first U.S. Wild and Scenic Rivers—and to the Pine-Popple State Wild Rivers Area and hundreds of other untamed rivers, as well as those subdued by dams to control flooding and create hydropower and recreational flowages.

We wish we could visit them all, in the way that Rick Kark paddled his 300th Wisconsin stream in 2007, a quest that began with a trip on the St. Croix in 1969. This book sets out to explore the state's largest and most significant rivers, which have a way of leading to other streams, lakes, and wetlands, in the way that one trip completed leads to many new adventures dreamed.

These streams draw us all, with their lapping current flowing ceaselessly to the horizon. A river is always going somewhere, a grand attraction for a restless spirit like me. The constant, gentle yet irrevocable change stills me, calms me in a life that does not always seem to head in a predictable, sane direction. Like the blood coursing through our veins, the river connects us to our physical world and assures us that this solid planet is here for us and hopefully for many generations to come.

The river has always been a metaphor for life, nourishing us, much like Mother Earth and Father Time. When we are one with the river, we are connected to all other lives and life forms, flowing endlessly, never stopping but forever changing. When we are at our best, we are one with the river, a piece of the moving, evolving universe.

When we linger too long away from the river, we wither and wait for the day we can return to its soothing shores. The river whispers a personal language, like the individual symbols of our dreams, confiding in all who travel its shores or skim its changing surface. The river reflects our own intent and destiny.

Nothing so defines a land as its rivers. Forests may be cut away, and mountains leveled for roads or reshaped by mining. Moraines are turned into landscaped developments. Only rivers remain generally as they've lain since the glaciers receded from the continent. True, waterfalls have broken down, channels have shifted, and dams have been built and torn down. Yet, through it all, the flow remains, from hidden springs and primordial wetlands to seas unseen.

This book presents one path — perhaps the book version of a "Wisconsin Rivers Trail" — to get to know the state's rivers. It's not intended to be encyclopedic and it's cast in the time it was written. As I finish this sentence, phone numbers are changing, new websites are appearing, and river developments and protection efforts are being launched. This guide is imperfect and all errors are mine. Yet, it's a start, an effort to gather the state's rivers between the covers of one book.

In Wisconsin, the river is always close at hand, whether you're a stone's throw from the Menominee in Marinette or live near the Wisconsin, anywhere along the 400-mile journey from its source at Lac Vieux Desert to its half-mile-wide mouth near Prairie du Chien. Consider this book your invitation to explore the state's rivers — not to learn all there is to know about them, but to get to know them up close and personal, to adopt them as stalwart friends, and to celebrate their energy and soul.

CHAPTER 1

St. Louis

The short, 23-mile section of the St. Louis River that marks Wisconsin's northwest boundary with Minnesota makes an enormous statement for its size. The broad lower river provides recreation for anglers, paddlers, and powerboaters. Yet, the twin harbors of Superior, Wisconsin, and Duluth, Minnesota, nurture a shipping- and industry-based economy.

Businesses, citizen groups, and public agencies have worked together to balance the needs of all these groups and plan for the best use of the lower St. Louis valley. The result is a richly variegated gathering of cosmopolitan neighborhoods and natural areas preserved for birds, wildlife, and wildlife viewers. People live close to the earth here, side-by-side with hundreds of species of resident and migrating birds and other animals along the sand dunes, marshes, and shorelines of Lake Superior and the St. Louis River.

Superior's largest tributary springs to life northeast of Hoyt Lakes, Minnesota, flowing 179 miles to its mouth. The St. Louis changes direction twice. The upper section runs through Seven Beaver Lake and generally southwest. The river turns to the southeast at Floodwood, Minnesota, and then northeast below Minnesota's Jay Cooke State Park.

Its valley was shaped by ancient lava flows and more recent glacial advances. North of the watershed, middle Precambrian ores form the Mesabi Iron Range. Argillite (a hard clay rock similar to shale and slate) and greywacke (a conglomerate of pebbles and sand) underlie the river's upper stretches. Its midsection flows

Looking to the mouth of the St. Louis from Wisconsin Point

over the silts and clays of glacial lakes. At Jay Cooke State Park, underground pressures broke and folded the argillite and greywacke layers, which now stand more spectacularly vertical than horizontal. Molten rock forced through the fractures cooled into black diabase dikes you can see in the riverbed. The lower St. Louis descends the Duluth escarpment and broadens into a 12,000-acre estuary; Lake Superior drowns the final section of river valley.

As a southern Wisconsinite, I usually view I-94 coming from Chicago, or occasionally I-90 from Rockford, as the state's front door. But for many northwestern citizens, the front door is undoubtedly Superior. And the harbor is certainly a more welcoming entrance hall than the concrete lanes, barriers, and billboards of the Interstate.

A long, divided sand spit protects the harbors and estuary from Lake Superior's thrashing waves. Wisconsin Point extends 3.5 miles west from Moccasin Mike Road in Superior to form Allouez Bay at the mouth of the Nemadji River. Minnesota Point reaches 7.0 miles east from Duluth at the mouth of the St. Louis. Together they form the longest freshwater sandbar in the world. The Superior Entry is a natural break in the bar and a shipping route to Superior. On the Minnesota side, ships reach Duluth through the man-made Park Point Ship Canal.

From Wisconsin, you can drive across **Duluth's Aerial Lift Bridge** to Minnesota Point and follow Minnesota Avenue to catch a view of the river mouth. You can soon glimpse the harbor between the houses that line the western end of the avenue. To reach a trailhead and enjoy a short hike to the end of the point, continue to drive through the **Park Point Recreation Area** toward the Sky Harbor Airport and park outside the airport fence. Look for the beginning of the 2-mile Park Point Trail, which begins as a gravel path, taking care to avoid the patches of poison ivy. At the water pumping stations, follow the right fork into the old growth pine forest remnant. On the left, look for the foundations of cabins built by early settlers. At 1.25 miles, follow the right trail to the bay and a view of the Burlington Northern Ore docks, flour mill, and grain elevators. Another half mile brings you to the remains of an 1855 lighthouse, designated a National Historic Monument in 1975. At the tip, you are standing only a few hundred yards from Wisconsin Point and looking at one of the busiest shipping entries on the Great Lakes.

The easy route back to your car is to retrace your steps along the 2-mile route. For a challenge involving some rock-hopping at the breakwater, follow the Lake Superior beach along the sand. Rock hounds can search for agates, jasper, and water-smoothed pebbles of glass.

One of the first Europeans to see this harbor was Daniel Greysolon, Sieur du Lhut, namesake of the city of Duluth. He first traveled to this region in 1679 and made his historic second trip to the Bois Brule-St. Croix rivers waterway a year later. At the time, the St. Louis was the principal route, with portages, from Lake Superior to the upper Mississippi River and Vermilion Lake in what is now Minnesota.

How did the St. Louis get its name? One theory is that the name refers to Pierre Gaultier de Varennes, Sieur de La Vérendrye, who explored areas west of Lake Superior and received the Cross of St. Louis from King Louis XV of France in 1749. Another more likely explanation is that early French explorers named the river in honor of King Louis IX, canonized as Saint Louis.

After Ojibwe (Chippewa) tribes ceded the area to the United States in the La Pointe Treaty of 1854 and the railroad came to the region, lumbermen arrived and settlers moved in. Towns like Brookston, Forbes, Peary, and Zim grew as railway villages. Lumber cut in the St. Louis River valley also supported the westward expansion.

Following 1890, as mining reshaped the northeastern Minnesota landscape, iron ore was transported to Duluth for shipment to the world, and industry grew along the banks of the St. Louis. Water quality surveys in 1928, 1948, and 1973 recorded increasing contamination from a U.S. Steel plant and other industrial activities, as well as failing village wastewater systems.

Today the U.S. Steel location is a federal Superfund site. The International Joint Commission, an advisory commission on U.S.-Canadian border water issues, has also named the lower St. Louis River one of 42 Great Lakes "areas of concern" due to severe pollution. In recent years, Wisconsin and Minnesota have issued consumption advisories about eating fish taken from the area; specific risks are for mercury in walleye and polychlorinated biphenyl (PCB) or pesticides in trout and salmon.

The good news is that the Superfund designation has meant some funding for clean-up efforts, and local citizens groups have worked to control pollution sources and repair the damage from earlier industrial and shipping activities. Both Wisconsin and Minnesota are studying the river and bays, monitoring the health of fish species and the level of pollutants they contain. In addition to walleye, the Wisconsin Department of Natural Resources collects and analyzes channel catfish, yellow perch, small mouth bass, bullhead, and northern pike. Other fish caught here include lake sturgeon, black crappie, rock bass, and pumpkinseed. A Wisconsin fishing license permits you to fish the St. Louis River, as does a Minnesota license.

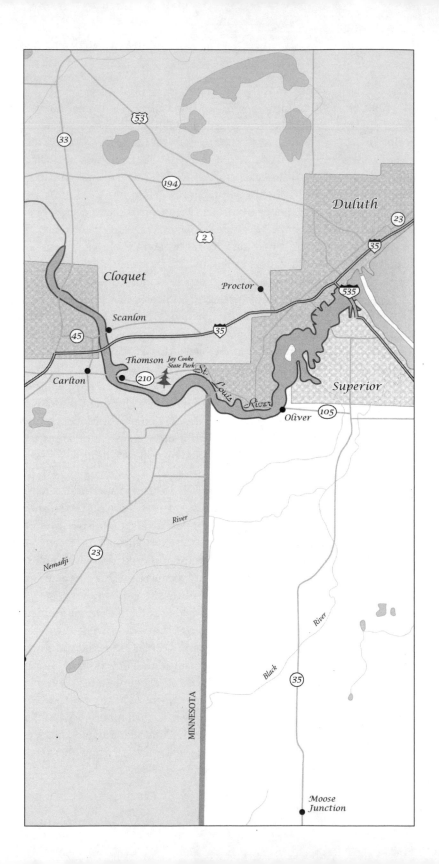

The St. Louis estuary is as known for the birds that fly over it as the fish that swim in it. The estuary serves as a bird sanctuary for species as varied as the majestic bald eagle and the tiny pine siskin. While development has endangered this habitat, public and private agencies again have worked to address the threat. The Wisconsin Department of Natural Resources has enhanced habitat for common terns, a state endangered species, on Wisconsin Point. It has also sought ways to support potential piping plover and great blue heron nesting sites.

Wisconsin Point and **Allouez Bay** already provide habitat for the blue-winged teal, merlin, least bittern, and northern harrier. In spring, the area welcomes a large variety of migrating birds. Watch for common loons and red-necked grebes in May and, in summer, buff-breasted sandpipers and ruddy turnstones. If you seek a brushy blind, note that Wisconsin Point, like Minnesota Point, contains many patches of poison ivy.

Besides birding, the estuary offers many ways to experience the Lower St. Louis. Paddlers of all skill levels can find trips to meet their abilities, with access from three landings in Superior north of 28th Street, in Oliver, and near the Wisconsin-Minnesota border off Minnesota State Highway 23, as well as several landings in Duluth. One caveat: either avoid the Duluth harbor or beware of big ships!

Campgrounds and trails also introduce thousands of explorers to the region annually, despite — or perhaps because of — its proximity to civilization, hotels, and restaurants.

At 4,400 acres, the Superior Municipal Forest is the third largest forest located within a U.S. city. Its maze of trails (take your compass!) follows the northern edges of Kimballs and Pokegama Bays on the St. Louis, provides spectacular views, and winds through a boreal forest containing white and red pine, balsam, cedar, black spruce, white birch, and aspen. Trails are open for hiking and mountain biking in summer, and for skiing, showshoeing, and snowmobiling in winter. (Get a skiing permit from the city of Superior, 1316 North 14th Street, Superior, WI 54880. Phone: (715) 395-7270. Website: www.ci.superior.wi.us.) There are two parking areas: 1) North 28th Street and Wyoming Avenue, and 2) off Billings Drive north of U.S. Highway 105.

Dwight's Point and Pokegama Wetlands State Natural Area, located within the Superior Municipal Forest, helps preserve the boreal forest, marsh, and wet clay flats at the confluence of the Pokegama and St. Louis Rivers. You can hike up to overlook the estuary from Dwight's Point.

South of the forest, the **Oliver-Wrenshall Trail** runs from Oliver, Wisconsin, to Wrenshall, Minnesota, skirting the St. Louis River Streambank Protection Area and sidling along the Pokegama at the state line.

On the Minnesota side of the lower St. Louis, the 5-mile **Western Waterfront Trail** skirts the foot of Spirit Mountain and edges the coves and points of the estuary. To the north, Duluth's Hartley Park provides a number of trails; look for those east of Old Hartley Road to find routes overlooking the St. Louis and Lake Superior.

Upriver, **Jay Cooke State Park** preserves a river stretch highlighted by gorges and rock outcrops, featuring 50 miles of hiking trails in addition to cross country skiing and snowmobile trails. The paved Willard Munger Trail begins in Hinckley, skirts the northern edge of Jay Cooke State Park, and follows the St. Louis into Duluth. Website: www.munger-trail.com.

While the drops and gorges make most of Jay Cooke State Park dangerous to paddlers, they create multiple breathtaking views, and you can drive or walk to campsites near the river. History buffs will want to check out **Thomson Pioneer Cemetery.** If you go, don't miss the swinging bridge. For more information, visit www.dnr.state.mn.us.

For campsites closer to the cities, try one of the following:

- South of Duluth, **Indian Point Campground** offers 71 tent and full-service campsites nestled on the point. Indian Point rents out canoes, kayaks, and outboard fishing boats, as well as bikes. In an unusual juxtaposition of wilderness and urban services, the campground also offers free wireless Internet connection. Indian Point is owned by the city of Duluth and managed by the Willard Munger Inn, located nearby at the trailhead of Minnesota's Willard Munger Trail. Website: www.indianpointcamp ground.com.

- Nearby, the privately owned **River Place Campground** at 9902 Hudson Boulevard, Duluth, lies adjacent to Boy Scout Landing. In addition to overnight camping, River Place has monthly and weekly rates. For reservations, call (218) 626-1390.

- **Spirit Mountain Campground** overlooks the estuary and, in the far distance, Lake Superior. Seventy-three tent and full-service campsites, plus 10 walk-in sites, nestle in the mountain forest. In winter, Spirit Mountain is an active ski hill; in summer, a variety of events spice up camp life. Watch for the Spirit Mountain exit on I-35 south of downtown Duluth. Phone: (800) 642-6377 or (218) 624-8544, or visit www.spiritmt.com.

For a river that spends so little of its length in Wisconsin, the St. Louis offers myriad ways to get to know it.

Vista Fleet Cruises operate from mid-May to mid-October, offering narrated trips to explore the harbors, the lower St. Louis River, and Lake

Waterfalls: Open Books on Geology

Waterfalls lure and lull us, drowning out other sounds and mesmerizing us like a bonfire on the verge of getting out of hand. Tall or broad, small or loud, Wisconsin's waterfalls are all destinations. We hike to them, portage around them, kayak in their foaming ponds, and swim and fish in less turbulent pools.

A few of the state's largest falls lie southwest of the St. Louis.

Amnicon Falls State Park opens like a book where you can read this geology. A billion years ago, the dark basalt foundation of the Upper Falls erupted as lava from deep in the earth. In contrast, the park's Lower Falls drops over red sandstone created mere millions of years ago when sand settled in a large shallow lake that spread across northern Wisconsin. The reason for this different composition lies between the two falls: About 80 feet in front of the Upper Falls, a line of broken rock crosses the river and marks the Douglas Fault.

This 500-million-year-old crack in the bedrock extends from east of Ashland, Wisconsin, to near St. Paul, Minnesota. South of the fault, the bedrock moved north and upward. If the Douglas Fault had never occurred, the basalt would today still lie beneath the sandstone. In addition to Upper Falls, Amnicon's Snake Pit Falls and Now and Then Falls also formed at the fault, as did Big Manitou Falls, located to the west on the Black River in **Pattison State Park.** At 165 feet, Big Manitou is the highest waterfall in Wisconsin — not to mention the fourth highest east of the Rocky Mountains.

Long after the Douglas Fault formed, succeeding glaciers pushed over northern Wisconsin, melted, and retreated. The rushing meltwater carried rocks that wore potholes in the basalt where the water whirled them around. When the river level is low, you can see several of these potholes in Amnicon State Park.

Superior, weather permitting. Docks are located in both Superior (Barker's Island off U.S. Highways 2 and 53) and Duluth (Harbor Drive near the Duluth Entertainment Convention Center). Sightseeing, brunch, lunch, dinner, pizza, moonlight, and special event cruises available. Phone: (219) 722-6218. Website: www.vistafleet.com.

The nonprofit, volunteer-run **Lake Superior & Mississippi Railroad** in Duluth offers daily 1.5-hour trips along the estuary, Spirit Lake, and Mud Lake from June to October. Admission: $9.25 adults and $6.25 children (free for children three and under). It's your choice to travel in a historic coach or an open-air flatcar originally built for the Northern Pacific Railway. The railroad is located at Grand Avenue and Fremont Street, across from the Lake Superior Zoo. Phone: (218) 624-7549. Website: www.lsmrr.org.

Superior Whitewater Rafting, 950 Chestnut Avenue, Carlton, MN 55718, leads 2.5-hour guided trips down the St. Louis for individuals age 12 and older. It operates daily, May through September, and can be found off exit 239 of I-35 and just south of Minnesota State Highway 61. Call to reserve your trip. Phone: (218) 384-4637. Website: www.minnesotawhite water.com.

Whatever your preferred outdoor activity, the **Willard Munger Inn,** 7408 Grand Avenue, Duluth, MN 55807, provides easy access to both the trail of that name and the river — plus a free pass to the nearby Lake Superior Zoo. Fireplace and jacuzzi suites offer needed pampering at the end of a long trek or paddle. The inn's staff is accustomed to answering travelers' questions and easily directed me to Ely's Peak Tunnel on a city trail once owned by the Duluth Winnepeg and Pacific Railroad — but that is another book. Phone: (218) 624-4814 or (800) 982-2453. Website: www.mungerinn.com.

CHAPTER 2

Bois Brule

A spa for outdoor lovers, the Bois Brule River runs clear and trash-free for 44 miles, from a boggy watershed divide in east central Douglas County to its mouth at Lake Superior. This is the "just right" river for many anglers, bird watchers, trekkers, and paddlers, whether you're a relative novice like me or a whitewater enthusiast.

The Bois Brule beckons with a rippling current and a steady flow, showcasing the efforts of conservationists and private landowners alike to protect fisheries from beaver, run-off, and over-fishing. At the heart of the 41,000-acre Brule River State Forest — and 12,000 privately owned acres within it — lies the finest trout stream in the Upper Midwest, varied forests, weathered estates, and a historic portage trail.

As the glaciers receded 10,000 years ago, the Brule had a different appearance, not to mention a different direction. Torrents from rapidly melting ice in glacial Lake Duluth cascaded south, carving one river valley where the Bois Brule and upper St. Croix Rivers flow today. When the ice sheets receded and the rush of water slowed, a broad ridge, an ancient uplift between the Bois Brule and St. Croix watersheds, emerged to block the southerly flow. Fed by springs in the high ground, the Bois Brule switched directions and began flowing north to Lake Superior.

When French explorers arrived a few hundred years ago in the wake of a fire, they called the river Bois Brulé (pronounced "bwa broo-lay"), "Burned Wood," a translation from the Ojibwe name, Wiskada Sepi, "Burning Pine River." The British called it the Burntwood. Today an Anglicized version of the French name is generally pronounced "bwa brool." But its friends call it simply the Brule.

Though the French found two rivers where there had been only one waterway thousands of years earlier, they learned from the Indians that the

Paddling the Bois Brule

distance between the source of the northward-flowing Brule and that of the southward-flowing St. Croix could be portaged. The French soon were using the ancient Indian trail to transport furs and trade goods along this route, which connected the Great Lakes to the Mississippi River.

You can still hike this early trail today, see the geography for yourself, and visualize the story of the people who tramped this ridge over the passing centuries. The portage trail is easily accessible, thanks to the efforts of the Claude Jean Allouez Chapter of the Daughters of the American Revolution (DAR). They rescued the trail from oblivion and marked it in the 1930s, in cooperation with the Superior and Solon Springs garden clubs. Today, the **Brule-St. Croix Portage Trail** is on the National Register of Historic Places. It is also a segment of the North Country Trail, which, when complete, will stretch from Allegany State Park in New York to the Missouri River and Lake Sakakawea State Park in North Dakota.

Access the portage trail from County Road A northeast of Solon Springs, just south of its intersection with County P, as County Road A bends around the north end of Upper St. Croix Lake. Look for the historic marker on the west side of the road. Drive a bit farther south to the driveway into the St. Croix picnic area, boat launch, and parking lot. The trail, about 2 miles long, begins across the road on the east side of County Road A.

How closely the modern trail follows the ancient portage remains unknown, but it's probably pretty close — although the starting point at the St. Croix end would have been about where the boat launch, locally known as Palmer's Landing, is today. The portage follows the edge of a ridge of glacial drift overlooking a wooded bog that stretches for 10 miles and contains the headwaters of both the St. Croix and the Bois Brule rivers. A bronze plaque on the east side of County Road A marks the beginning of the trail, and a short incline takes you up onto the ridge.

As you follow the trail northeast, you encounter a series of small markers placed by the Daughters and their garden-club partners, memorializing a string of notable European explorers in the Bois Brule's history. (Maybe one day, they will add markers memorializing the Indians who used this portage for centuries, perhaps millennia, before the Europeans arrived.) The markers are in reverse chronological order from the St. Croix end of the portage, and the first one you'll encounter reads "NICOLAS AND JOE LUCIUS 1886." Joe Lucius was 15 when his family arrived in White Birch (now Solon Springs) in 1886. He became a guide, and designed and built

Near source of the Bois Brule at the end of the St. Croix-Brule Portage Trail

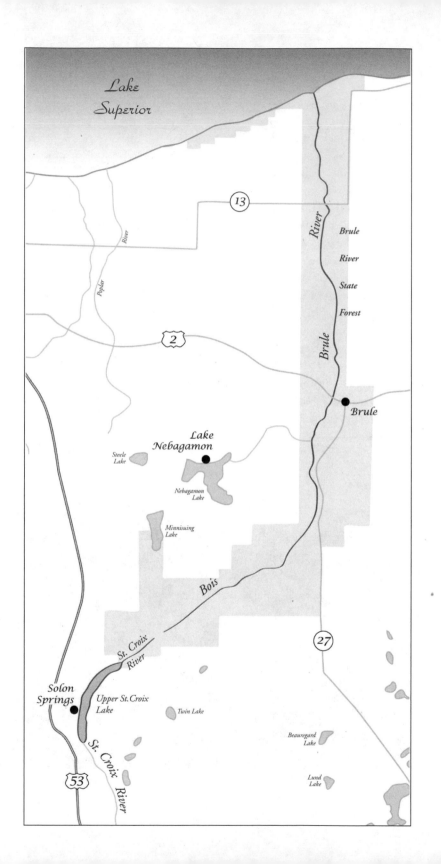

unique Brule River boats. Hybrids between canoes and round-bottomed rowboats, they first appeared in 1895 or 1896 and were used by Brule fishermen for many years.

Near the next marker, for U.S. Indian agent and explorer Henry Schoolcraft, you can still see signs of an August 2000 hailstorm that devastated 5,000 acres. Loggers salvaged usable trees, and plantings and natural regeneration are slowly restoring the forest.

About a half mile from the beginning, near a marker for Michael Curot (a fur trader who passed this way in 1803 and wrote about his trip), the trail ascends a crest overlooking the bog. Here you'll find a most welcome bench, provided by the **Brule-St. Croix Chapter of the North Country Trail Association** (www.northcountrytrail.org/bsc/).

When the DAR and its garden club allies marked the trail, the forest here and across most of northern Wisconsin had been logged away. Then, from this high point you would have seen the countryside for miles around: southwest down the length of Upper St. Croix Lake, north across the bog to the West Fork of the Bois Brule, and south to Lake of the Woods, just outside the boundary of the state forest. Today the second-growth mixed deciduous and coniferous forest has grown and closed in. White cedar, black spruce, balsam fir, silver maple, white and yellow birch, black ash, alder, and poplar give a hint, but only that, of how the land once looked.

The trail next descends into the small ravine that holds Lake of the Wood and re-ascends along the ridge. Then it levels out and passes above the spring-fed headwaters of the St. Croix above Upper St. Croix Lake, just under a mile from the starting point. For many years, in fact since the French exploration of the area in the late seventeenth century, local lore had it that the St. Croix and the East Branch of the Bois Brule flowed out of opposite ends of Big Spring. This hydrologically improbable tale may have originated when beaver dams raised water levels, mixing the flow from separate springs.

A Wisconsin Conservation Department stream-improvement work crew put the question to rest in 1936 when it located Brule Spring at the head of the Bois Brule's east fork and demonstrated that it had no connection to Big Spring, some 500 yards to the southwest. The crew built a stone wall and birch railing around the spring and planted spruce trees around it as well. The birch railing is long gone, but the intrepid hiker, well anointed with mosquito repellent, may yet descend into the bog at this point (just over a mile from the beginning of the trail) and find the spring.

Though hard to imagine from this vantage point, the imperceptibly low rise between the two springs is a continental divide, separating the

Old Indian Trails

Much of the Native American commerce flowed through the Great Lakes region in dugout and birchbark canoes. Some also moved on overland trails, in heavy packs partially supported by tumplines over the bearers' foreheads. These old Indian trails were no primitive, narrow tracks through the wilderness. They were really dirt roads, wide and devoid of vegetation, packed hard by centuries of tramping feet. Being dirt roads, though, they were fine in the summer and snowshoeable in the winter, but impassable rivers of mud in the wet seasons.

In time, these routes were taken over by the European newcomers, and many now lie beneath modern streets and highways. Some, however, did not thrive and were eventually bypassed and abandoned. One such was the **Old Bayfield Trail,** which ran from Chequamegon Bay to the mouth of the Saint Louis River. A fragment survives today as part of a hiking trail within the Brule River State Forest (access and parking off Clevedon Road, about 3 miles north of U.S. Highway 2).

Mississippi River basin from the Great Lakes, St. Lawrence River, and the Atlantic Ocean. As you gaze back west and southwest across that divide, you are looking at a salient fact of North American geography, for you are not standing on a mountain. The vast interior of North America is drained by four great systems: the Mississippi, the Great Lakes/St. Lawrence, the numerous rivers flowing into Hudson's Bay, and the Mackenzie River, flowing into the Arctic Ocean. The key feature of this geography is that these drainage systems are not separated by continental divides atop great mountain ranges. Rather, the divides are low and for the most part easily traversed glacial moraines and uplifts, like the one between the Brule and St. Croix.

Long before the Europeans arrived, these waterways and the portages between them became the highways of an extensive commercial network centered on the Great Lakes. Into and out of this region poured the stuff of commerce: ceramics, utilitarian wares of wood and tree-bark, bone and stone implements and projectile points, animal hides, dried and smoked meat and fish, marine products (including ornamental seashells from the Atlantic and Pacific coasts), wild rice, agricultural produce (especially the Three Sisters: corn, beans, and squash), and even copper and lead.

The tribes surrounding the Great Lakes prospered as middlemen in the trade that passed through their territories. This trade engendered competition, diplomatic maneuvering, and, sometimes, open warfare. These issues intensified with the arrival of Europeans, their manufactured goods (especially firearms and steel tools), their demand for beaver and other pelts, and their national conflicts. Tribes fought even harder to maintain their positions. As Europeans explored farther westward, tribes closer to the expanding European settlements and outposts did their best to dissuade or forcibly prevent their new trading partners from contacting other tribes farther inland.

Daniel Greysolon, Sieur du Lhut, the French soldier-diplomat, revisited the Lake Superior region in 1680, this time to the Bois Brule in the summer of 1680. Du Lhut's mission was to negotiate a peace treaty between the warring Dakota (Sioux) and Ojibwe, open direct trade with the Dakota who controlled most of Minnesota and northwestern Wisconsin, and get the tribes to focus on supplying furs to French traders. The Ojibwe then controlled St. Mary's River, linking Lakes Superior and Huron at the strategic Sault Ste. Marie. They had expanded westward and largely controlled the Lake Superior shoreline. This had brought them into conflict with the Dakota, who were at a disadvantage because the Ojibwe had direct access to French firearms and other steel tools and weapons.

When du Lhut's presumably Ojibwe guides introduced him to the Brule-St. Croix, the shortest route between Lake Superior and the Mississippi, he promptly claimed possession in the name of King Louis XIV and later built the first European fort in Wisconsin, on the portage or possibly on Upper St. Croix Lake. The French then controlled this key route until losing the French and Indian War, and their North American empire, to the British in 1763. Despite the temporary success of du Lhut's peace mission, the Ojibwe and Dakota conflict resumed by 1736 and they remained generally at war until the mid-nineteenth century.

Du Lhut's memorial marker is the last of the series along the portage trail, not far from the trail's end. Just beyond, the trail divides. Follow the left fork down a slope into a marshy area and the clear, cold waters of the East Fork of the Bois Brule. Downstream about a quarter mile, the east and west forks join to form the main stream. This spot is a good place to lean on your walking stick and daydream of the lithe explorers who kicked through these marsh grasses 300 years ago.

Reverse your steps to retrace your path past the headwaters of the St. Croix and the series of markers. The 2-mile return trek to your car will likely seem shorter than the hike out, now that you're familiar with the trail.

If, instead of following the left fork to the headwaters, you take the right fork, you'll pass through woods edging the Brule River Bog on the North

Country Trail. Short boardwalks will take you across an ash bog to Jerseth Creek. The trail continues through pine and popple groves. After 5.2 miles, you'll reach a trailhead near the Highland Town Hall off County Road S approximately 5 miles west of State Highway 27. From here, the North Country Trail proceeds northeast, leaving the Brule River State Forest at Bayfield County, south of U.S. Highway 2.

Another trail worth checking out is the 1.7-mile **Stoney Hill Nature Trail,** which begins and ends across Ranger Road from the **Brule River Campground.** Parking for the Stony Hill Nature Trail is near the recycling/waste station. The loop trail climbs to the site of a former fire tower. Try to plan your trek for a sunny day and bring the binoculars to fully enjoy the river valley vista.

Outside the nearby 1930's-era ranger station, we picked up a fistful of useful brochures, forest guides, and maps from a weathered literature rack before heading into the Bois Brule River Campground.

At the campground, we parked near the river and walked to the landing, our friendly black Lab, Rumpus, towing us forward. When we reached the landing, the reason for her eagerness was clear: a group of kids and dogs splashing in the cold water of the Brule. To prevent any altercation, no matter how unlikely, we tugged Rumpus reluctantly away. In addition to the swimming hole, the landing offers a handicap-accessible fishing pier and a picnic area.

The well-maintained campground provides 18 back-in sites and two sites right on the river, accessible by canoe or a short walk through the forest. If you stay here on a clear night, peek from your tent or camper in the wee hours to stargaze. On clear summer nights, even the fainter Pleiades are easily visible, framed between the tops of the tall pines.

In the morning we drove north on Highway 27, turning west on Highway 2 in Brule and stopping to explore the rustic wayside on the west edge of town. Rumpus led the way down the rough path to the river and the old highway bridge that, in its day, surely carried millions of travelers across the chilly trout stream.

North of Highway 2, County Road H sidles along the river until it intersects with State Highway 13, which runs almost to the Brule's mouth. Before reaching Lake Superior, the highway takes a right angle to the east toward Port Wing, Cornucopia, and Bayfield. Yet, the gazetteer revealed a thin, red artery stretching from Highway 13 to the mouth and a boat landing. We were aiming for that red line.

North of Highway 2, we counted three roads in quick succession leading from County Road H to angler access areas. Each offered a parking area and short trail to the river.

Though seldom crowded, the Brule nevertheless welcomes 33,000 anglers annually. They stalk the river's resident brook, brown, and rainbow trout, as well as lake, brown, and rainbow (steelhead) trout and Chinook and Coho salmon that migrate up the Brule from Lake Superior. From late March through May and again from mid-August through late November, anglers fish for steelhead, sometimes wading from snow-covered banks. Beginning in July, they use spinners and spoons to take Chinook salmon. Coho migrate up the Brule from late August to late November and are often caught in areas where the river flows more slowly.

The last of the three access points leads to the Brule's Boxcar Hole (apparently named because it's large enough to hold a boxcar), which is closed to fishing from July 15 through October 31. Two other areas have added restrictions, and anglers may use only artificial baits on the Brule south of Highway 2. The special regulations support the river's fisheries and allow trout to reproduce at least once before being available to anglers.

We continued north and passed Kauppi Road before scouting for Park Road on the left. It was well-marked, and soon we were rolling into **Copper Range Campground** and Landing. Fifteen rustic campsites surrounded the pit toilets on a loop off Park Road.

Both Copper Range and Bois Brule campgrounds offer registration on a first-come, first-served basis, so plan to arrive early on prime summer weekends. Or, you can opt for backpack camping, though you must hike with your gear a minimum of 1 mile from where you park your vehicle and camp 100 feet from any trail and out of sight of any water body. Get a free Special Camp Registration Permit from the Brule River State Forest Station before heading out to camp. Popular trails for backcountry camping are the 26-mile snowmobile trail between Brule and St. Croix Lake and the North Country Trail between Highway 27 and St. Croix Lake.

At Copper Range, we walked along the campground loop to find the trail near campsite #35 that leads to the canoe landing. As we descended the steep trail, voices and laughter floated above the unmistakable gurgling of the river. When we reached the Brule, we spotted thimbleberries on the bank and three canoes floating into view. Their occupants bantered back and forth like birds on a winter feeder. We watched them go with a sigh. Maybe next year we'll canoe this stretch, but regret would waste this golden day.

West of the campground, Park Road ends past a one-lane bridge over the Brule. At the bridge, daisies bobbed above the bank grasses and we watched as three more canoes approached and bounced toward a Class I rapids. Young women piloted this flotilla, with most of the canoes containing two paddlers apiece, but one squired a woman in the center, who lay back with the sun on her face and hands drifting in the water.

The group's canoes were marked "Brule River Canoe Rental," which offers canoes and kayaks to rent, as well as guided kayak tours to the Squaw Bay sea caves on the Lake Superior shore near Cornucopia. Address: P.O. Box 145, U.S. Highway 2, Brule, WI 54820. Phone: (715) 372-4983 or (715) 392-3132. Website: www.brulerivercanoerental.com. E-mail: spacejet21@aol.com.

Paddlers often begin their trip at Stone's Bridge Landing upriver from here at County Road S, where there's plenty of parking and easy river access. If you put in there, you're soon floating through a dark, cavelike passage of cedar, spruce, tamarack, and balsam.

Two miles downstream, look for McDougal Springs on the right. Beyond the spring, the Brule winds through several private tracts, and approximately 3.5 miles from Stone's Bridge you can't miss Cedar Island Estate. Footbridges lead to the island and connect cedar-sided buildings on both sides, all part of the 4,000-acre estate that secluded three presidents — Calvin Coolidge, Herbert Hoover, and Dwight Eisenhower. Ulysses Grant and Grover Cleveland stayed elsewhere on the Brule. Clearly, they all knew how to pick a river.

The Bois Brule at Pine Tree Landing

Experienced paddlers seeking easy whitewater can put in at Pine Tree Landing north of Copper Range Campground and paddle to the river's mouth. The river picks up speed in its lower 18 miles, falling 328 feet between Copper Range and its mouth. Upriver above Copper Range, the drop in elevation is less than 100 feet.

For a shorter day, skilled paddlers often begin downriver at the Highway 13 Landing. Two miles into this 8-mile route to Lake Superior, a portage trail on the west bank goes around a lamprey dam.

This barrier protects lake trout and other fish from the parasitic, non-native, sea lamprey. These look like eels, but they lack jaws and have a skeleton of cartilage instead of bone. During their adult phase, sea lamprey attach to fish, taking nutrients from their prey and eventually killing them. The barrier consists of a dam blocking three-quarters of the river and a fish ladder that trout and salmon can jump but lamprey are unable to negotiate.

Our goal was the reverse: to traverse the woods downstream to the Brule's mouth.

We followed County Road H to Highway 13 and then followed Highway 13 north to Brule River Road and turned west. Despite the dust billowing up from this gravel washboard road, we left the windows down. A mature bald eagle soared over us, its white head silhouetted like a tiny cloud riding a dark airplane.

Along the left side of the highway, four angler-access parking areas offer trails into the **Brule River Boreal Forest State Natural Area.** Stands of white pine, white spruce, and balsam fir march up its steep slopes, while black ash, red maple, and alder line the river terraces. In addition to eagles, residents include the ovenbird, hermit thrush, and black-throated, green, pine, and Nashville warblers.

The Wisconsin Department of Natural Resources has established one other natural area on the river. The **Brule Glacial Spillway State Natural Area** is situated upstream near the Stone's Bridge Landing. You can paddle in or access the area from the North Country Trail. Look for nesting olive-sided flycatchers, golden-crowned kinglets, and Lincoln's sparrows.

Observers have recorded more than 200 bird species in the Brule River State Forest, more than any other similarly sized northern Wisconsin region. If you're lucky, you might spot some of the forest's rarest birds — the black-backed woodpecker, white-winged crossbill, merlin, great gray owl, and goshawk.

But on our drive that day, we saw only the eagle. Moving restlessly behind us, Rumpus smelled the big lake long before we caught the cool, fishy scent.

We pulled into the parking area and stared at the grassy, windswept terrain before getting out and striding past a picnic table to an overlook. I strained to hear crashing rollers. But on the day we visited, the biggest American inland sea was a gently rocking, gray-blue expanse that might have lulled to sleep a stressed writer on deadline as readily as a child.

A sign at the overlook commemorates the exploration of Daniel Greysolon du Lhut and notes that the American Fur Company once operated a fish camp nearby. Two hundred years after du Lhut's discovery, English immigrants settled on the spot, planning to catch fish and pack them in wooden barrels manufactured here for shipping to points east. But this attempt — and their community — failed in 1884. At the turn of the twentieth century, entrepreneurs built a logging dam a half mile upriver, sorted the logs at the mouth, and rafted them to Duluth sawmills. A few short years later, intrepid homesteaders flagged down the Duluth-Ashland ferry here, when they needed to go to one town or the other.

Selfishly, I felt grateful that all these activities were short-lived, and that the coast remains relatively wild. I'm also indebted to Frederick Weyerhaeuser, who in 1907 decided to move his lumber interests to the Pacific Northwest and deeded 4,320 acres to the state, forming the core of the Brule River State Forest. Wisconsin received additional adjacent land in the 1930s. The farmers who had followed the lumbermen could not eke a living from the barren cutover lands during the Great Depression, and in lieu of delinquent taxes, counties received many acres, which were eventually transferred to the state. Later acquisitions extended the boundary of the Brule River State Forest to the river's mouth.

The mouth was serene but not empty. A couple searched for driftwood and agates on the sand spit separating the river channel from the lake. Their kids swam off the protected, sandy beach of the river above the mouth.

Mike kept a tight hold on Rumpus' leash as we headed down to the rock-strewn beach. Across the river, another family explored the opposite bank. Their little dog saw Rumpus, barked ferociously, and lunged into the water. Could that small dog swim all the way over here? But, no, it turned and bounded back to its family.

We did likewise, turning our backs on that loud miniature terror and strolling along the lakeshore in the opposite direction. When a hundred yards separated us from the mouth, we found ourselves alone on this stretch of beach and Mike let Rumpus off leash. She sailed off with a bound, dancing in and out of the waves at the water's edge and following scents we could only imagine.

The Bois Brule River

Soon, Rumpus returned, tongue lolling, and took up a pace by our side briefly, before tearing away again. She repeated the game several times before finally tiring. Mike clipped her lead in place and we turned to trek back to the top of the overlook. Before crossing the parking area to the car, we all paused for a final glance at the North American lake that's as expansive as time itself.

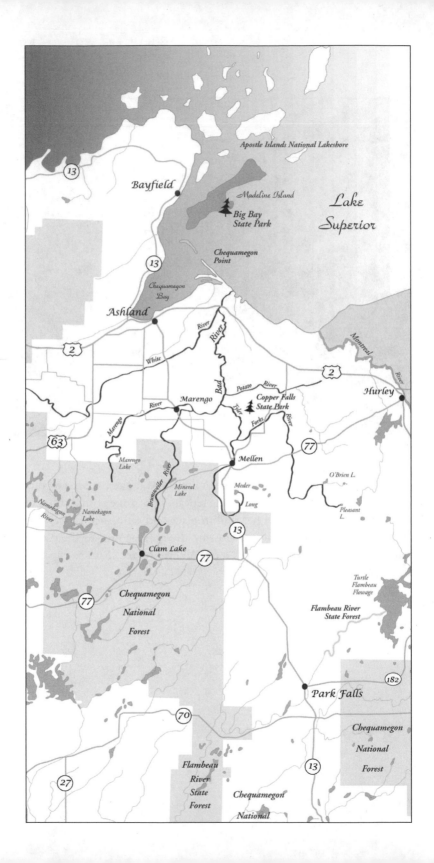

CHAPTER 3

Bad

≋

More than many, the Bad River — with four major tributaries, a deeply undulating midsection, and fanlike delta — presents a complex water system. I tried to trace the twisting, 76-mile stream on a road map from its source at Caroline Lake in east central Ashland County to Lake Superior, but its squiggling lines were hard to follow. The tributaries of this broad watershed reach from central Bayfield County all the way east to within a few miles of the West Branch of the Montreal.

We located the headwaters at shallow Caroline Lake in the Winegar Moraines near the southern rim of the Lake Superior basin. From here, the river flows north, down through the Gogebic-Penokee Iron Range, ending in an extensive wetland at Lake Superior.

I used the gazetteer to locate the four major river tributaries — Marengo (including its major Brunsweiler River tributary), Potato, Tyler Forks, and White. Several of these wilderness streams exhibit waterfalls. Each features rapid currents and whitewater running over basaltic beds through northern hardwood forests.

The Bad River plunging through Copper Falls

Each also babbles in perfect harmony with birdsong and the wayward wind.

The Bad cuts steep, crooked paths through ancient lava beds in its upper reaches. At **Copper Falls State Park,** the riverbed consists of once-molten lava that solidified eons ago after flowing up from fissures in the area now occupied by Lake Superior. A half mile downstream from its confluence with Tyler Forks River, the Bad slices through first conglomerates and then shale that once settled atop the lava as layers of rocky sands and mud. You can see these conglomerate layers, tipped almost vertical, at Devil's Gate in the park.

Travelers have visited this region for many years. A decade before Copper Falls was established as Wisconsin's 11th state park in 1929, veterans returning from World War I constructed trails and bridges here. During the 1930s, the Civilian Conservation Corps expanded and improved these efforts, often making use of the readily available slate and boulders in bridges, buildings, and walkways.

Hiking is the best way to see the scenic wonders of Copper Falls State Park. Designers of the National Park Service's **North Country Scenic Trail** knew what they were doing when they plotted the trail through the park. This trail segment displays exceptional views of the Bad and Tyler Forks rivers, colorful cliffs with variegated rock layers, and deep woods canopies. Mike and I, with our black Lab, Rumpus, combined a short walk along the North Country Scenic Trail with park trails to complete a 1.7-mile circuit that crosses both rivers, providing several different perspectives of Copper Falls, Brownstone Falls, and Tyler Forks Cascades. A short loop to the west

Tyler Forks tributary at Copper Falls State Park

encompasses a nature trail and leads to an observation tower providing eagle-eye views of the convoluted Bad River.

During the late nineteenth and early twentieth centuries, miners endeavored to duplicate here the success found in the booming copper mines of upper Michigan. They diverted the Bad River between Copper and Brownstone Falls to keep their diggings from flooding, but for all their labors they extracted only small amounts of the mineral.

Logging in the 1920s and 1930s also changed the appearance and environment of the Bad River watershed. Today old growth forest remnants can be found only along the Lake Superior shoreline. Most interior forests, including those in the park, have re-grown on cutover lands.

North of Brownstone Falls, the North Country Scenic Trail crosses Little Creek. South of the falls, it follows the park road past a campground and the east shore of tiny Murphy Lake. From there, it continues to the larger Loon Lake, where the trail currently ends, not far from the park office.

You, however, can keep hiking if you have a mind — and the strength — to, along the figure-eight-shaped **Red Granite Falls Area Trail.** It heads south from the main parking lot, with the middle of the "eight" sliding between two parcels of private land and the final loop skirting a short, straight section of the Bad River. Alternately, bird-watchers will want to walk slowly along the Trail of the Valleys to listen and look for blue-headed vireos, hermit thrushes, blackburnian warblers, and other species to add to their life list.

Another completed section of the North Country National Scenic Trail, the 4-mile Marengo River segment, entails a moderately challenging climb to the **Marengo Overlook.** The trailhead, with parking for three or four cars, lies on Fire Road 202 off County Road D in the Chequamagon National Forest east of Cable and south of Grand View. When completed, the North Country National Scenic Trail will stretch from upstate New York to the middle of North Dakota.

The eventual route of the trail between Hurley and Copper Falls State Park hasn't been finalized, but a path through the **Potato Falls Recreation Area** would certainly give hikers tremendous terrain to explore. The state-operated recreation area near State Highway 169 offers views of the falls via an easy trail along the top of the cliff, a stairway to a wooden viewing platform, and a longer descent to the river where the entire 90-foot length of the upper and lower falls stretches below you.

South of Copper Falls, Mellen boasts the **Three Rivers Park, Hike, and Bike Trail** with access from East Tyler Avenue. In case you're wondering, the three "rivers" are Montreal Creek, City Creek, and the Bad River.

We set up base camp for a few days at **Wildwood Haven Resort and Campground** on Long Lake near Mellen. All the wooded campsites and cabins are situated on a hill rising above the lake. Wildwood offers a sand beach and rents a pontoon boat, fishing boat, canoes, and even a rowboat. Phone: (715) 274-6136. Website: www.wildwoodhaven.com.

Counting Copper Falls State Park, all three public campgrounds on the Bad River and its primary tributaries are located at waterfalls. **Upson Community Park** welcomes visitors to **Upson Falls,** which cascades over dark basalt 18 feet into the Potato River northwest of town. Hickory, oak, and spruce frame both the falls and the park, with campsites, electrical outlets, picnic area, pavilion, and fireplace. To get there from Mellen, drive east on State Highway 77 to State Highway 122. Drive north on Highway 122 into Upson, turn west on Upson Park Road, and follow it to Upson Community Park. You can see the falls from the parking lot.

Downstream, **Potato Falls Recreation Area** provides tent campsites, toilets, and picnic tables at the top of red clay cliffs, along with the trails and, of course, the falls. In fact, the picnic area overlooks the falls, its liquid notes both lulling and invigorating. Drive north on Highway 122 to U.S. Highway 2 to arrive at the recreation area. Follow Highway 2 west to State Highway 169 and turn south. Continue through the small town of Gurney and turn west on Potato River Falls Road. Follow the road about 1 mile to the Potato River Falls Recreation Area.

If you're looking for waterfalls, you'll want to check out **Foster Falls,** located off Highway 122 north of Upson Falls. From Upson Park Road, drive north on Highway 122 approximately 2.5 miles to Sullivan Road. Turn west on Sullivan and in about 2 miles, as you approach the river, watch for a dirt road to the north. Turn onto this road and follow it to the end, where you can park and walk a short path to Foster Falls.

Downstream, the Bad broadens and flows over sandstone through steep clay banks as it enters the reservation of the Bad River Band of Lake Superior Ojibwe. Sediments from bank erosion and the river's tributaries run into the Bad and enlarge **Lake Superior's Chequamegon Point,** as well as Kakagon and Bad River sloughs. All these areas provide important wildlife habitat.

Sometimes called Wisconsin's everglades, these sloughs contain wild rice beds that Indians have harvested for thousands of years. Now in late August, the Bad River Band welcomes the public to its annual Menomin (wild rice) Powwow, held in Odanah to celebrate the harvest.

The Bad River Band kept approximately 124,000 acres, including 200 acres on Madeleine Island in the La Pointe Treaty of 1854, after the Ojibwe successfully resisted removal to lands west of the Mississippi River. The treaty also established reservations at Lac Court Orielles and Lac du Flambeau. The Bad River Band has preserved its lands, and more than 90 percent of its acreage remains undeveloped.

Because the **Bad River Band** emphasizes land preservation, it maintains a no-access policy, other than on public roadways and at business establishments. The single exception occurs in winter, when a snowmobile trail runs from the east along Lake Superior to the Bad River Lodge, Casino and Convention Center.

Located on U.S. Highway 2 near Odanah, the lodge offers a limited number of free RV electrical hook-ups in addition to rooms and suites. Phone: (715) 682-6102 or (800) 795-7121. Website: www.badriver.com.

Just west of Odanah (pronounced "Oh day' nuh"), we pulled over to read the historical marker explaining the derivation of the Bad River's name, which seems a misnomer for this beautiful stream. Early French travelers named the Mauvaise (Bad) River, according to the marker, due to the difficulties of its navigation. The Ojibway name translated to "Marsh River," which seems more apt.

In addition to the no-trespassing policy of the reservation, long sections of the Bad River's tributaries are protected from development through the environmental commitment of public and private landowners. The headwaters of the Marengo lie within the Chequamagon National Forest, and the river runs predominantly through woodlands before entering the Bad River Indian Reservation. The Potato River, which begins high in the Penokee Range south of Upson and runs west to the Bad, is also largely forested. And the White River runs through both the **White River Marsh State Wildlife Area** and the **Bibon Swamp State Natural Area** west of the Bad River reservation.

Both paddlers and anglers can find plenty of streams to explore within the publicly accessible sections.

With proper water levels, experienced paddlers have found adventure canoeing the Bad from Fire Road 184 in the Chequamagon Forest northeast to Mellen. This section features Class I and Class II rapids, as well as varying water levels.

A more popular run is on the White River, beginning at Maple Ridge Road Bridge 1.1 mile east of U.S. Highway 63, and winding 13 miles through numerous Class I and Class II rapids to the dam at State Highway 112. This trip offers enough challenge to be interesting, continuous woodland brightened with wildflowers, and, in the latter half, gravel-bar rest areas.

The Bad River winds through Dr. Gilman Park in Mellen

Upriver, the White offers canoeists access to Bibon Swamp State Natural Area, the largest wetland in Bayfield County. If you choose this paddle, bring your scope: The swamp provides cover for bobolinks, boreal chickadees, evening grosbeaks, golden-winged warblers, ruby-crowned kinglets, redhead ducks, veeries, and a variety of other northern species.

Anglers find plentiful trout in the Bad River. From Copper Falls State Park to Minnie Creek approximately 2 miles from Caroline Lake, the Bad River is rated a Class II and Class III trout stream, containing rainbow, brook, and brown trout. Tributary rivers and streams provide additional trout habitat.

However you decide to experience the Bad River — at the end of a line, in a canoe, or on a trail — adding a short auto tour to your itinerary can provide a wide-angle view of Wisconsin's northern geology and history.

Begin at the Dr. Gilman Park on the Bad River in Mellen. Besides the usual grills, picnic tables, shelter, and soccer field, find the three large blocks of black granite. Note their scars: old drill marks made when they were cut from a nearby quarry.

From **Dr. Gilman Park,** proceed south on State Highway 13/77. Approximately 2.5 miles to your left (east), **Mount Whittlesey** soars 1,866 feet toward the clouds, making it the second highest point in the state.

Continue south, crossing the Bad River. From the bridge, its headwaters lie about 7 miles to the northeast at Caroline Lake. Follow Highway 13/77 to the wayside on your right (west). A plaque marks the **Great Divide,** which rises 1,550 feet above sea level and separates the states' two primary drainage areas. Water falling to the north runs toward Lake Superior, through the Great Lakes, and finally down the St. Lawrence River 2,000 miles to the Atlantic Ocean. Water falling to the south runs to the Chippewa River, into the Mississippi River, and eventually into the Gulf of Mexico. To the east side of the highway are the headwaters of the East Fork of the Chippewa River.

Continue south on Highway 13/77, turning west on Highway 77 when the two highways diverge north of Glidden. This section of Highway 77 is the **Great Divide National Scenic Highway,** wending westward through the Chequamagon National Forest into the upper Chippewa River basin.

In Clam Lake, turn north on County Road GG and enjoy the remote forest, lake, and stream wilderness. If you can, time this drive for dusk, and be on the alert for wildlife crossing the road ahead, or ranging or grazing alongside.

Northeast of Mineral Lake, stop at the **Penokee Overlook** for a magnificent view of this Wisconsin-Michigan range. Now you know what eagles must see. Continue on County Road GG to return to your starting point in Mellen.

Finally, for a view from the top of Mount Whittlesey, proceed east on Highway 77 to State Highway 122. Head north to the point where Highway 122 turns left and County Road E forks to the right. Follow County Road E about 2 miles to Whitecap Mountain Ski and Golf Resort on Weber Lake. Walk around and admire the view, poke your head into the shop, and maybe have a bite to eat at the restaurant. To learn more, visit: www.skiwhitecap.com.

Return outside for a last look at the view, and take a moment to fix it in your mind. To the north, Lake Superior and the Apostle Islands float in the distance. I hope that your memory can hold onto this scene and replay it often.

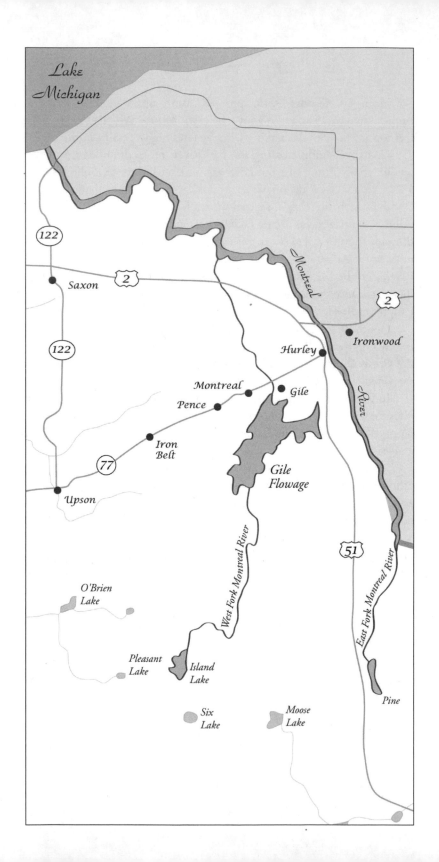

CHAPTER 4

Montreal

For a small river, the Montreal makes a big noise. Its 40-mile length encompasses seven wild waterfalls and innumerable rapids, riffles, and rock gardens. Interrupted by dams, the river's fast current powers three Xcel Energy hydro plants. Its roaring canyon also marks part of Wisconsin's boundary with Michigan.

Given the lower river's deep gorge and turbulence and the fact that large sections run through private lands, getting close to the Montreal can be challenging. Geology is to blame for this inaccessibility — and for its beauty. The East and West forks of the Montreal rise from elevated granitic lakes approximately 4 miles apart. The West Fork rises from Island Lake and flows north through Gile Flowage to Hurley. The East Fork springs from Pine Lake east of U.S. Highway 51 and flows north, forming the Michigan-Wisconsin border from a point just west of the Underwood State Natural Area. The two forks meet north of U.S. Highway 2, giving rise to the Montreal River and continuing as the state border another dozen miles to Lake Superior.

The river slices north through the **Penokee Range** (also known as the Gogebic Range) that stretches 80 miles east from southern Ashland County into Upper Michigan. North of Hurley, the midsection of the Montreal cuts through dark volcanic basalt, and farther downstream, through sandstone conglomerate. All along the lower river, sheer cliffs and rock formations tell ancient, geologic stories from a time when the earth was much younger, more malleable, and a less friendly place.

In its last mile the river widens, the cliffs drop and disappear, and islands sprout in the slower current above the Superior Falls dam. Below the dam, dark igneous rock and stands of conifers and birch frame the 90-foot falls. From the base of the falls, the Montreal slides over ledges and around rocks, widening and worming around the sandbar at the river's mouth.

Secluded Superior Falls on the Montreal

No doubt the most popular way to get close to the Montreal is to undertake an auto tour of its waterfalls. Be warned: in some cases, "auto" tour is an overly optimistic misnomer. If you plan to reach every falls, consider a truck or four-wheel-drive tour. Leave the low-slung Mustang convertible in the driveway.

We loaded up on information from the visitor center on Highway 2 at the west edge of Hurley and set off, once more with Mike driving, me attempting to navigate, and Rumpus, our Lab, riding shotgun in the backseat. Considering the number of maps, brochures, and notes we'd accumulated, I knew that finding the falls would be easy.

We began upstream and worked our way north to Lake Superior. I pointed to our first destination, **Spring Camp Falls** (also called Montreal Falls), on the map and we headed southwest from Hurley on State Highway 77. At County Road C, we turned south and drove over the Gile Flowage causeway, with Rumpus calling our attention to the fishermen onshore and in boats spread across the water on both sides of the road. So far, so good.

Created by damming the West Fork in 1941, the 3,384-acre reservoir has a 26-mile shoreline marked by bays and rock outcrops. Anglers vie for walleye and small mouth bass, plus northern pike, muskellunge, and a variety of panfish. To sustain the fishery, the Wisconsin Department of Natural Resources has worked with Xcel Energy to moderate its seasonal drawdowns of the flowage and preserve the river's volume and shoreline habitat. The DNR has also educated boaters about the spiny water flea (bythotrephes cederstroemi). This invasive crustacean, no more than a half inch in length, likely migrated to the Great Lakes on European freighters. It competes with small fish for zooplankton, and many larger fish can't eat the flea because of its barbed, spiny tail. Boaters are urged to clean their boats and equipment before leaving the flowage and take other steps to prevent the spread of the flea.

While Spring Camp Falls is only 1.2 miles upstream, a glance at our directions showed that we would drive considerably more miles to reach it. At the end of the causeway, Mike set the trip odometer and measured 1.5 miles, at which point County Road C right angles east. Carefully following directions, we did not follow C but instead turned west onto a gravel road and drove 1 mile to East Branch Road. At East Branch Road, we headed south, proceeding for 2.6 miles, scanning the right shoulder for signs of an unnamed dirt road. (What would we do without trip odometers? Lots of arithmetic, I decided.) We found the two-wheel track and bumped along it for another mile, with Rumpus whining behind us: she knew we were heading for a park. At last we spotted a turnaround and small parking area, empty of other vehicles.

The path plunged into the woods, and at first all I could see were trees and Mike's back. But abruptly we arrived at the West Branch. Spring Camp Falls cascaded 20 feet in a gentle decline over basaltic rock. While Rumpus pulled Mike to the bank where she sniffed at the water, I photographed the falls and its isolated glen, wishing we could return in fall when it must be spectacular with red, gold, and evergreen trimmings.

We came up empty on our search for the next waterfall on our list. Several guidebooks noted **Gile Falls,** but their directions, leading us from Kokogan Street to Gile Falls Street in Gile, ended in defeat. Piles of felled trees blocked the trail when we finally located it, and a sign read, "Trail Closed." When we asked at the Hurley visitor center, we learned that this small falls is on private land and no longer accessible. Although some brochures describe an alternate trail to the falls, it's a moot point given the landowner's decision.

Our next destination, also on the West Fork, proved easier to find. **Kimball Falls** stars as the shining centerpiece of **Kimball Town Park.** From Hurley, Mike drove us west on Highway 2 approximately 3 miles from U.S. Highway 51 and turned south on Park Road. We continued 0.2 miles and then turned west on Town Park Drive, crossing a one-lane bridge to enter the park near the bottom of the10-foot falls.

I watched Rumpus pull Mike toward the rocks at the riverside before I walked back over the bridge to get a shot upstream. The falls were no more

Interstate Falls

than a layered, eight-foot drop, but the river swung around a very pleasant picnic area, complete with pavilion, drinking water, and pit toilets.

Encouraged by our quick success, we moved on to **Peterson Falls** and **Interstate Falls** on the East Fork. These falls are located just north of the beginning (or end) of Highway 51's journey through Wisconsin, Illinois, Kentucky, Tennessee, Mississippi, and Louisiana to (or from) Lake Pontchartrain at New Orleans. When you've satisfied your urge for river travel, there's always the option to explore Highway 51, where you can complete an Official Highway 51 Passport with stops at 15 Wisconsin destinations. For information, call (866) HWY-51-WI or visit www.ExploreHwy51.com.

Following Highway 2 west of Highway 51, we soon spotted the giant Ero Nasi Construction sign and turned right (north) onto a one-lane gravel road. The moment we slowed and hit the gravel, Rumpus perked up and began to whine for the park. I reached into the back seat to pet and calm her, but all I succeeded in accomplishing was to increase her excitement. She was standing now, her front paws on the armrest between Mike and me, her tongue in my hair. Thankfully the road soon came to a dead end, no more than a third mile from the highway. We parked in a lot that has room for maybe three cars and followed our now routine hike to the falls, Rumpus, as always, in the lead. This time we needed the insect repellent on the third-mile trail that ended at the top of Peterson Falls. It was an impressive sight: an iridescent torrent plummeted 25 feet into a clear, evergreen-fringed pool. Foam and spray billowed up from its base. Rumpus insisted that we scramble down to explore the area, and when we arrived, she plunged into the shallows as far as her lead would allow. Somehow, we all got wet. Interstate Falls is about a half mile downstream of Peterson Falls.

As we moved toward the Montreal's mouth, the falls grew bigger. The last two, Saxon and Superior, are among the state's highest and drop more than 75 feet over a basalt brink. Both also power hydro plants. At 90 feet, Superior Falls is the larger of the two, nearer the mouth, and easier to get to.

Saxon Falls lies ensconced in the Montreal gorge near a dam and powerhouse about 3 miles upstream from **Superior Falls.** Using the gazetteer, I issued loud directions to Mike in order to be heard over the canine comments from the backseat. We followed County Road B to Saxon Falls Road, proceeding north on Saxon Falls Road until we came to a sign proclaiming "Saxon Falls Hydro." We followed the gravel drive to the plant, but failed to see an easy trail to the river. We then followed the road upstream a short distance, but that did not pan out either. The sun was slanting westward and we wanted to see Superior Falls before dark, so, disappointed, we moved on.

Only later we realized that we should have looked more closely downstream of the hydro plant.

At least Superior Falls allowed us to end the day on a 90-foot high note. We returned to Highway 122, north of Highway 2 and Hurley, and followed the state road over the bridge across the Montreal into Michigan. We watched for the sign to the falls and took the second gravel road on the left. Soon, we were happily pulling into the power plant lot, where we parked and walked to the **Montreal River Scenic Overlook.** The contrast from the deep woods and cradled falls we'd been viewing all day to Lake Superior's broad, azure expanse momentarily stunned me. The sun's lengthening rays burnished the breakers as they rolled in. Only Rumpus appeared unaffected by the sight of the rolling, rhythmic surf.

She pulled Mike to a steep, roughly paved trail with a rope handrail strung along its left edge, and we began the descent. I held the rope with my left hand, my right cupped protectively about the camera swinging from its neck strap. We passed a lone woman plodding up the trail and moved to allow her to hug the rope side as she trudged upward.

The paving ended on Superior's rocky shore and we glanced around this world, so different from the cliff top. The plain of small boulders spread out around us, ending in a vast inland ocean ranging in tone from indigo to gray. To our left, the broad Montreal mouth hosted father-and-son anglers, each casting from atop a large rock. Within the river's cover, protected by a gravel bar, a family swam and played in the slightly warmer water of the Montreal.

We hiked upriver for a better view of Superior Falls as it thundered through a darkening, 150-foot-deep gorge. The roar echoed in the canyon, and we approached so close that the entire image no longer fit in my viewfinder. I lost myself in the tumult, as if standing before a bonfire, but, eventually, came out of my trance. Mike had already turned back toward the lake and the bluff trail, and reluctantly I followed, to return to our car, dinner, and day's end.

Later we learned that the steep trail from mouth to bluff top is part of the old **Flambeau Trail,** a portage through the Penokee-Gogebic Range southeast to Long Lake just north of Mercer. The Flambeau Trail began on water at La Pointe, Madeline Island, and then followed the Lake Superior shore to the Montreal. From Long Lake, Indians and later voyageurs followed this paddle-and-portage route to Lac du Flambeau settlements and the Mississippi River. They cached their canoes at Saxon Harbor, shouldered their packs, and followed the old portage trail from the east side of the Montreal's mouth inland. They climbed the rugged, steep-gorged range and finally reached the continental divide located at the north end of Long Lake. This "120-pause" portage had 120 rest stops and took anywhere from two and a half to seven full days to cross. Today, two Wisconsin Rustic Roads (6 and 100) follow sections of the Flambeau Trail southwest of Long Lake.

Following the end of the fur trade, the Penokee-Gogebic Range endured the lumber rush and then one of Wisconsin's several mining booms. But unlike the short-lived lumber era, mining continued here until well past the middle of the twentieth century. Hurley, the center of the action along the Wisconsin-Michigan border, roared in its early years with saloons, wealth, and wild abandon. You can still find vestiges of its past on **Silver Street** and in **Hurley's Heritage District,** where a "lower block" once sheltered gaming operations in the basements of legitimate establishments. Early each winter, the annual Red Light Rally welcomes 1,500 snowmobilers to town and includes a snowmobile parade down Silver Street. In contrast, Little Finland on Highway 2 preserves a different sort of heritage — that of Finnish immigrant miners; the attraction showcases a traditional homestead with fish-tail log construction.

Today, more kayakers than carousers probably visit Hurley. The town has become a mecca for outdoor enthusiasts year round. Spring through fall, experienced paddlers find plenty of cliffs, conifers, birch, and maple to admire in the Montreal canyons, when they have time to look up. Numerous stretches of Class II and, in higher water, Class III or IV rapids keep all eyes focused on the turbulent currents, rocks, and ledges. Once on the river, there's no turning back in the steep-walled chutes, unless you stop, or get stuck, on a gravel bar in low water.

Besides paddling, there are only a few public long views of the Montreal. In addition to short treks near the publicly accessible falls, the 15-foot **Rock Cut Falls** on the West Fork about 3 miles from Hurley is visible from the former railroad bridge on the **Iron Horse ATV and Snowmobile Trail.** In Hurley, an ATV/snowmobile trail also runs along the river for a few blocks. To the southwest, the **Pines and Mines Mountain Bike Trail** runs near the western shore of Gile Flowage, following the river south to the east edge of Island Lake. In Michigan, the **Montreal River Gorge Trail,** another section of the Pines and Mines Trail System, follows the river north of Highway 2 in Ironwood.

The only campsites on the Montreal River are actually in the river, specifically, on the islands of **Gile Flowage.** Gile County Park, located west of Hurley, offers related amenities — picnic tables, fireplaces, drinking water, toilets, playground, swimming beach, and a pavilion where you can play board games if rain rolls in. A boat launch provides the means to get your gear to the primitive campsites located on all the islands of the flowage.

If you like your camping more civilized, Saxon Harbor County Park, west of the mouth on Lake Superior, contains a small campground with electrical hook-ups and pump-out facilities. In addition, it features a picnic area with drinking water, fireplaces, shelter, and toilets, as well as a playground and swimming beach. A busy marina provides more than 50 boat slips with an adjacent restaurant and bar.

But if you long for a soft mattress and in-room cable, **Rippling River Lodge** off Highway 2 in Kimball offers riverside rooms year-round. It provides accommodations for groups of two to 16 people and is a short distance from the Iron Horse ATV and snowmobile trail. Phone: (800) 434-6208.

Whitecap Mountain Resort, on Weber Lake west of Hurley, presents another option for those interested in more active sports. Spring through fall, Whitecap Kayak provides trips and instruction, plus accommodations. In winter, Whitecap Mountain offers downhill skiing comparable to Colorado's slopes. Phone: (715) 561-2227. Website: www.whitecapkayak.com.

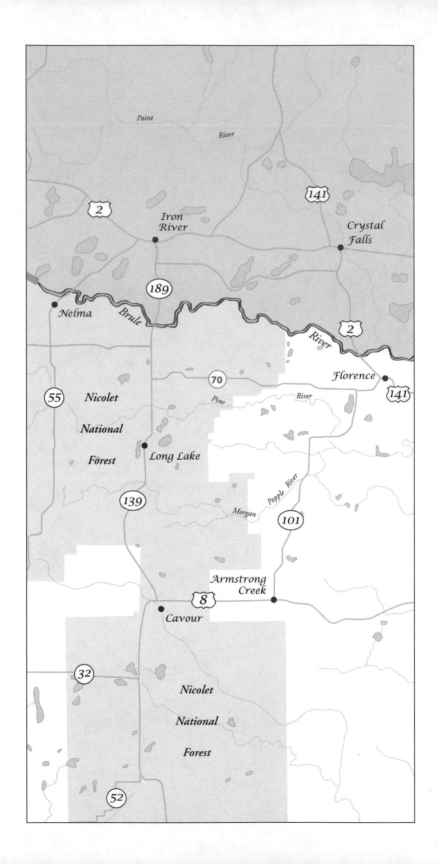

CHAPTER 5

Brule

This Brule launches from Brule Lake in Michigan's Ottawa National Forest, east of Lac Vieux Desert and Land O' Lakes. Sometimes called the "Border Brule," to differentiate it from the Bois Brule, this wilderness river's entire length forms part of the Wisconsin-Michigan border.

If, before I began researching this book, you had asked me about Wisconsin's **Treaty Tree,** I might have guessed that it could be found near Prairie du Chien or maybe at Keshena, both sites of treaty signings between Indians and early American soldiers. In fact, a sign now marks the position of this generally forgotten, long toppled tamarack at the headwaters of the Brule River.

The tamarack marked both a treaty signing and a point along the state's northern border. Captain Thomas Jefferson Cram, U.S. Corps of Topographical Engineers, came up the Menominee and Brule Rivers and set the Wisconsin-Michigan boundary in 1840. En route to the Brule headwaters, he counted 59 islands in the river and saw several Indian campgrounds. When he reached the headwaters and the north side of Brule Lake, Cram met an Ojibwe chief, who proclaimed that these hunting lands belonged to the tribe.

Beneath the tamarack, Cram inscribed a treaty on birch bark. He provided gifts to the Ojibwe chief and pledged that all future surveyors would also present gifts in order to continue passage beyond this point. Nearby, Cram set mile post zero, as the beginning of the overland portion of the Wisconsin-Michigan border, between Brule Lake and the Montreal River.

Seven years later, when William Austin Burt arrived at the treaty tree to revise and officially establish the state line, the local Ojibwe produced the birch bark treaty. Burt duly provided tobacco and other supplies for safe passage westward. He also inscribed on the tamarack the words: "Wm. A. Burt; June 2, 1847; State Boundary."

Though the historic tree is gone, you can hike to a sign at its old base and to a survey marker on the state border. From Florence, drive west on State Highway 70 to State Highway 55. Turn north on Highway 55 and cross into Michigan, where Highway 55 becomes Michigan State Highway 73. Drive 7.5 miles to Hagerman Lake Road. Turn west and proceed 3 miles to West Brule Lake Road. Continue west for 2 miles; then turn south and follow West Brule Lake Road another 2 miles to the parking area. Look for signs to Brule Lake Historical Site. The third mile, wooded path to the Treaty Tree sign begins at the edge of the parking area.

From Brule Lake the river runs 47 miles to its meeting with Michigan's Michigamme. Together these two northern rivers form the beginning of the mighty Menominee. The Brule-Menominee waterway flows through expansive forests and wetlands open to recreational use. The Brule flows between Wisconsin's Nicolet-Chequamegon National Forest and Michigan's Ottawa National Forest. The upper Menominee forms the eastern edge of Spread Eagle Barrens State Natural area and runs through many acres of We Energies holdings open to fishing, paddling, hiking, and camping.

Generally, the Brule is more isolated, though you can still explore it both on foot and by canoe. If you paddle the Brule River, you are guaranteed to

The Brule leaves Brule Lake

see wildlife. The upper river, from the Brule River Campground to State Highway 139, is also flat, so you have the opportunity to watch for great blue herons, eagles, beaver, otter, bear, and deer without worrying about the next sharp bend or rapids. With few exceptions, the lands enveloping the Brule are publicly owned, so there are few cabins, piers, or other developments to interrupt your wilderness views. The banks are largely forested with stands of pine, cedar, maple, and elm, interspersed with marshlands.

From Highway 139 to its confluence with the Michigamme, the Brule features a number of rapids, rock gardens, and bridges to enliven your journey. Be alert when the water is high for sufficient clearance underneath the bridge at Fire Road 2446, and be aware that portages are available (for instance, on the Michigan side around Two-Foot Falls, east of Pentoga).

In summer, **Ski Brule** rents rafts, tubes, and canoes for trips on the Brule River, and offers horseback rides and a sporting clays course. Ski Brule is located south of Iron River, off Michigan Highway 189 (Wisconsin Highway 139). Phone: (800) 362-7873. Website: www.skibrule.com.

We ventured away from the immediate river bank to explore the river's environs on foot. On the Wisconsin side, **Brule River Cliffs State Natural Area** offers a glimpse of rare habitat on north-facing, shaded dolomite outcrops rising more than 30 feet above the river. A wide variety of ferns, including the rare green spleenwort and Braun's holly fern, make a comfortable home in the cold, wet region.

To get there from Florence, drive west on Highway 70 to Fire Road 2152 (Daumitz Road). Go north 2.3 miles to a T-intersection, where Fire Road 2152 jogs west following Wisconsin Creek Road for 1 mile before resuming its northward course. Follow Forest Service signs to the Brule River. Stop at the boat landing for a glimpse of the river, then backtrack to walk east about three quarters of a mile toward the west edge of the cliffs, hiking through old farm fields and past an abandoned, roofless log enclosure, likely a former animal pen. There is no clear trail and the river is invisible through the dense trees. But you won't get lost if you follow the edge of the field and the sound of rippling water. Watch for the varied ferns at your feet.

Also west of Florence, **Whisker Lake Wilderness** lies between the Brule to the north and Highway 70 to the south, with Fire Road 2150 forming its western boundary. This designated federal wilderness area is accessible primarily by foot, and trails meander through thick woods, over ridges, and around several small lakes, including Whisker, Riley, and Camp Thirteen. To learn more, call the U.S. Forest Service in Eagle River at (715) 479-2827.

Backcountry camping is available in Whisker Lake Wilderness, but the Brule River area has limited established campgrounds. Paddlers can stop at

View from the boat landing at Brule River Cliffs State Natural Area

primitive canoe campsites, and the Nicolet-Chequamegon National Forest does provide one riverside campground. Nestled in a balsam fir and red pine grove, the **Brule River Campground** contains 11 sites and offers canoe access, drinking water, pit toilets, fire rings, and peaceful solace, despite easy access from State Highway 55 north of Nelma.

Determined to see the mouth of the Brule, Mike and I drove — not quite in circles — through the back roads northeast of Florence. After a few wrong turns, we located the canoe landing near the Brule's juncture with the Michigamme. A sign at the landing announced "reduced maintenance" at the landing due to low usage. However, it did provide picnic tables, grills, and toilets.

The sight was worth the search. Golden light from the setting sun glinted off the wide and quiet Brule, and the **Michigamme River Falls Dam** was visible on the left. Deer and raccoon tracks marked the sandy bank. Our impatient search ended in a place of great patience and serenity.

From the intersection of Highway 70 and U.S. Highway 2/141 in Florence, drive 2.9 miles east on Highway 2/141. Turn north (left) at Cross Cut Road and drive 0.7 miles to an unmarked road (Montgomery Lake Road).

Turn right on Montgomery Lake Road and proceed 0.4 miles to Camels Clearing Road. Turn left on Camels Clearing Road and drive north for 1.6 miles to a Y intersection where there are three black mailboxes (at least they were black in 2006). Bear left and drive 0.9 miles to the canoe landing. If, instead of bearing left, you drive right, you are on Florence Town Road I. The Michigamme dam is also accessible in Michigan; follow Swanson Road west from State Highway 95.

During our northeastern Wisconsin trip, we stayed on **Lost Lake** in the Nicolet National Forest west of Florence. Located east of Highway 70/139 on Fire Road 2156 (Chipmunk Rapids Road) south of Tipler, Lost Lake deserves more attention than it receives.

In addition to more than a dozen primitive campsites, eight cabins stand clean, neat, and unchanged since the Civilian Conservation Corps constructed them in 1938. We used the available wheeled cart to transport our sleeping bags and other gear down a short trail to our cabin above the lake. It was spacious for the three of us; Mike, Rumpus, and I each had our own set of bunk beds, with springy steel springs and thin mattresses. At the end of each set of bunks, a footlocker, marked "YCC" (Youth Conservation Corps) provided storage. A picnic table and two separate wooden benches completed the furnishings. On the table, a notebook and pencil invited comments from visitors, and these ranged from weather reports to accounts of hikes, fishing excursions, and animal sightings.

Friendly hosts Mary and Marty Taps welcomed our questions and explained the history of the campground. Due to U.S. Forest Service funding and maintenance issues, a recreation hall, filled with 70 years of history, was closed to visitors.

The campground offers a picnic area, swimming beach, and boat landing; only non-motorized boats are permitted on the 86-acre lake, which is stocked with smallmouth bass, as well as brown and rainbow trout. A trail circles the lake and connects to the **Lauterman National Recreation Trail** system and **Chipmunk Rapids Trail** on the Pine River, a tributary of the Menominee. Near the Lost Lake parking area, the **Assessor's Trail** runs for a mile through an impressive stand of 150-year-old hemlock and pine. An easy hike, this trail offers benches at the half-way point and interpretative signage along the way. Wherever you wander in the Nicolet National Forest, you are never far from isolated lakes, fast-running rivers, and alert wildlife.

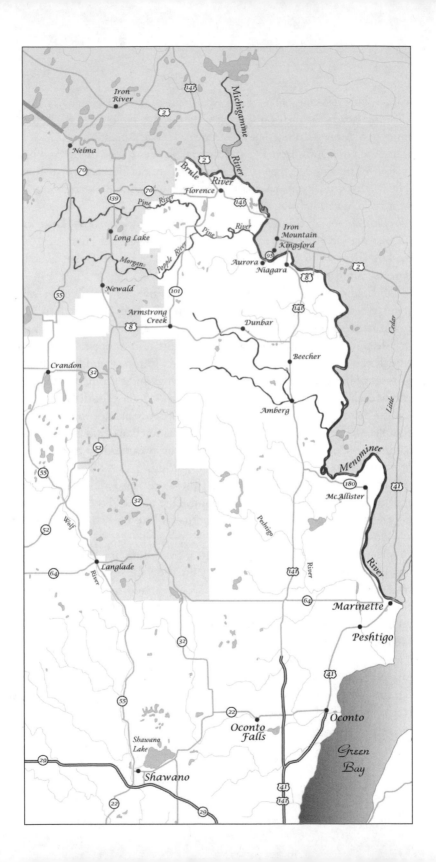

CHAPTER 6

Menominee

Astalwart workhorse of a river, the Menominee drains 4,070 square miles in northern Wisconsin and Upper Michigan and defines a long section of Wisconsin's northeast boundary. It also hosts 10 hydroelectric plants and several paper mills along its 118-mile journey from the confluence of the Brule and Michigamme to its mouth at Lake Michigan between the twin ports of Marinette, Wisconsin, and Menominee, Michigan.

The upper Menominee figures prominently in the **Great Wisconsin Birding and Nature Trail,** a highway-based route that highlights several hundred great birding spots. The Lake Superior Northwoods Region of the trail encompasses the **Spread Eagle Barrens State Natural Area,** which shelters upland sandpipers, northern harrier, and warbling vireo. Also keep an eye out for Nashville, chestnut-sided, pine, and mourning warblers throughout the grassland and scattered stands of pine, scrub oak, and aspen.

The Menominee forms the eastern boundary of Spread Eagle Barrens, and the lower Pine River runs through it. Several access routes lead to parking areas on the edge of the barrens. From Florence, drive east 2 miles on U.S. Highway 2/141 to Condroski Road. Turn south on Condroski, following it to Old Highway 69. Turn east on Old Highway 69 and drive to Lake Anna Road. Follow Lake Anna Road south for 0.8 miles to Overlook Road. Continue south on Overlook Road for 1 mile to the parking area. Or, approximately 7 miles east of Florence, turn south on West Ellwood Lake Road and follow it 1.2 miles to the parking area. To reach the south edge of the barrens, drive south from Florence on County Road N for 8 miles to Roach Fire Lane Road. Follow Roach Fire Lane Road 2.9 miles to a parking area on the left. Black bears, fishers, badgers, coyotes, red fox, and deer also live in the barrens.

Look for the same species in the Menominee River State Natural Resources Area to the south and add gray wolves — a.k.a. timber wolves —

Wisconsin Wild Rivers Act

Governor Warren Knowles signed **Wisconsin's Wild Rivers Program** into law in 1965, designating the Pike River in Marinette County and the Pine and Popple in Florence and Forest counties as Wisconsin Wild Rivers. The goal of the program is to maintain free-flowing rivers and preserve scenic and habitat values. Wisconsin was the first state in the nation to enact legislation protecting its wild rivers.

to your list of creatures to watch for if you explore the **Pine-Popple State Wild Rivers Area.** These two Menominee tributaries afford many outdoor opportunities. The lower river is marked with Marinette County parks, waysides, and, nearing the mouth, city parklands. All of these areas were created with you — and your children and grandchildren — in mind.

Expert paddlers also sometimes seek out the Pine River tributary of the Menominee, which offers several falls and rapids — and portage opportunities — above LaSalle Falls. Below the falls, even beginners can enjoy a wild river experience, and tubing the section from Oxbow Landing to Ellwood Lake Landing is a growing attraction.

You can also hike t0 the 20-foot **LaSalle Falls,** located above the flowage and dam. From Florence, drive 9 miles south on County Road N to County Road U. Continue south on County Road U and proceed about a third mile to County Road C. Turn west (right) on County Road C and drive 1.9 miles to LaSalle Falls Road. Turn north (right) and drive a short distance to a fork in the road. Bear left at the fork. The distance from County Road C to a parking area on the right is 2.6 miles.

A trail, about a mile in length, leads to the top of LaSalle Falls. A Wild and Scenic River Corridor sign at the parking area shows a map of the trail, which also leads to a canoe portage around the falls.

While the Menominee used to be viewed as unwelcoming to paddlers, We Energies, canoeing organizations, and local outfitters have worked with the National Park Service to improve the situation. The **Menominee River Watershed Canoe Trail** comprises over 200 river miles along the Menominee, Brule, Michigamme, Paint, and Pine Rivers. You can pick up maps indicating parking areas, boat landings, dams, portages, and primitive campsites for a small fee from the Wild Rivers Interpretive Center, at the intersection of U.S. Highway 2/141 and State Highway 70/101 in Florence. Phone: (888) 889-0049. Website: www.florencewisconsin.com.

The Brule meets the Michigamme

The campgrounds all have pit toilets; six have drinking water. We Energies owns 40,000 acres in Wisconsin and Michigan along the Brule, Paint, Michigamme, and Menominee Rivers. The utility has developed 15 primitive campgrounds with a total of 89 campsites along the four rivers. Three of these campgrounds are in Wisconsin: one above the White Rapids Dam on the Menominee east of Amberg, and two on both sides of the Pine River Dam at the end of the flowage west of Kingsford.

West of the Menominee River, **Chipmunk Rapids Campground** lies on the south bank of the Pine River in the Nicolet National Forest immediately downriver from the Class I-II rapids. A popular canoeing destination, the Pine features several additional rapids and falls before flowing into the Menominee southeast of Florence. Experts can run Meyers Falls and Bull Falls, but everyone must portage around LaSalle Falls.

Anglers also head to the Pine (as well as the Popple, Pemebonwon, and Brule) to fish for trout. And Fisher Creek, which runs into the Brule just above its confluence with the Michigamme, is well-stocked and a popular spot for children to learn to fish for trout.

Unless the weather is uncooperative, most visitors add hiking to their itinerary. **Chipmunk Rapids Campground** provides access to a 3.3-mile loop trail that edges the river and connects to the Assessor's Interpretive Trail (see Brule Chapter 5). Another nearby path, **Ridge Trail,** leads to an overlook of the Pine River north of Lost Lake.

If you're set on paddling, Northwoods Wilderness Outfitters, in Iron Mountain, Michigan, can prep you for a trip down the Brule, Menominee, Pine, or Michigamme rivers, whether you have little or lots of experience. The firm rents a cabin, canoes, and kayaks; offers a shuttle service to get you on the river and back to your vehicle at trip's end; and guides fishing, scenic, and adventure trips. Fishing trips are geared to muskie, walleye, bass, and trout. Women-only trips generally last three or four hours. A couple's getaway package includes two nights at the cabin. And one easy, two-hour trip features dinner at The Blind Duck restaurant in Kingsford, Michigan. Northwoods Wilderness Outfitters sells a full line of paddling, camping, hunting, fishing, and fly-fishing accessories, plus snowshoes, topo maps, archery, ski-joring, and sled dog equipment. This is also a spot to pick up a Menominee River Watershed Canoe Trail map, as well as river, fishing, and hunting reports. To learn more, call (800) 530-8859 or visit www. northwoodsoutfitters.com.

The **Blind Duck** restaurant is situated on Cowboy Lake, adjacent to the Menominee River and near the Ford Airport north of Kingsford. The popular lunch and dinner spot serves American, Mexican, and Italian fare. Phone: (906) 774-0037.

A few miles north, on the east bank of the river at the Highway 2/141 Bridge, **Edgewater Log Cabin Resort** offers 60-year-old log cabins renovated for twenty-first-century travelers, with cable TV, laundry facilities, and boat slips. In addition to Wisconsin travel attractions, the folks at Edgewater can clue you in on Michigan waterfalls, trails, boating, and fishing opportunities. For more information, phone (800) 236-6244 or visit www. edgewaterresort.com.

Head downriver to Niagara for excellent views of the Menominee along Highway 141. Parkland and flower gardens line the highway. Benches offer a marvelous view of the dark bluffs towering above the Michigan side of the river, and the Riverside Trail System is open to hikers, bikers, and skiers. The trailhead is off Highway 141 on Washington Avenue.

Straddling the Menominee in Niagara, the former Stora Enso North America plant and its **Little Quinnesec Falls Hydro-Electric Project** loom above the river. East of the plant, turn north from Highway 141 onto

Clark Street, which almost immediately turns into Will Street. A small park and boat landing is on your left, offering a view of the plant and toilets, as well as river access. Purchaased in 2008 by NewPage Corporation, Stora Enso once produced coated printing paper from this plant and owned a total parcel of 800 acres in Michigan and 400 acres on the Wisconsin side of the river.

To me, the most beautiful section of the upper Menominee runs through Piers Gorge, where flat docks of basaltic rock extend into the river. A hiking trail runs along the river for 1.5 miles, providing access to Misicot Falls and other rapids. Access is from the Michigan side of the river. Drive across the border on U.S. Highway 8 east of Niagara. Watch for the Piers Gorge Scenic Area sign on the left. Turn west onto Piers Gorge Road. Drive to a fork in the road. Take the left fork and at the second fork, bear right. Proceed to the parking area and a well-marked trailhead. While also approachable by whitewater rafters and expert paddlers, this Class IV to V whitewater section is more broadly — not to mention safely — viewed from the trail. In fact, the first half mile leading to the eight-foot drop of Misicot Falls is wheelchair accessible. Beyond Misicot, the trail turns rugged and eventually climbs to an outcrop, providing another panorama of the river. An island upstream marks Sand Portage Falls, with the falls tumbling five feet along the north side of the island. The trail ends with a loop to the north of the river, or you can turn around and retrace your steps for a quicker return march.

What's so special about Piers Gorge? Maybe it's the way the rock plateaus enable you to climb close to the roaring waters, or the way the river roars through rocky chutes. There's something about the blending of river and rock that enhances both. They stand in sharp contrast, and even I can read the geology here.

The upper Menominee, along with the Brule, flows through the heart of the northern Wisconsin/Michigan iron region, mined heavily from 1880 into the Great Depression. Complex, folded layers of volcanic rocks with slate and greywacke pressed between two iron formations lie atop layers of dolomite and quartzite. You can see the dark volcanic rocks here and you can walk on the dolomite layer to the west in the Brule River Cliffs State Natural Area.

J. C. Morse first filed an iron ore mining claim on the Michigan side of the Menominee in 1873. Three years later, the Menominee Mining Company organized, and the Chicago Northwestern Railroad began construction on the Menominee River Railway, extending the line to the

Florence Vulcan Mine two years before mining began there in 1879. The original Vulcan Mine had opened 9 miles east of Iron Mountain, Michigan, in 1870. Peak year for the Florence operation was 1920, and the Vulcan finally closed in 1945 at the end of World War II.

The Michigan Vulcan Mine, now called **Iron Mountain Iron Mine,** remains open to visitors. From June 1 to October 15, you can don a hard-hat and yellow slicker and board a mine train to view the underground tunnels, stopes, and timbering. The attraction is located off Highway 2 in Vulcan. Phone: (906) 563-8077; in the off-season: (906) 774-7914. Website: www.ironmountainironmine.com.

Downstream, the Menominee flows largely through sand and gravel glacial outwash over dolomite. Falls, dams, and islands punctuate the swift current; and you can see many of these features on foot, as well as by boat.

The highest in Marinette County, Long Slide Falls is on the North Branch of the Pemebonwon River, another Menominee tributary. From Niagara, drive south on Highway 141. Approximately 4.5 miles north of Pembine, turn east on Morgan Park Road. Follow Morgan Park Road 1.6 miles to the entrance drive to the parking area. A short trail leads to the top of the 50-foot falls.

Twelve Foot Falls Park provides a dozen campsites on the North Branch of the Pike River, which enters the Menominee northeast of Wausaukee. Follow U.S. Highway 8 west of Highway 141. Turn south on Lily Lake Road and then west on Twin Lake Road to Twelve Foot Falls Road; follow the signs to the park. A brief hike takes you to both Twelve Foot Falls and Eight Foot Falls. About 1 mile north of the park, Eighteen Foot Falls is located down a narrow, unpaved road off Twelve Foot Falls Road. A short, rugged trail leads from the parking area to Eighteen Foot Falls.

East of Pembine, you can find **Quiver Falls** on the Menominee, off Highway 141 east of Pembine. Follow County Road R (Kremlin Road) to Pemene Dam Road and drive approximately a half mile to the Quiver Falls Dam parking area. A path leads to an overlook of the falls and remnants of an old dam.

Roughly a mile downstream, the half-mile **Pemene Falls Hiking Trail** leads to an overlook of these Menominee falls, with options to continue along a 0.8-mile loop, follow a short side trail to a riverside campsite, or explore the entire 1.9-mile oval path. The falls drops 10 feet between cement remnants of an old dam. The trail winds partly along old logging roads, through large pine stands with some rocky outcrops. Generally an easy hike, this trail nevertheless contains several steep and rocky sections. To reach the parking area, from Highway 141 south of Pembine, turn east on County Road Z and proceed 10.7 miles to Verhayen Road. Turn north on Verhayen, which quickly becomes a dirt track entering the Menominee River State Natural Area, following it to the parking area.

For a view of **Pemene Falls** from the east side of the river, follow County Road Z across the bridge into Michigan and take the first left to the north on State Road W2, a gravel road. Drive 0.6 miles to the Gerald Welling Access Site, which offers a view of the falls and old dam. Welling was a Michigan conservation officer who died in the line of duty in 1972. This site, which is below the falls, has a grill and toilets. To get to the top of the falls, continue on State Road W2 a short distance to the Pemene Falls sign and parking area. A steep trail and a stairway both lead to the falls.

Between Quiver Falls and Pemene Falls, the **Menominee River State Natural Resources Area** offers additional primitive campsites, including two on the river shore and on state-owned islands, where the maximum stay is one night. These sites provide a cleared space to pitch a tent and usually have a fire ring. Trash must be packed out.

The **Four Seasons Resort** pampers guests on Miscauno Island located south of County Road Z in the Menominee at the mouth of Miscauno Creek. The resort features cottages, 55 suites, a dining room, swimming pool, sauna, whirlpool, and massage therapist. The resort's Island Golf Course offers multiple views of the Menominee River. The original Miscauno Inn opened in 1905, connected to the mainland by a branch of the Wisconsin and Michigan Railroad. Renamed the Four Seasons Club in 1920, it burned to the ground three years later. In 1925, a new club was built around the original fireplace. For many years the club was owned by John Ross, and then by his son Walter until 1976. Contrary to rumor, while the club hosted many famous people, Al Capone was not one of them, but the U.S. Treasury Department did take over the club in 1990 from a group of owners who were charged with fraud and racketeering. The current owners purchased the club from the Treasury in 2002. Phone: (715) 324-5244 or (877) 324-5244. Website: www.thefourseasonsclub.com.

Dave's Falls County Park is almost as easy to find as the Four Seasons; certainly it's easier to discover than Pemene or Quiver falls. It's located on Highway 141, on the west side of the highway less than a mile south of Amberg. Named for a young lumberman who died while breaking up a log-jam, the park preserves an area of woodland and outcrops along a sweep of the Pike River including the 30-foot Dave's Falls and another 15-foot drop upstream. The walk from the parking area to the falls involves a short stairs and a moderately steep upward slope. The park features picnic tables, toilets, drinking water, fireplaces, and a playground, and provides river access to anglers in search of trout.

The easiest access to Bull Falls, downstream from Dave's Falls, is from County Road K. Drive east on County Road K from Highway 141 for 0.3 miles, and pull to the side of the road at the power lines. Walk north down a slope to the river and the 15-foot cascade. Marinette County's parks and waterfalls seem to go on forever, but a long weekend usually provides enough time to explore most of them.

South of Wausaukee, turn east off Highway 141 to follow State Highway 180 generally along the Menominee all the way to Marinette.

Roughly 6 miles to the east, Bear Point Boat Landing presents another access to this remote river. Walk to the bank and look for animal tracks or mussel shells left by lunching raccoons.

To venture deeper into this isolated area, follow County Road JJ east off Highway 180 to Caylor Road. Turn north on Caylor Road and then east at the quarry to reach Grand Rapids Road. Follow Grand Rapids Road to the dam and flowage where stumps stand sentinel over the secluded lagoon. If

The circle of life at the Grand Rapids flowage

no other people are around — and chances are, your group is alone — ask everyone to remain quiet for a few minutes. Walk to the water's edge and breathe deep. Sometimes, in the stillness, you can almost absorb nature's wildness.

Menominee River Park's 65 acres extend along the east bank 13 miles north of Marinette. Follow Highway 180 north to County Road X, turning east on County Road X to Park Place Drive. A canoe campsite and boat landing awaits paddlers at the north end of the park, which also offers picnic facilities, pit toilets, and drinking water. Anglers take advantage of the boat landing and try their skill along the riverbank. Children head for the playground and run across the footbridge over a small stream. Families make themselves at home around the fireplaces and picnic tables. And everyone heads for the shelter if raindrops threaten.

Crystal Springs Wayside Park at Wickham Road and **Twin Island Wayside** offers other stopping points along Highway 180. Twin Island provides a picnic table plus access to the stony, reed-lined banks of the broad, island-studded lower Menominee.

Menominee Indians occupied regions along the lower river, along with Ojibwe groups, when explorers and fur traders visited beginning in 1670. The first white settler known in the region, Stanislaus Chappu (also

View from Twin Island Wayside

"Chappee"), built a trading post on the west side of the Menominee's mouth in 1794 and operated it for 30 years, until forced out by William Farnsworth, who had established a post nearby in 1822. Farnsworth's Native American, common-law wife, Marinette, eventually took over operation of the post, while her husband helped establish a sawmill, which opened in 1832.

The northern lumber boom was long and loud in Marinette, one of Wisconsin's largest cities in 1900. Initially, lumber companies targeted the area's vast pine forests, since pine could be floated downriver with relative ease. By the end of the nineteenth century, the pine was largely gone. Lumbermen next felled the region's hardwoods, transporting the logs on the railroads built to service the mining industry.

To see a miniature replica logging camp and learn more about "Queen Marinette," visit the **Marinette County Historical Society Logging Museum** on Stephenson Island near the mouth of the Menominee. Open varying hours, Tuesday through Sunday, from Memorial Day through Labor Day. Phone: (715) 732-0831. When we visited, we saw ducks on the river and crawfish shells sprinkled on the lawn, possibly the litter left from a raccoon's lunch. Be sure to take the pedestrian bridge back to the Wisconsin Welcome Center, where you can pick up more information on the history and culture of the lower Menominee.

Marinette offers birders excellent viewing opportunities for many species of ducks, swans, hawks, plovers, sandpipers, gulls, terns, woodpeckers, flycatchers, warblers, and more. The paved Menekaunee Walkway runs south from the river along Green Bay, offering glimpses into the lives of cormorants and shorebirds, not to mention bank swallows, which nest in the large piles of sand near the mouth. Finally, the half-mile **City of Marinette Nature Walk** pokes like a periscope into the environs of a variety of marsh birds.

On the Michigan side, check out the Chappee Rapids Learning Center on River Road about 5.5 miles north of Menominee for bluebirds, bald eagles, Cooper's hawks, osprey, and warblers during migration periods. In Menominee, Tourist Park on Harbor Drive east of First Street is a hangout for migrating shorebirds. Follow Harbor Drive to Lighthouse Pier Walkway, where you might spot gulls, terns, grebes, and loons.

No doubt the biggest fish story on the Menominee is that of the sturgeon. Though the sturgeon population on the river is among the highest in the Lake Michigan basin, so many have been caught in recent years that in 2006, Wisconsin and Michigan agreed on new, stiffer rules. The two states agreed to cut the sturgeon fishing season in half, basically to the month of September, rather than September and October. And they enacted a catch-

View from Menominee River Park

and-release-only policy for sturgeon fishing below the Hattie Street/
Menominee Dam in the twin cities of Marinette, Wisconsin, and
Menominee, Michigan. Finally, fishermen intending to keep a sturgeon must
now pay for a tag — $20 for a resident or $50 for a non-resident — and register the catch.

If you'd like someone else to catch and prepare your meal, both
Marinette and Menominee offer water's edge dining and lodging options.
The Landing, 450 First Street, Menominee, mixes great steaks and seafood
with big-windowed views of the harbor and lighthouse. Phone (906) 863-
8034. On Green Bay, **Schloegel's Bayview Restaurant,** 2720 10th Street
at Highway 141, Menominee, is known for its Swedish pancakes with lin-
gonberries, in-house bakery goodies, and local whitefish. Phone: (906) 863-
7888. Across the river, the **Best Western Riverfront Inn,** 1821 Riverside
Avenue, Marinette, offers 120 rooms. Ask for one of the 60 rooms facing the
Menominee River. Phone: (715) 732-0800.

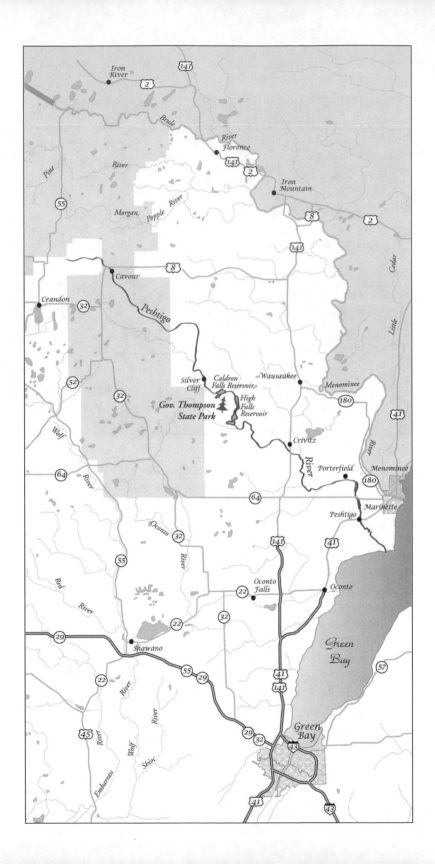

CHAPTER 7
Peshtigo

≈≈≈

The "Pesh" is a rafter's river, a kayaker's delight. But it's also a muskie haven, a historic waterway, and a prominent producer of electric power. Along with the Menominee, Oconto, and Fox Rivers, the Peshtigo drains Wisconsin's northern highland, as well as the sandstone lowland of its central plain. Slow and easy at its beginning and end, the river's midsection drops sharply and provides power at five hydroelectric dams.

Rising in Forest County, the South, Middle, and West Branches meet to form the Peshtigo River near Crandon. While the West and Middle Branches rise in the middle of marshland, you can see the more precise

Clouds reflected in Peshtigo Lake

source of the South Branch at Peshtigo Lake from the boat landing east of State Highway 32/55, just north of Crandon.

Within the **Nicolet National Forest**, the upper Peshtigo meanders slow and shallow through sandy marshland and mixed forests. Fallen trees lay across the current, obstructing paddlers and providing fish habitat.

Half a dozen miles south of Cavour, the current picks up. The river roils with rapids, ledges, and waterfalls. Over thousands of years, floods of glacial meltwater, grit, and gravel flowed here, plowing the river's channel through sandstone to granite and other hard igneous bedrocks.

Below the CCC Bridge and Landing north of Fire Road 2131, paddlers come to take on several Class I and Class II rapids. The longest of these is Preserve Rapids, containing half a dozen pitches, many interspersed by quiet pools. Rapids gradually intensify, with Michigan Rapids appearing below the mouth of Armstrong Creek. Paddlers often take out on the right and follow the trail to scout the upper pitch of this escapade or portage around it.

Portages aside, this general area of Nicolet National Forest offers several trails for landlubbers who want to get close to the river. The 2-mile **Michigan Rapids Hiking Trail** is fairly challenging, covering rocky, uneven ground. But the lasso-shaped trail, with a long, narrow loop at its end, offers views of Michigan Rapids, islands, rock formations, and the mouth of Armstrong Creek. Be alert for wet areas in the spring and poison ivy at the far end. To get to the trailhead from the **Peshtigo River Trail,** continue east on Fire Road 2131 for about 7.5 miles (12 miles from Laona) to Fire Road 2134. Turn right on Fire Road 2134 and drive south a half mile. Immediately beyond the Burnt Bridge crossing of the Peshtigo, watch the left side of the road for the trailhead and a parking area for three vehicles.

Hiking trails abound in Marinette County, and its 231,000-acre forest also contains numerous hunter trails, miles of ATV and snowmobile trails, and three hiking trails. One of these swings close to the river near Taylor Rapids and Strong Falls. The **Peshtigo River Walking Trail** runs 8.75 miles through the forest south of the river. To get there from U.S. Highway 141, turn west on Benson Lake Road north of Wausaukee at Amberg. Travel west on Benson Lake Road, cross County Road I (Parkway Road) and continue to Swede John Road. Turn southeast on Swede John Road and look for Fire Road 1512 on the right. Turn right to reach the trail.

Soon after the river enters Marinette County, the whole family can explore **Goodman County Park.** Thanks to the Depression-era efforts of the Civilian Conservation Corps (CCC), this park provides some of the best campsites on the upper river. It contains 15 sites, as well as the historic caretaker's cabin, which accommodates up to eight people. You can also rent a large and a small shelter at the river's edge.

A plank walkway and bridge span the river, providing a clear view of Strong Falls and, in low water conditions, a look at several potholes carved into granite rocks planted in the riverbed. In addition to the rocks, mini-islands project out of the river. Tall red pines tower over the park, and in fall the understory burns with color. Note: The day-use fee for access to all Marinette County parks is $3. To drive to the park, head west from Pembine on U.S. Highway 8 and drive to County Road I (Parkway Road). Turn south (left) on Parkway and drive to Goodman Park Road. Follow it to the park.

South of the park, pull off the Goodman Park Road at the sign marking the **Marinette County Beech Forest,** a Wisconsin State Natural Area, to admire the woods dominated by sugar maple, yellow birch, and hemlock, as well as beech.

Not far downstream, **McClintock County Park** offers several excellent picnic spots, as well as 10 campsites and three footbridges that take you over the rock-strewn river to two islands and the west bank. Walking from the parking area, you descend a CCC stairway to the floodplain. The first bridge you set foot on climbs 40 feet above the river and inclines sharply upward.

A bridge at Goodman Park

Strong Falls, Goodman Park

Beneath you, the river ripples around hundreds of random rocks, scattered like seed from a giant hand. Both islands hold grills and picnic tables, and the second also has a shelter. The 320-acre park is located off Parkway Road about 15 miles north of County X.

Downstream, one of the Peshtigo's most notable sections, **Roaring Rapids**, attracts serious paddlers from around the world. It stretches approximately 4 miles and encompasses rapids, drops, and Five Foot Falls. Expert paddlers put in near the mouth of Otter Creek at Farm Dam Landing, off Farm Dam Road and County Road C, and they generally take out at Boat Landing 12, about 0.67 miles downstream of the County Road C Bridge.

Kosir's Rapids Rafts offers rentals and owns the private landing just south of the bridge. The company also offers rafting trips on the Piers Gorge section of the Menominee River and has a large fleet of funyaks (one-person, easily maneuverable inflatable boats). You can purchase a video of your river trip and stay in the campground or a riverfront log cabin. To get there, drive north from Crivitz on County Road A to County Road C. Turn west (left) on County Road C and follow it 10 miles to Kosir's. Phone: (715) 757-3431. Website: www.kosirs.com.

> **Two other outfitters offer tubing, rafting, canoeing, and kayaking trips on the Upper Peshtigo:**
>
> - **Thornton's Whitewater Rafting Resort and Campground** leads 5-mile, guided raft trips on the Peshtigo. Funyaks and trip videos are also available, not to mention camping, cottages, mountain bike rentals, and two paintball courses. Thornton's is located on Parkway Road, 5 miles north of County Road X. Phone: (715) 757-3311. Website: www.thorntonsresort.com.
> - **Wildman Whitewater Ranch** features rafting trips, sea kayaking trips, tubing, ATV and snowmobile tours, horseback riding and a high ropes challenge course, plus a golf course at the Menominee River and blues entertainment on summer Saturday evenings. This Western-themed resort also offers campsites on the river, along with a lodge and cabin accommodations. Phone: (888) 813-8524 or (715) 757-3311-2938. Website: www.wild manranch.com.

Caldron Falls and High Falls flowages feature lake-like paddling, with many bays and channels waiting to be explored. Powerboaters and jet skiers also use these flowages, and Caldron Falls is a Class A muskellunge fishery, where anglers also catch large and smallmouth bass, walleye, rock bass, yellow perch, black crappie, bluegill, and pumpkinseed. High Falls Flowage features similar species, though less muskie and walleye. Anglers also head for the 5-mile stretch downstream of Johnson Falls Dam, a designated trout fishery, where northern pike, walleye, and smallmouth bass are found.

Thunder River Rearing Station is open to the public from 8:00 a.m. to 3:30 p.m. daily during the summer. The station rears brown trout in the spring and summer, and Coho salmon in the fall and winter. Call ahead to schedule a tour, at (715) 757-3541. Rest rooms and picnic area available. Drive to the rearing station from Crivitz, following County Road W west to Caldron Falls Road. Turn north on Caldron Falls Road and proceed to Hatchery Road. Turn west (left) and follow Hatchery Road to the station.

The popular flowages, of course, owe their existence to dams on the Peshtigo. **High Falls Dam,** the first on the river, was completed in 1911 to generate power for northeast Wisconsin. Johnson Falls Dam began operating in 1924, and Caldron Falls Dam began producing electricity a year later. The Potato Rapids Dam began operation in the late 1950s.

Following the Federal Energy Regulatory Commission's 1998 relicensing of the Wisconsin Public Service Corporation (WPS) to operate the dams, the utility opted to sell considerable acreage to the state as parkland. In 2001, the state began acquiring land from the WPS to establish the

> **When you're finally ready to come indoors and relax, there are any number of dining and lodging options to choose from, especially in the region surrounding the Caldron Falls and High Falls flowages.**
>
> - **Peshtigo River Resort and Supper Club** provides rental condominiums and riverside dining, on an outdoor deck if weather permits. Located off Parkway Road between Caldron Falls and High Falls Flowages, the resort also features special events including a spring walleye tournament and July canoe race. Phone: (715) 757-3741 or (715) 757-3991. Website: www.peshtigoriverresort.com.
> - **Pine Acres Lodge and Resort** provides housekeeping cottages and larger vacation homes on High Falls Flowage and offers boat, canoe, and paddle boat rentals. It's located on Parkway Road, north of County Road X. Phone: (715) 757-3894 or (715) 757-3402. Website: www.pineacresresortinc.com.
> - **Popp's Resort** offers motel suites, cottages, and rental homes on High Falls Flowage, on County Road X next to Boat Landing 4. Next to the resort, Rene's Supper Club serves lunch and dinner seven days a week. Popp's rents paddle boats, canoes, boats and motors, and pontoons up to 28 feet in length. Phone: (715) 757-3511. Website: www.poppsresort.com.

Peshtigo River State Forest. Wisconsin's 10th state forest today encompasses more than 12,000 acres, including 70 miles of river frontage. The state also purchased 200 acres on the south shore of Caldron Falls Reservoir from the utility plus 1,987 acres from the owner of Paust's Woods Lake Resort to form the main parcel of Governor Thompson State Park. WPS sold another 400 acres as lakeshore lots on Peshtigo flowages.

When we visited **Governor Thompson State Park,** a staffed park office welcomed visitors, but much work remained to be done. You can access 6.2 miles of maintained trails from the visitor center and from the boat launch on Caldron Falls Flowage. Uncounted, undesignated, wild trails also crisscross the property, which contains 6.5 miles of undeveloped shoreline. A word of caution if you're traveling with children: Stick to the developed trails and keep youngsters away from cliff edges. Future plans envision campsites, picnic areas, and a restored pine barrens.

The park is easy to find from Crivitz: drive northwest on County Road A (briefly along the Peshtigo River) to County Road X. Turn west on County Road X and continue over the High Falls Reservoir Bridge to Parkway Road. Turn north on Parkway Road and drive a half mile to Ranch Road. Turn west on Ranch Road and proceed 1 mile to Paust Lane. Turn north on Paust Lane to the main entrance. If, instead, your destination is the boat landing, stay on Parkway Road proceeding north from Ranch Road until you reach Boat Landing 13 Road. Turn west and drive roughly 20 miles to the boat landing.

The nearby **Peshtigo River State Forest** offers hiking in summer and cross-country skiing in winter. Both the **Spring Rapids Trail** (5 miles) and the **Seymour Rapids Trail** (3 miles) feature steep hills and good views from the west side of the Peshtigo River. In winter the two trails are linked through a cooperative network of ski trails over public and private lands.

Drive to Spring Rapids Trail from Crivitz by heading west on County Road W for 5 miles to Kirby Lake Lane. Turn northwest and follow Kirby Lake Lane to the trailhead, which will be on your right, immediately before the road turns straight west. Drive to Seymour Rapids Trail from Crivitz by following County Road W past Kirby Lake Lane. Continue on County Road W when it turns north. At the intersection with Bushman Road, County Road W turns west. Follow Bushman Road north to County Road 1634, which leads to the trailhead.

There's no shortage of campgrounds in the area, and we found three other excellent choices near the Pesh:

- **Veterans Memorial Park** offers 15 campsites on the Thunder River, a tributary of the Peshtigo. The park also provides picnic tables, fireplaces, toilets, drinking water, and a playground. But its best feature is Veterans Falls, visible from a footbridge over the river. The park is open from May 1 through deer season. From Crivitz, drive north on Highway 141 and turn west on County Road X, crossing the Peshtigo River to Parkway Road. Turn south on Parkway Road to reach the park.

- **Peshtigo River Campground** contains cabins, as well as camper and tent sites, for a total of 100 sites. The campground provides river access, canoe rentals, tubing trips, and floating coolers, in addition to the usual private campground amenities, plus pavilion, game room, and convenience store. It's easy to find, 2 miles south of Crivitz on Airport Road off Highway 141. Website: www.peshtigorivercampground.com.

- If you don't mind a walk to your tent site, **Big Joe Campground and Landing** is an undeveloped campground in the Nicolet National Forest providing three sites and pit toilets on the Upper Peshtigo. From Crandon, drive east on U.S. Highway 8, following the highway as it turns north in Laona, to State Highway 139. Continue north on Highway 139 approximately 1 mile to the drive into the parking area on the west side of the highway.

The Peshtigo River State Forest features three canoe campgrounds plus **Old Veteran's Lake Family Campground,** which remains open year-round. It provides 16 sites, pit toilets, hand pumps, picnic tables, and fire rings. Old Veterans Lake lies just west of the river, separated from it by two narrow strips of land. A hiking trail rings the lake. To get there, drive north on U.S. Highway 141 from Crivitz and turn west on County Road X. Drive west on County Road X, crossing the Peshtigo River to Parkway Road. Turn north on Parkway and drive about 3.5 miles to the campground.

Many campgrounds and trails along Wisconsin rivers abound with signs of the past, and the Peshtigo is no different. History still lingers along this river, impossible to ignore.

Humans first walked into the Peshtigo River region as the glaciers receded some 10,000 years ago, to explore the streams and lakes left by the melting mountains. No signs of human life remain from that period, but there are signs of human activity dating to 5500 B.C.

Mike and I stopped at **Copper Culture State Park** to learn about the lifestyle of early inhabitants who left a burial ground (not mounds) here thousands of years ago. This earliest known cemetery in the state, located on Paust Lane off State Highway 22 at Oconto, was placed on the National Register of Historic Places in 1966. The 48-acre park features a short-grass prairie, woodland hiking trails to the Oconto River, and the Charles Werrenbroeck Museum, open on weekend afternoons from Memorial Day to Labor Day.

Built in 1924 as a Belgiam homestead, the brick museum overflows with photos, maps, and Copper Culture artifacts excavated from the surrounding acres in the 1950s. Copper awls, spear points, fish hooks, a knife, and a bracelet make this one of the oldest archaeological sites in North America showing evidence of metal use. Archaeologists also dug up a whistle crafted from the leg bone of a swan, a clam shell from the Mississippi River, and a shell found only in the Atlantic Ocean offshore from North Carolina to Florida.

If you go, there's little cost. A state park vehicle sticker is not required; however, the museum appreciates visitors' donations.

The **Peshtigo Fire Museum** on Oconto Avenue north of U.S. Highway 41 in downtown Peshtigo records a much more recent, terrible history. Though long before my time, my stomach still tightens when I contemplate the awful Peshtigo Fire. Disaster struck a town that was both prosperous and totally unprepared.

In the fall of 1871, the region boomed with the growing lumber industry. People lived in scattered communities like Crivitz and Peshtigo, connected

Stairs lead to the river at McClintock Park

by the river and rudimentary roads. With a population of 1,700, Peshtigo boasted Catholic and Congregational churches, a school, a woodenware factory, a sash and door factory, a foundry, a boarding house for workers, saloons, and many homes.

On Sunday, October 8, the town disappeared, turned to dust and ashes by the horrendous fire that swept across 2,400 square miles of northern

Wisconsin and Michigan on tornado-force winds. Compared to the Peshtigo fire, the Chicago fire on the same date seems almost trivial, though it's the one recorded in most history books. The Peshtigo fire leveled the village and killed more than 1,000 people, 800 immediately and more than 200 in the days following the inferno. Many of those who perished simply could not reach the river before being overtaken by flames. When the survivors waded out of the Peshtigo in the chill, early morning hours of October 9, the only structure standing on the west bank was a brick kiln. Corpses marked the paths of former streets. The survivors warmed themselves at piles of smoking debris and began their search for loved ones.

One survivor walked 6 miles to Marinette for help. Soon tents, food, and other supplies arrived. The injured were treated and carried to Marinette, where a hotel was converted to an extra hospital. Several hundred of the dead were unidentifiable and buried in a mass grave.

The first marker authorized by the State Historical Society of Wisconsin still stands at the Peshtigo Fire Cemetery on Oconto Avenue. And to commemorate the date of the inferno, the Peshtigo Fire Museum ends its season on October 8 every year. Though memories and scars of the great fire would never be eradicated, the city was rebuilt and prospers still.

Peshtigo Harbor

The city today invites you to experience the river. A water trail, the **Peshtigo River Trail,** begins downtown and runs 11 miles to Lake Michigan. It takes you past an upland hardwood forest and through the marshy estuary near Green Bay.

Near the river's mouth, the **Peshtigo Harbor Birding Trail** begins on the west side of Harbor Road, approximately a half mile south of Hale School Road. There is a parking area and a gate at the trailhead just off the road. The trail loops 4 miles through varied terrain — forest, marsh, and the Green Bay shore. Bring your binoculars and expect to spot an equally varied palette of birds and to hear a cacophony of calls. More than 100 species have been recorded in the area — common loon, double-crested cormorant, great egret, green heron, hooded merganser, belted kingfisher, eastern phoebe, red-eyed vireo, and rough-winged swallow, to name a few.

The Hemlock Curve Nature Trail circles within an oxbow on the lower river in the Peshtigo Harbor Wildlife Area. To get there from Peshtigo, drive south on Hale Road to Harbor Drive. Turn east on Harbor Drive, which soon turns southeast along the river. Turn east on Badger Road to reach the trailhead.

The river ends at Peshtigo Harbor as quietly as it began. Once a busy lumber port, the site of a giant steam sawmill and a village of 500, today the wild harbor welcomes primarily anglers, hikers, and birders. The only reminders of its boisterous past are the remains of dock pilings and a commemorative sign erected by the Marinette County Historical Society.

However you choose to explore the Pesh — tracing its course through history, dipping a paddle into its currents, casting a fly overhead, or snapping a shot of a heron on the wing — this river will satisfy. Chances are, it will also center you and grant you peace.

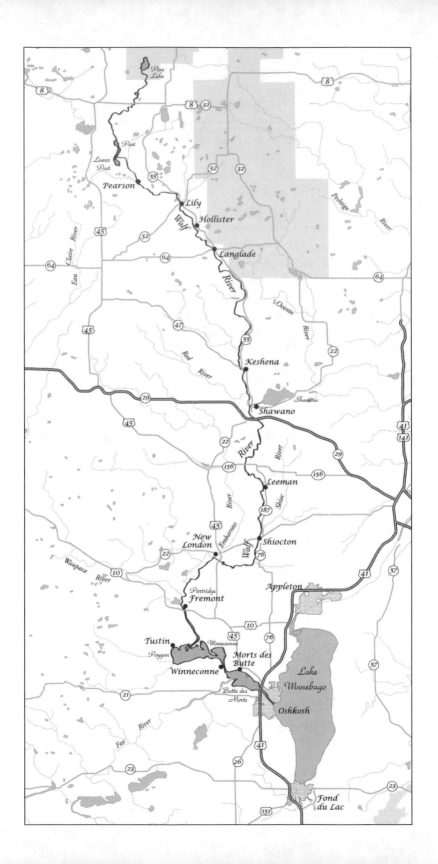

CHAPTER 8

Wolf

≋

The Wolf begins as a small, quick brook rushing over a rocky bed, launching from the south edge of Pine Lake in Forest County. When we visited, we observed a tundra swan, a band encircling its neck, swimming and catching fish near the outflow of the Wolf. From here, the river flows free as a bird, largely unfettered and undammed above Shawano, attracting enthusiastic whitewater paddlers and trout anglers from around the globe.

I am grateful to a vast parade of people who have preserved the Wolf River over the past two hundred years. One of Wisconsin's first National Wild and Scenic Rivers, the Wolf maintains its unspoiled beauty while growing in volume along its 204-mile voyage through Lake Poygan and

Tundra Swan at Pine Lake, the headwaters of the Wolf

Lake Winneconne to Lake Butte des Morts and the Fox River in Outagamie County. The Wolf River basin expands thanks to large and small tributaries — most significantly the Embarrass River, Little Wolf River, Shioc River, Tomorrow River, and Waupaca River.

The Wolf River batholith forms the bedrock of an area stretching roughly from Lakewood south to Waupaca and from Oshkosh west to near Wausau. This granitic mass formed 1,450 million years ago through volcanic action, as magma rose under pressure from deep within the earth.

Ten thousand years ago, when the last of the glaciers receded from North America, the Wolf River helped drain Glacial Lake Jean Nicolet. While the retreating glaciers left moraines and kettles over much of the batholith, you can still see the underlying granite along the river. Most of the watershed is hilly and forested, cratered with lakes and bogs. The southeastern section lies in a lower plain, partly a remnant of a glacial lakebed, and now a prime agricultural region.

Near Crandon and the headwaters of the Wolf, mining interests sought to create a copper and zinc mine during the last quarter of the twentieth century. But environmentalists — perhaps remembering the damage pollutants have caused to the lower Fox River — argued that improper disposal of wastes from the proposed underground and pit mining operations would pollute the Wolf. Others contended that, although the mine might bring jobs to the area for a 25-year period, prosperity would be temporary, followed by economic decline when the mine inevitably closed.

After years of costly public and legal wrangling, the controversy was resolved in 2003. The Forest County Potawatomi and the Mole Lake Sokaogon Ojibwe banded together to purchase the 5,000-acre mine site from the Nicolet Minerals Company for $16.5 million, permanently removing the area from mining consideration. Paddlers, anglers, hikers, and other wilderness explorers heaved a collective sigh of relief.

While hikers and anglers often visit the headwaters area, fewer paddlers brave the Upper Wolf. Beset by beaver dams, beds of wild rice, and rocky shallows, the segment from the river's source at Pine Lake to Post Lake can be a challenge to canoe, especially in dry weather. Still, it offers a secluded wilderness setting and a hope to see a deer or a bear with little whitewater to worry about.

From below Post Lake Dam to Pearson and the Langlade County Road T Bridge, even beginning paddlers enjoy this 10-mile, often curvy stretch of quiet water. Occasionally weeds and marshland blur the banks, but this trip runs mostly through forest, the last segment flowing through a section of the Upper Wolf River State Fishery Areas.

Power boating on Post Lake

The next 38 miles present increasing whitewater challenges. If you put in at Pearson, the first serious Class II rapids is Wendigo, past the County Road A Bridge. An alternative to avoid these rapids is to put in at the landing on River Road, which leads south from County Road A. You next encounter the slightly more manageable Strauss Rapids, and 2.5 miles later, the outlet of Turtle Lake. You can take out on the right, downstream of the State Highway 52 Bridge.

From here to Menominee County, the river is increasingly for kayaks and rafts only — with several portages required. Popular put-in and take-out spots in Langlade County are at Hollister Road, Dierck's Landing (also known as the Irrigation Ditch) on the left with access to State Highway 55, the State Highway 64 Bridge, and the County Road M Bridge, as well as the landing at the Wild Wolf Inn on the left. The last few miles of this stretch are among the most popular in the state for whitewater aficionados in search of spray, thrills, and calculated risk.

The Wolf is the staging ground for many an adventure, though it pays to beware that during spring and periods of high water, rafting generally requires experience, not to mention wetsuits. Novices with good stamina and judgment can enjoy many summer trips. Since Wisconsin prohibits overnight camping on the river, all trips run one day or less.

Until a tornado destroyed Bear Paw Outdoor Adventure Resort at Langlade on June 7, 2007, it offered exceptional trips, instruction, and accommodations. Owners Jamee Peters and Shirlee Roché may yet manage to resurrect the business. Stay tuned by visiting their website: www. bearpawoutdoors.com.

Expert whitewater instruction can also be found at **Wolf River Guides,** owned by Jen and Mike Wild, west of Langlade. Phone: (715) 882-3002. Website: www.wolfriverguides.com.

Not far to the south, **Buettner's Wild Wolf Inn** has a well-deserved reputation and a long history of welcoming tired travelers. It overlooks Gilmore's Mistake Rapids, which has its own singular history. During the lumber era, Gilmore reported to his employer that logs could not be sent through the narrow rapids, but then a competing lumber company dynamited the riverbed and was able to successfully float logs downstream, proving Gilmore wrong. You can find the inn on Buettner Lane, on the east side of Highway 55, just north of its intersection with Highway 64. Phone: (715) 882-8611. Website: www.wildwolfinn.com.

Herb's Rafts, allied with Buettner's Wild Wolf Inn, coordinates trips on the upper Wolf from Hollister to County Road M. Ask for a sack lunch if you'll be on the river more than a couple of hours. Phone: (715) 882-8611. Website: www.wildwolfinn.com/raft.htm.

Nearby, **Jesse's Historic Wolf River Lodge** has earned recent praise from magazine travel reviewers and ordinary travelers. The sprawling, comfortable complex tops a bluff surveying the Wolf River below Larzelere Rapids. Take your choice of accommodations including rooms in the main lodge, log cabins, a tree house (the "Nuthouse"), and a cabin down by the river. The quilts and happy conglomeration of antiques add a sense of history to family reunions and anniversaries. Directions: From the intersection of Highway 64 and Highway 55 in Langlade, drive north on Highway 55 for a short distance to Taylor Road. Turn north (left) on Taylor and the inn will soon appear on your left. Phone: (715) 882-2182. Website: www. wolfriverlodge.com.

Wolf River Camping (or River Forest Wolf River Camping) provides wooded campsites and special rafting packages, plus canoe, paddle boat, and mountain bike rentals. It's located at the intersection of Highway 55 and County Road WW south of Highway 64 in Langlade County. Phone: (715) 882-3351. Website: www.wolfrivercamping.com.

The largest campground within the Nicolet National Forest showcases signs of the last glaciers. **Boulder Lake** provides 89 single-unit campsites, six sites large enough for six to 16 people, and four sites that can accommodate up to 30 people each, in addition to a boat landing, swimming beach, showers, and flush toilets. You can see large boulders left by the last glacier by hiking the boardwalk of the 2-mile **Boulder Lake Campground Trail.** The 362-acre lake lies between the Oconto and Upper Wolf Rivers. To get to the campground from Langlade, drive south on Highway 55 for 5 miles to County Road WW. Turn east (left) on County Road WW and continue a half mile to Fire Road 2166 (Campground Road) and follow it to Boulder Lake.

Below these campgrounds and accommodations, the Wolf flows free and fast, rumbling over granite terraces and slicing through the rocky dells in the heart of today's Menominee Nation.

The Menominee did not always live along the Wolf. When the first Europeans arrived on the scene during the 1600s, they met Menominee bands living at the mouth of the Menominee River and at Green Bay. For many years the Menominee and Europeans interacted through the fur trade. Following the War of 1812 and the end of the fur trade, the United States increasingly pressured the Menominee to give up lands east of the Wolf. In an 1848 treaty at Lake Poygan, the United States mandated that the Menominee move to Crow Wing County, Minnesota.

But 2,500 Menominee refused to leave northeastern Wisconsin, and just six years later their persistence was rewarded. The Treaty of 1854, signed at Keshena, acknowledged their right to the lands they still hold today. Like the Lake Superior Ojibwe who stayed near the Bad River and Yellow Thunder and the other Ho-Chunk (Winnebago) who refused to be removed from the Dells (see Middle Wisconsin Chapter 13), this group of Menominee peaceably but insistently retained their place along the river — and Wisconsin is the richer for their culture, history, and strength.

The Menominee also share with other Wisconsin tribes a tradition of protecting their lands and rivers for future generations. Despite the efforts of lumber barons, the tribe has sustainably harvested its timber for almost 150 years. Menominee County today remains an island of green in a cutover landscape. The Menominee harvest a great diversity of trees — ash, black cherry, butternut, cedar, white pine, and yellow birch, to name a few of the 33 species found in the county. Cutting cycles are carefully gauged, with the result that today the amount of standing timber, 1.5 billion board feet, remains the same as the initial estimate done in 1854!

For a small sense of the history of this successful industry that today provides work for some 300 employees, visit the **Logging Museum of the Menominee Nation,** off State Highway 47 on County Road W West, just north of Keshena. Thanks to a teenager who worked as a cook's helper in Upper Michigan logging camps and went on to amass and give away an incredible collection of logging artifacts, the museum provides an in-depth view of the lifestyles of the lumbermen. You will not be bored; neither will the kids. Among seven log buildings are a cook shanty with a hash chopper, a bunkhouse with a side-loader or muzzle-loader bunk, a 26-foot bateau used on the river, and a collection of horseshoes including mud shoes, bog shoes, and sore-hoof shoes. If you can't wait to learn more, take the online tour: www.menominee-nsn.gov/tourism/logMuseum/museum.php.

To experience the signature section of the Wolf, drive through Menominee County on the 24-mile stretch of Highway 55 that hugs the river's east bank.

If you drive on Highway 55 from north to south, you will note a pull-out on the left soon after entering Menominee County. Turn in and stop to admire the rock-strewn river and the lone evergreen sprouting from a cleft in one of the midriver boulders. Be still and wait a bit. Mike and I watched a group of rafters bouncing downstream, and spotted an osprey winging overhead.

Shotgun Rapids comes up a couple of miles ahead on Highway 55 (roughly 25 miles north of Shawano), along with the site of Shotgun Eddy Raft Rental. The eddy (actually a rock garden) comes at the end of a long Class II rapids. **Shotgun Eddy Raft Rental** offers half- and full-day trips for experienced and inexperienced rafters. Riverside campsites (only for rafters) and a camp store complete the amenities. Phone: (920) 494-3782 or (715) 882-4461. Website: www.shotguneddy.com.

Approximately 5 miles south of Shotgun Eddy and a bit more than a mile past County Road B, we found Indian Route (IR) 34 leading eventually to **Sullivan Falls.** We turned west on IR 34, a bumpy dirt road with exposed ledges of granite bedrock, and drove 1.2 miles to Ducknest Rapids. From the parking area, we easily located the short, wooded trail to the river's edge and the 300-foot rapids that ends in a six-foot dive through steep rock walls. Feeling more relaxed by the minute, we returned to the car and drove another half mile until the road dead-ended at the parking area for Sullivan Falls. This is a fee area of the Menominee Nation. When we visited on a warm, sunny weekend, we bought a soda from the refreshment stand and lingered to watch the rafters and kayakers plummet over the seven-foot drop. While paddlers can sign up for river trips in Menominee County, fishing is off-limits except to members of the tribe.

Teakettle Rapids and the **Dells of the Wolf River** follow less than a mile downriver — though the distance by car is at least 5 miles. From Sullivan Falls, retrace your path to Highway 55, turn south (right) and continue to Indian Road 53. Watch for signs indicating **Big Smokey Falls** and "Wolf River Rafting." Turn west on IR 53 and continue past the road to Big Smokey Falls until the road dead-ends at a parking area. This site, also a fee area, lies at the beginning of Teakettle Rapids and just above the Dells. It serves as a take-out point for paddlers who are not continuing on through — and over — the Big Smokey Falls.

Return to the short road to Big Smokey Falls and follow it to the parking area "paved" with bedrock granite. An island divides this seven-foot drop into two very differently conformed descents. The east channel is choked with huge boulders and often with broken tree limbs. The west channel presents a sharp plunge over a rock

Purple loosestrife shares a split rock with a cedar tree

ledge to daredevil kayakers and rafters. You can walk to the island for a small fee and get a close look at the rafting route. **Big Smokey Falls Rafting** is the final take-out point on the river in Menominee County. Phone: (715) 799-3359.

Continue south on Highway 55 for 5.1 miles from the intersection with IR 53. The rough road to **Big Eddy Falls** can be a challenge to find. It lies on the west side of Highway 55, a short distance north of Dickie Road, which heads east. (If you spot Dickie Road, turn around and drive to the first opening on the west.) You may want to leave your car on the roadside and hike the quarter mile along the rugged trail to the falls. We noted a bear track in the hardened mud of this trail when we trekked here one September. Proceed south on Highway 55 for 3 miles to the Historic Marker installed by the Wisconsin Historical Society in 1963. It points out Spirit Rock and tells a legend about the past and future of the Menominee people.

North of Keshena, a sign marks Keshena Falls Road (Formerly County Road C), which leads to a bridge over the river and eventually to Highway 47. At the bridge there is a parking area and a sign commemorating the history of the Menominee and the spring sturgeon runs:

Here the sturgeon stopped on their upstream spawning runs each spring, until construction of two downstream dams blocked their annual return. It is said there is an underwater drum at the foot of the falls. In spring, high water beats the drum, calling the sturgeon home from Lake Winnebago.

View from the top of Big Eddy Falls

Depending on your itinerary and your preferences, take your pick from the following possibilities:

- **Kuckuck Park** in Shawano features a picturesque view of the river, as well as a playground, shelter, and picnic area.
- **Shawano's Sunset Island Park** offers a boat dock, shelter, grills, and rest rooms, plus accessible fishing piers on the Wolf River channel leading to Shawano Lake. It's located two blocks off Highway 47/55 at the end of North Franklin Street.
- If you're up for a swim — or a nap on the sand — **Wolf River Beach** provides an expanse of shoreline, with rest rooms, changing room, and showers. It's located in downtown Shawano on the east bank of the river at West Green Bay Road.
- The **Mountain-Bay Trail** crosses the Wolf from the west near the edge of Shawano, tracks through the downtown, and passes south of Shawano Lake, before continuing eastward. The trail's name indicates its beginning and end points: it tracks 83 miles from Rib Mountain to Green Bay. Trail passes are not needed for hiking or walking dogs (on leash only), but they are needed for biking or horseback riding. Pick up a daily pass at self-registration stations on the trail or an annual pass from the County Clerk's Office, County Courthouse, 311 North Main Street, Shawano, WI 54166, or from the Shawano Country Chamber of Commerce. Phone: (800) 235-8528 or (715) 524-2139. Website: www.shawanocountry.com.
- **Shawano Lake County Park and Campground** contains 90 campsites with electricity, showers, play equipment, an indoor roller rink, camp store, and fish cleaning facilities. Another section of the park offers a picnic area, tennis and basketball courts, softball field, volleyball court, and rest rooms. A 300-foot sand beach and boat launch are popular summer attractions. Drive east of the city on County Road H to the park on the north side of the lake, which flows into the Wolf River via the Shawano Lake Outlet.
- **Waukechon Riverside Park**, south of Shawano, provides picnic tables, grills, docks, and boat landing. To get there from State Highway 29/47/55, drive east to County Road K and turn south (right). Go along County Road K to County Road CCC. Turn west (right) on County Road CCC to the park and boat landing on the east bank of the Wolf.
- **Hayman Falls Shawano County Park** contains several wooded trails, including one along the rugged bank of the Embarrass River, which runs into the Wolf east of New London. The park also offers picnic tables, a shelter house, drinking water, grills, toilets, and a playground. From State Highway 29 at Shawano, turn west on County Road M. Proceed on County Road M to County Road CD. Turn west (right) on County Road D and continue for 1 mile past Pella. Turn south and drive a half mile, following the signs to the park.

The bridge at Keshena Falls

Like Big Smokey, an island divides the river into two prongs at Keshena Falls. The Wolf cascades around the isle as it gradually drops about 20 feet in a roaring turbulence.

South of Menominee tribal lands, the lower Wolf runs slower and wider, offering more leisurely boating and fishing adventures. Shawano area public parkland provides many additional camping and hiking opportunities.

Downstream from Shawano, the Wolf abounds with trails where hikers — or in winter, skiers and snowshoers — can get off the beaten track but still be close to civilization. Survival gear is not required, only sturdy boots or shoes and an interest in exploring the outdoors.

Navarino Nature Center stands near the south boundary of the 15,000-acre Navarino State Wildlife Area about 10 miles south of Shawano. Navarino maintains 14 miles of trails for hiking from spring through fall, and skiing and snowshoeing in the winter. If you want to try snowshoeing without making a commitment to the sport, the center rents snowshoes. Visitors have reported sightings of badgers, beaver, bear, coyote, deer, fishers, mink, muskrat, otters, red fox, and other mammals, as well as a variety of amphibians. And the center, which organizes canoe trips, birding hikes, and crane counts, has compiled a bird list of 239 species, including egrets and four other herons, 18 species of duck, 10 types of flycatchers, 12 hawks, 24 sandpipers, and 31 warblers. Phone: (715) 758-6999. Website: www.navarino.org.

To drive here from Shawano, proceed east on Highway 29 to the intersection with Highway 47/55 and County Road K. Turn south (right) on County Road K and follow it through the Navarino State Wildlife Area to Navarino Road. Turn east (left) on State Highway 156 and Navarino Road. When Highway 156 turns south, bear north on McDonald Road, proceeding into the wildlife area.

Mosquito Hill Nature Center fronts the Wolf east of New London. It provides 5 miles of hiking trails and 5 miles of snowshoe trails on its 430-acre property, as well as organized hikes and canoe excursions. One segment of the snowshoe trail runs along the river. One hiking/snowshoeing trail leads to the hilltop overlooking the Wolf River and its bottomland forest. As at other Outagamie County parks, pets are not allowed on the trails. The nature center, which features indoor wildlife exhibits, is closed on Mondays. Phone: Outagamie County Parks Department, (920) 832-4790. Mailing address: N3880 Rogers Road, New London, WI 54961. Directions: From U.S. Highway 45, drive east on County Road S to the park.

In Outagamie County, the Wolf shapes the identities of river towns like New London and Fremont, where beaches, parks, and landings serve as the communities' back yard. Under the State Highway 10 Bridge, **Fremont's Wolf River Crossing Park** features a boat landing, picnicking, volleyball, basketball, and a lagoon, the site of the annual Fremont Area Law Enforcement Children's Fishing Tournament. Partridge Lake Park (locally known as Fremont Beach) offers swimming, a raft, picnic tables, grills, shelter, and rest room. New London's River Trail gives an unusual, semi-urban view of the Wolf as it wends through the town.

To the west, the **River Ridge Trail** runs through and around Waupaca. Segments edge the Waupaca River, which flows into the Wolf at Lake Butte des Morts.

A little farther to the west off Highway 54, **Hartman Creek State Park** remains open year-round. With more than 100 campsites sheltered by either red pines or a mix of apple and other hardwoods, you can usually reserve a place in the shade. Kids — and their parents — like the programs led by volunteer naturalists, and the park contains two shelters that can be reserved. Hartmann Creek eventually flows into the Waupaca Chain O' Lakes and Waupaca River, which empties into the Wolf east of Weyauwega.

On the Little Wolf tributary north of Waupaca, the Millstone restaurant in Iola showcases a restored mill and offers soups, salads, sandwiches, draft root beer, and homemade ice cream. Tom and Melody Fucik own three historic buildings that once comprised the 1860 Wipf Mill. In addition to the restaurant, the Fuciks are restoring a museum on the property that had lapsed into serious disrepair. The couple has already restored the mill turbine and it now provides electricity to power the complex, located on Main Street.

At the end of the Wolf's long journey, several public landings and parks are situated around Lake Poygan. Between Poygan and Lake Butte des Morts (part of the Fox River channel), Lake Winneconne Park provides a landing and mooring protected by an island, as well as a beach, dressing rooms, picnic tables, shelter, playground, and areas for playing horseshoes, baseball, and volleyball. In Winneconne, follow State Highway 116 to Third Avenue. Turn north on Third Avenue and proceed to the park.

But the best way to view the final destination of the Wolf might be aboard the **Fin N Feather Showboat II,** an excursion boat based in Winneconne. Typical cruises motor into Lake Butte des Morts, Lake Winneconne, and Lake Poygan. You can sign up for one of the scheduled two-hour cruises, which include a lunch or dinner buffet, or with a minimum of 30 people, book your own trip. Find the boat at 22 West Main Street, on the Wolf River in Winneconne. Phone: (920) 582-4305. Website: www.fin-n-feathershowboats.com.

Rafting the Wolf

Sturgeon Viewing

Sturgeon-watching has developed into a seasonal sport in northeast Wisconsin, and growing opportunities exist to observe sturgeon spawning, usually for several days between mid-April and mid-May. Lake sturgeon, which live in the Mississippi River, Lake Michigan, and Lake Superior, as well as Lake Winnebago, move from Lake Winnebago up the Wolf as far as Shawano to spawn. Their fertilized eggs land on rocks, in crevices, and on other surfaces where they adhere until they eventually hatch and grow into tiny sturgeon. A few places to scout for sturgeon activity:

- The State Highway 29 Bridge at the Shawano Dam offers a good viewing stand. Sturgeon Park at the end of Richmond Street provides benches and paved trails.
- At Shiocton, visit the old State Highway 54 Bridge over the river, near Bamboo Bend.
- The Wolf River Sturgeon Trail offers both viewing and in-season fishing near Muckwa Wildlife Area, along County Road X west of New London. This new Waupaca County Parks paved trail edges a restored spawning ground.
- Within the city of New London, Pfeiffer Park also offers good viewing. From Highway 45, turn west on Waupaca Street and follow it to Embarrass Drive. Turn left and drive to the park. Walk along the bank of the Embarrass River to find the dancing and rolling sturgeon.

To find out when the sturgeon are active, call the Department of Natural Resources: (920) 424-3050.

Would you like to volunteer as a sturgeon guard? Each spring, the Department of Natural Resources organizes volunteers to protect the spawning fish, which are oblivious to humans and vulnerable to poachers. If you sign up for a 12-hour shift, you will begin by checking in at Sturgeon Camp near Shiocton, where you will receive a meal, an orientation, an identification hat that you can keep, a sack lunch, and directions to an assigned site. To register, call (920) 303-5444 or e-mail DNRSturgeonGuard@wisconsin.gov.

If you'd prefer seeing a sturgeon captured and in your hands, you can fish for sturgeon in the fall hook-and-line season on the Wolf below the Shawano Paper Mill Dam. There's also a short February spearing season on Lakes Winnebago, Butte des Morts, Poygan, and Winneconne, with a limited number of tags available for the latter three lakes.

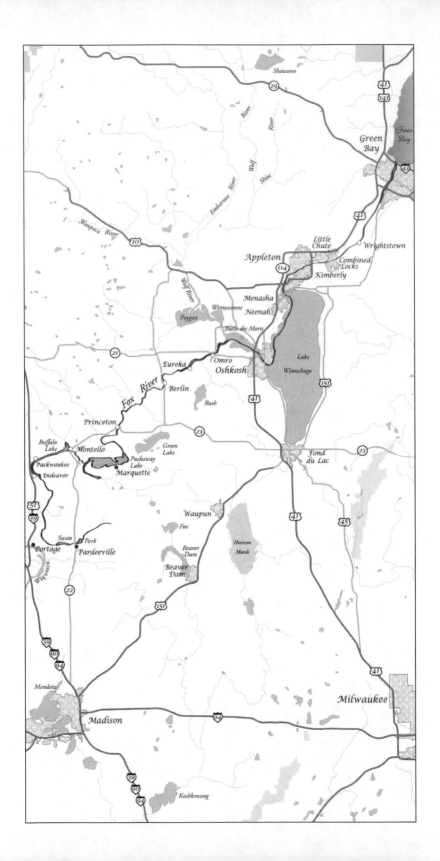

CHAPTER 9

Fox

~~~~~

In its upper reaches, the Fox River almost circles back on itself, rising from Green Lake County not far south of the Grand River, which flows into the Fox southeast of Montello. The incipient river courses southwest through wetlands, through sandy soil, and 50 to 100 feet above sandstone bedrock. You won't find rocky outcrops here near the southwestern edge of Wisconsin's once glacier-covered lands.

At Pardeeville, site of the upper river's first hydroelectric dam, the Fox widens to form Park Lake. The village makes the most of this landscaping at Chandler Park, more or less surrounded on three sides by the lake.

East of Pardeeville, the Fox broadens once more, into the larger Swan Lake. Immediately downriver from the lake, the 1,670-acre **Swan Lake State Wildlife Area** covers most of an extensive wetlands area that provides habitat for deer, small mammals, sandhill cranes, and many species of waterfowl. To observe the birds here, drive south from Portage on U.S. Highway 51 to County Road P. Turn east on County Road P and watch for Swan Lake State Wildlife Area signs.

Mike and I stopped at the large riverbank wayside on the north side of State Highway 33 near the point where Jacques Marquette and Louis Jolliet stepped from the Fox to begin their 1.28-mile historic portage to the Wisconsin River. At the behest of Jean Talon, a high-ranking official in Louis XIV's New France, Marquette and Jolliet left the Straits of Mackinac in two birch bark canoes during the spring of 1673. Their mission: find a route to the Mississippi River. After staying for a time with the Menominee Indians on Green Bay and then at a town made up of 3,000 Miami, Kickapoo, and Mascouten Indians, Marquette and Jolliet followed two Miami guides along the upper Fox to reach this spot on June 14.

Marquette's journal reports that they walked 2,700 paces from the Fox to the wide, sandy Wisconsin. From here, the two explorers paddled down the Wisconsin to enter the Mississippi three days later. Other explorers followed, among them Daniel Greysolon, Sieur du Lhut, and Jonathan Carver, who reported a bustling fur trade at the portage in the late 1700s.

Laurent Barth sold furs and built the first cabin near the portage in 1793. Almost two decades later Pierre Pauquette began operating a trading post here for Joseph Rolette, as traffic along the Fox-Wisconsin route continued to grow.

In the wake of fur trading, as lead miners and settlers moved increasingly into Indian lands, violence erupted sporadically on the Wisconsin frontier. In 1826, Ho-Chunk Chief Red Bird heard a rumor that two Ho-Chunk had been killed at Fort Snelling (near today's Saint Paul, Minnesota) for a murder they did not commit.

The same year, a white family making maple sugar on Ho-Chunk lands was murdered. Then on June 28, 1827, Chief Red Bird and three of his companions killed two farmers, Solomon Lipcap and Registre Gagnier, and seriously injured Gagnier's infant daughter at Prairie du Chien. Two days later a band of Ho-Chunk fired on the keelboat Oliver Perry on the Mississippi near the mouth of the Bad Axe River, killing two men.

The Ice Age Trail flanks the east bank of the Portage Canal

To prevent a larger war, Chief Red Bird surrendered near the portage on September 2, 1827. The brief uprising prompted the construction of Fort Winnebago near today's Highway 33 wayside in the fall of 1828.

Major David E. Twiggs, who would later serve as a general in the Confederate Army, supervised construction of the fort. It lay equidistant from Fort Howard at Green Bay (116 miles to the northeast) and Fort Crawford at Prairie du Chien (115 miles to the southwest). A man who would become a more famous Confederacy legend, Lieutenant Jefferson Davis, also served here after graduating from West Point.

The army manned the fort until 1845, and just a year later it was destroyed by fire. The Surgeons' Quarters, originally purchased by the army from the fur trader, still stands on the hill across the highway from the site of the former fort. Now restored, the Surgeons' Quarters and an adjacent 1850 school house are open to the public from May 15 to October 15 (fee). Phone: (608) 742-2949. Website: www.wsdar.com/surgeons.

The fort guarded the portage trail, which followed what is now Highway 33 and a Portage city street, **Wauona Trail**, to the Wisconsin River. During periods of flooding, a fork in the low-lying portage trail ascended Ketchum's Point and offered an alternate path to the Wisconsin.

The Surgeons' Quarters near the site of Fort Winnebago

This high trail is where Red Bird walked in 1827. Wearing white elk skin and bearing a white flag, the Ho-Chunk chief marched with his men along the ridge to surrender at the U.S. Army camp on the Fox River. As he walked, Red Bird sang his death song. He had expected to be killed but was instead imprisoned at Prairie du Chien, where he died a year later. A marker commemorating his surrender is located where Highway 33 and Cook Street diverge east of Jackson Street.

A short distance upstream, the **Old Indian Agency House** was built in 1832 by the U.S. government for Indian Agent John Harris Kinzie and was placed on the National Register of Historic Places in 1972. Kinzie occupied this white shuttered home with his wife, Juliette Magill Kinzie, who wrote *Wau-Bun, the Early Day in the Northwest,* recording her experiences at the portage and elsewhere. Wau-Bun means "early day" or "dawn" in Ojibwa.

The Old Indian Agency House stands near the Portage Canal, completed in 1851 to provide a navigable waterway between the Fox and Wisconsin rivers. Envisioned years before, the canal had seemed an obvious step, especially when the flooded Wisconsin created a sporadic navigable channel between the two rivers. In the end, the canal never fully lived up to its early promise of efficient, affordable transportation from Green Bay to the Mississippi, due to various navigation barriers along both rivers, and to the rise of the railroads. Still it carried a good deal of commercial and recreational traffic until it was finally closed by the U.S. Army Corps of Engineers a century after it had opened.

Today it remains a monument to Wisconsin history and serves as a recreation corridor. We watched a canoeist maneuver through a section of the restored canal, and hiked a segment of the Ice Age National Scenic Trail, which flanks its eastern bank. Occasional benches proffered rest and suggested reveries of Red Bird and Wau-Bun. The trail twice crossed footbridges to the other side of the canal and Agency House Road.

We walked along the canal to the site of one of its two locks. Today, all that remains of the Fort Winnebago Locks near the former fort are several old iron baffles, rusting in the water. The trail, the canal, and Indian Agency Road are all accessible from East Albert Street, a Wisconsin Rustic Road that runs just west of the fort site and northeast off Highway 33.

On the opposite side of Highway 33, a brown-painted log sign reads, "Historic Portage Canal Recreational Corridor." We walked the short corridor that offers hiking and cross-country skiing along the canal. Near its end at the railroad tracks, two deer loped away from us into the brush.

Portage Canal Lock at the Wisconsin River end of the canal

We followed the old canal as closely as possible along city streets and discovered the Wentworth Grain Elevator, established in 1861 and now called Canal Seed and Feed. It still backs up to the canal at the corner of Mullet Street and Thompson Street. From 1864 to 1874, Robert Wentworth, who also owned the Portage & Green Bay Transportation Company, shipped grain to Green Bay by steamboat. This grain elevator and two dozen other sites are part of the Historic Portage Downtown and Waterfront Walking Tour area, bordered on the south by Edgewater Street.

Next we located Lock Street, which heads south of Highway 33 near the Wisconsin River, and drove to the dead end at the Portage Locks. The first lock built in 1851 was simply a guard lock to prevent sand and debris from flowing into the canal; it was rebuilt in 1892–1893 as a lift lock. The steel gates now stand, restored and partially open, behind a steel railing. Restoration and development of the lock, the canal, and trails along the city's waterways began in 2006 with help from state and federal funding.

At 506 West Edgewater Street, the Zona Gale Home presides over a view of the Wisconsin River. A Portage native, the author is best remembered for her 1920 novel, *Miss Lulu Bett;* its dramatization earned her a Pulitzer Prize a year later. Gale built this home for her parents in 1906, reserving for herself a study on the second floor. Owned by the Women's Civic League, this distinctive home with its Greek revival exterior and Craftsman interior can be toured by appointment (fee). Another Gale home (the William L. and Zona Gale Breese home) today houses the Museum at the Portage, 804 MacFarlane Street. This home also contains a Gale study, as well as many early city artifacts. To learn more, call (608) 742-6700.

Though not from Portage, John Muir grew up on a nearby farm. Born in Scotland in 1838, he emigrated to Wisconsin with his family in 1849, attended the University of Wisconsin, and frequently walked the lands along the Wisconsin River. His travels through the western United States, writings, and advocacy led to the establishment of Yosemite National Park and the national park system.

Portage has significant park land, including the **Wisconsin River Levee Walk.** In our short trek along this high bank, we encountered many other wayfarers — joggers, bicyclists, roller bladers, and a couple ambling hand in hand.

Showy gardens, a pond, a miniature waterfall, footbridges, shelters, and gravel paths sculpt Pauquette Park into a series of outdoor rooms. This manicured site once contained a landing and a ferry service started by Pierre Pauquette about 1830. The legendary Pauquette — trader, ferryman, farmer, and interpreter — got into an argument in 1836 over payment for provisions with a Ho-Chunk named Mau-ze-mon-e-ka, or "Iron Walker," according to Richard Durbin in *The Wisconsin River: An Odyssey Through Time and Space.* Over time, the dispute grew, and at one point Pauquette beat up Iron Walker. Iron Walker started carrying a gun. When he next met Pauquette, Iron Walker drew his weapon and the ferryman challenged him to fire. Iron Walker fired, killing Pauquette. At Iron Walker's trial the judge ruled the killing an act of self-defense.

From Pauquette Park, the Portage Canal and Marquette segments of the National Ice Age National Scenic Trail run in opposite directions. Hiking the Marquette segment offers one way to experience the Fox below Portage. The river runs through a few wooded areas, as well as grasslands and marsh.

Whether you are hiking, paddling, or driving along the river, **Governor's Bend County Park** offers a pleasant picnic and fishing area with soothing views of the grass- and tree-lined river. Governor's Bend takes its name from a long-ago visit by Nelson Dewey, the state's first governor. From Portage, follow Highway 33 east to County Road F and proceed north on County Road F about 3 miles to Fox River Road. Turn left on Fox River Road and drive to Lock Road. Turn west onto Lock Road and follow it to the Columbia County park.

Roughly 2 miles downriver, the forests and marsh of the 3,176-acre **French Creek State Wildlife Area** spread out east of the Fox and contain French Creek Fen, designated a state natural area in 2007. This area features three fens containing calcium carbonate, mound springs, wet prairie, and sedge meadow near the confluence of French and Spring creeks. It's a haven for lesser fringed gentian, cespitose bulrush, and other rare plants, as well as birds including black tern, American bittern, and yellow-billed cuckoo. To get there by car, drive east from Portage on Highway 33 to County Road F. Turn north and follow County Road F for 3 miles to Clark Road. Turn east on Clark and drive three quarters of a mile to Dumke Road. Turn north again on Dumke and proceed about 1 mile to Monthey Road. Finally, turn east on Monthey and drive a half mile to a parking area on the north side of the road.

Marquette County contains only one county park, but it, along with the **Muir Park State Natural Area and National Historic Landmark,** beckons travelers to relax and reflect on the life of the co-founder of the Sierra Club. Located on County Road F north of French Creek and County Road O, John Muir Park takes in the lands surrounding the naturalist's boyhood home. It features a picnic area, ball diamond, and nature trail encircling Ennis Lake, called Fountain Lake in Muir's day but later renamed for another early settler.

This park began due to the efforts of another Wisconsin naturalist. A week before he died on John Muir's birthday, April 21, 1948, Aldo Leopold, author of *A Sand County Almanac,* had written to Ernie Swift, Wisconsin Conservation Department director, recommending that the Muir family homestead be designated the state's first natural area. But that honor went to Parfrey's Glen, Sauk County, in 1951.

Meanwhile, a grassroots effort was underway to create a county park on the site. Sylvester "Syl" Adrian of Montello advocated for the creation of John Muir Memorial Park, which was finally created and dedicated in 1957.

In 1972, Wisconsin set aside the state natural area with the diverse terrain — spring-fed kettle lake, fen, sedge meadow, open bog, prairie, and forests. Botanist and author of *The Vegetation of Wisconsin,* John Curtis monitored the prairie, and visitors still come to see the varied plant communities.

Nineteen years later, the National Park Service dedicated Fountain Lake Farm National Historic Landmark, embracing the 80-acre homestead. Originally proposed by Erik Brynildson in 1987, the farm's historic landmark designation won support from Wisconsin Senators Robert Kasten and William Proxmire, the Sierra Club, and the park service.

Hardly more than an hour's drive to the southwest, sandhill cranes gather along the Lower Wisconsin near our own land now, readying for their fall migration. Their numbers seem to grow every year — just like the individuals who have gathered together over time to protect Fountain Lake Farm and honor the man who made it famous.

Beyond the **Fox River National Wildlife Refuge,** the river flows around boggy Packwaukee Island and the marshy banks near Endeavor before slowing and widening into Buffalo Lake. The 11-mile lake curves first west, where I-39/U.S. Highway 51 brushes close to it, and then swings northeast, passing Packwaukee and many lakeside residences before reaching the Montello Dam.

Montello grew at the confluence of the Montello and Fox rivers, which still flow through the center of this city, once famous for its red granite. In fact, a section of Montello granite was selected for the tomb of President Ulysses S. Grant in New York City's Riverside Park. Today the city is equally known for the waterfalls in the old Montello Granite Company quarry, located on State Highway 23 downtown in Daggett Memorial Park. It also showcases the biggest tree in the state, a humongous cottonwood in the yard next to the courthouse.

East of Montello, the Fox runs through more wetlands before entering Lake Puckaway, a 9-mile long lake no more than five feet deep. It's popular with anglers and duck hunters and will accommodate most powerboats. It's also where I first ignominiously paddled a kayak.

I'd joined a group of 10 women on a two-day trip that ended at Princeton and involved a sprint across Lake Puckaway. The trip sounded easy enough. Who would have thought such a shallow lake could conjure up such titanic waves? With the wind against us, our group plowed across the lake. I tried to keep my eyes on our destination point across the lake, where we'd planned a rest stop, but the spray across my glasses blurred my vision. I could barely see the woman on my right, as she edged ahead and disappeared into the mist and waves. I hoped that with a water depth of only five feet, drowning would be unlikely if I flipped over and out of the kayak, though the wind and the waves argued otherwise. Eventually, of course, I reached the other shore, despite the fact that my kayak seemed determined to slip beneath a pier — the details of my graceful landing are better left untold.

The rest of our paddle down the Fox, past the mouth of the Mecan, around the Princeton Dam, and into town was a merry-go-round compared to Lake Puckaway.

Princeton impressed me. The historic town features a 7-mile-long canal that carried water from the Mecan River to a gristmill. The currents of the Fox were insufficient to power a flour mill, so the 10-foot-wide canal to the Mecan was constructed in the 1860s. Thanks to the canal and the Mecan, the mill became Green County's largest, reported Margaret Beattie Bogue in *Exploring Wisconsin's Waterways.*

The town also grew as a provider of goods and services to surrounding farmers. Beginning in 1869, a monthly cattle fair was held for more than 130 years, and today the Princeton Flea Market offers old stuff, new stuff, collectibles, antiques, arts and crafts, farm market items, and unexpected treasures weekly from late April to mid-October on the east side of town in the City Park on Highway 23. Early risers are welcome; the flea market generally opens before 6:30 a.m.

Downstream, the Fox flows slowly through more wetlands, and soon forms the southeastern boundary of the **White River Marsh State Wildlife Area.** Near its upstream border, an old lock and dam area attracts anglers. An island divides the Fox into two channels here. The dam, removed in 2003, was located in the western channel, with the lock in the eastern channel. The 11,093-acre wildlife area offers two canoe landings. Visitors also come to fish, pick berries and nuts, and watch for red fox, other small mammals, and diverse birdlife, including migrating sandhill cranes in the fall. Wisconsin Rustic Road 22 follows White River Road through this area, off County Road D north of Princeton. Also in this area, the Puchyan River enters the Fox from the east.

Larger than Princeton, Berlin displays the same kind of historic downtown charm, with several old homes and restored central city buildings filled with antiques, art, and gifts. Originally platted as the Fox River crossing of a road between Fond du Lac and Stevens Point, Berlin flanks both sides of the Fox and contains several riverside parks. Longcroft Park, on the west bank downtown, features a 190-foot-long pedestrian bridge over the river, a playground, picnic area, grills, and aquatic center. In winter, visitors enjoy outdoor ice-skating and the heated warming house. Riverside Park extends along the east bank on the city's north side. It offers lighted softball diamonds, volleyball courts, basketball courts, lighted horseshoe courts, playgrounds, shelters, rest rooms, and 25 campsites with electricity. There's also a double boat launch and over 2,000 feet of seawall with boat moorings.

The Berlin Locks south of the city are no longer used, but thanks to state and community efforts, the area was redeveloped in 2002 and now provides boat launches above and below the dam, a rest room, and a handicapped-accessible fishing pier. There are also plans to restore the old lock tender's house.

The only remaining operational lock on the upper Fox can be seen at Eureka. The state-regulated, 209-foot dam has a nearby small boat launch and a fishway constructed in 1989 to permit lake sturgeon, walleye, and other fish to move upstream to traditional spawning areas.

Omro has more miles of waterfront acreage than Venice, Italy, according to the city's website: www.omro-wi.com. It also boasts a historic downtown tour that you can drive, bike, or walk; brochures are available at the Chamber of Commerce office, Omro City Hall, and local businesses. Omro's parks line the riverbanks. Scott Park on Main Street features a gazebo with visitor information, in addition to fishing, boat docking, picnicking, and ice-skating. Near the Main Street bridge, Riverside Park provides an artesian well, picnicking, and fishing opportunities. Stearn's Park on Huron Street also has a gazebo, plus a boat launch and playground. Fred C. Miller Park on Kiwanis Street contains the Omro Family Aquatic Center, boat launch, sand volleyball court, shelters, and picnic areas. And the Fox and Hounds Park on East River Drive offers a boat launch and river views from the north side of town.

Named for French fur trader, blacksmith, and early resident Charles Omereau, the city was a lumber center in the mid-1900s. David Humes, its first settler, designed a grouser towboat to move logs from the Wolf River basin and Lake Butte des Morts to the new town. Using a steam-propelled tow and windlass, the boat could pull rafts larger than otherwise possible, according to Margaret Beattie Bogue.

Lake Butte des Morts lies roughly 3 miles downstream from Omro and received its name from a large hill that had served as an Indian burial ground. The Wolf River exits Lake Poygan and enters Lake Butte des Morts from the north, and the combined waters of the Fox and Wolf flow toward Oshkosh and Lake Winnebago, the state's largest inland lake.

With more than 150,000 adult sturgeon, Lake Winnebago boasts a sustainable sturgeon spear-fishing season. Sturgeon can grow to eight feet long and weigh over 200 pounds; the largest registered on Lake Winnebago was caught in 2004 and weighed 188 pounds. The Wisconsin Department of Natural Resources has created a website to track the history of sturgeon fishing on Lake Winnebago: www.winnebagosturgeon.org.

Thanks in part to the white pine of the Wolf River basin and its location at Lake Winnebago, Oshkosh became a significant lumber town in the nineteenth century, known as the Sawdust City. Even as the lumber era ebbed elsewhere, the city's Paine Lumber Company grew into the world's largest, employing 2,200 workers in 1929, Margaret Beattie Bogue reported.

You can still see several lumber baron mansions by walking through half a dozen historic districts, with maps available from the history pages of the city's website: www.ci.oshkosh.wi.us.

One mansion has provided a home to the **Oshkosh Public Museum** since 1924. Edward Sawyer, son of lumberman and U.S. Senator Philetus Sawyer, gave the home at 1331 Algoma Boulevard to the city in 1922. Phone: (920) 424-4731. Website: www.oshkoshmuseumorg.

Many years later, Nathan Paine initiated an art center, which his widow completed for the city after his death in 1947. Housed in the lumberman's former home at 1410 Algoma Boulevard, the **Paine Art Center and Gardens** showcases the work of current artists in the elegant home built by local craftsmen and skilled workers from Milwaukee and Grand Rapids, Michigan. Phone: (920) 235-6903. Website: www.thepaine.org.

Oshkosh presents a number of boat landings and other parks on the Fox. West of the Oshkosh Avenue bridge, the 17.1-acre Rainbow Park provides a boat landing, fishing, ice and roller hockey, picnicking, and rest rooms. A Wisconsin Historical Society marker memorializes Knaggs Ferry, operated by James Knaggs for 19 years. His notable passengers included Governor Henry Dodge, and in 1831, Knaggs ferried John and Juliette Kinzie en route to their Indian Agency assignment in Portage. South of the Ohio Street bridge, William Steiger Park, named for a U.S. Congressman, features a boat launch, dock, hiking trail, and picnic shelter. Carl Steiger Park, named for the congressman's father, is located south of the Ohio Street bridge and offers a trail and picnicking. Near the Main Street bridge, the 2.75-acre Riverside Park offers a boat mooring, picnic area, shelter, and rest rooms.

Part of a downtown redevelopment plan, Leach Amphitheater has been drawing people to Oshkosh's Riverside Park since 2006. Adjacent to the convention center, the outdoor amphitheater features diverse entertainment, and can accommodate 7,000 people on the lawn or brick terrace. For tickets, phone (920) 494-3401 or (800) 895-0071. Website: www.leachamphitheater.com.

Menominee Park, located on 110 acres along Lake Winnebago, offers any activity a family might want — a zoo, 30,000-square-foot volunteer-built playground, miniature train, merry-go-round, recreational trail, sailboat launches, beach, and sports fields. A bronze statue of Chief Oshkosh gives tribute to the man for whom the city is named.

When you're ready for a sit-down meal, **Fratellos Waterfront Restaurant and Brewery,** 1501 Arboretum Drive, offers fresh seafood, steaks, pastas, and sandwiches, plus its handcrafted beers and live music on Friday and Saturday nights. On sunny days, the outdoor seating area is usually crowded with boaters who have tied up at the dock, as well as customers who have arrived by car. Phone: (920) 232-2337.

Though never lighted to guide boats on Lake Winnebago, **Asylum Point Lighthouse** today leads visitors to a spot to relax, fish, and generally enjoy the outdoors. Built during the 1930s, the lighthouse was never used. Inmates from the Winnebago Correctional Institute renovated it in 2007, refitting windows and replacing the roof.

Nearby, **Asylum Point Park** provides a marsh wildlife area and a boat launch, as well as island picnicking, on the point of land where the Northern Asylum for the Insane once stood. Built in 1871, the asylum was later renamed the Winnebago Mental Health Institute; but the original name survived for the point and Asylum Bay beyond it. To drive here, follow State Highway 76 north of Oshkosh to Snell Road. Turn east on Snell Road and proceed to Sherman Road, following Sherman to the park.

Opposite the Fox River's outlet from Lake Winnebago, a 12-foot-high bronze statue of Ho-Chunk Chief Red Bird gazes northwest from a 200-foot cliff on its eastern shore. The nineteenth-century leader well knew these lands that still contain several conical and effigy mounds, including four panther mounds and two buffalo mounds, dating from about AD 800 to AD1300.

The statue and limestone cliffs are part of **High Cliff State Park** on the **Niagara Escarpment.** This limestone and dolomite ledge extends from Wisconsin to New York, where it forms the base of Niagara Falls. The ledge runs northeast by way of Lake Winnebago, Door County, and underneath Lakes Michigan, Huron, and Erie. It formed over 400 million years ago as a subtropical coral reef, from the deposits of decomposing shells and sea life skeletons. At that time, its inland sea covered what is now Lake Michigan and much of lower Michigan and eastern Wisconsin.

After Red Bird's time, a quarry and lime kiln occupied part of this land from 1895 to 1956. Remnants of the kilns, where limestone was heated to produce lime, are visible along the Lime Kiln Trail. The 0.3-mile Indian Mound Trail offers interpretive signage and is accessible to people with disabilities.

The park's 40-foot observation tower provides an even better vantage point, from which you can sometimes pick out the cities of Appleton, Kaukauna, Menasha, Neenah, and Oshkosh. High Cliff also features a marina, a beach (no lifeguard), camping, nature center, museum store (formerly the company store), picnic areas, and playground. The park welcomes flocks of warblers in the spring; ask for the bird brochure at the park office. The 1,147-acre park is located off State Highway 114 on State Park Road. From Menasha, drive east on U.S. Highway 10/State Highway 114, curving southeast on Highway 114 where Highway 10 continues east. Drive to Pigeon Road, turning south and driving 1.6 miles to State Park Road, which leads to High Cliff. Phone: (920) 989-1106.

Named for the man who was governor of both Wisconsin and Utah territories, Doty Island stands in the Fox at the outlet of Lake Winnebago, dividing the river into two channels. The Fox drops ten feet on either side of the island, and the twin Winnebago Rapids guaranteed development. James Duane Doty and Morgan L. Martin both purchased federal land in 1835 on the island and at the future sites of Neenah on the west bank and Menasha on the east bank.

Born in New York in 1799, Doty moved to Michigan in 1818, and two years later joined a mission to Wisconsin Territory with Michigan Governor Lewis Cass. Doty went on to serve as a judge and settled in Green Bay in 1824, where he promoted the city's development. Next, the ambitious Doty bought land and platted lots in Madison, successfully lobbying to locate the territorial capital there in 1836. He represented Wisconsin Territory in the U.S. Congress and served as its second territorial governor from 1841 to 1844.

When his term ended, Doty moved to Neenah and worked with his son Charles to promote the town site of Menasha. But he couldn't stay away from politics and served next as a delegate to Wisconsin's constitutional convention. After Wisconsin became a state in 1848, Doty was elected to the U.S. House of Representatives. After losing his seat in 1853, he returned to the home he had built on Doty Island.

This time, Doty stayed on the Fox River eight years until President Abraham Lincoln appointed him Superintendent of Indian Affairs for Utah Territory. Doty became governor of Utah Territory in 1863 and died in office two years later.

Another of Wisconsin's early movers and shakers, Morgan L. Martin formed the Fox and Wisconsin Improvement Company to build locks, dams, and canals, and to enhance the waterway for transportation. Thanks to his efforts and those of other entrepreneurs, boat traffic increased, though the railroads were soon carrying more goods.

State Highway 47/114 today crosses both channels of the Fox and the island, which is divided between Menasha and Neenah, with Doty's cabin standing on the Neenah side across from Kimberly Point. The cabin, large for its time and dubbed "the Grand Loggery" by Doty's wife, was moved from the east end of the island to the city's Doty Island Park in 1938. The one-and-a-half story, T-shaped cabin finally had to be torn down in 1948, but was reconstructed and added to the National Register of Historic Places. Besides the cabin, the park, 701 Lincoln Street, contains a shelter, gazebo, and picnic tables. The cabin is open from noon to 4:00 p.m. daily, June through August, plus Memorial and Labor day weekends. Costumed guides recreate the era when Doty lived at the Loggery. Phone: (920) 751-4614.

Beginning with the **Neenah Lighthouse** on Kimberly Point on Lake Winnebago, the southerly of the river's twin cities offers considerable parkland and riverfront development for visitors and locals to explore. Though not open for tours, the tower, also called Kimberly Point Lighthouse, still serves as a landmark for boaters. The accessible fishing deck and rest rooms at the point are open from spring to fall. To reach the point from Neenah, follow Highway 114 to the island and turn right onto East Wisconsin Avenue, following it to the lake and turning left on Lakeshore Avenue.

Spearheaded by Future Neenah, Inc., a nonprofit committed to economic and cultural vitality, the city has undertaken ambitious waterfront redevelopment. A 1.5-mile, barrier-free Neenah Riverwalk begins at Shattuck Park and stretches between the Commercial Street and Oak Street bridges crossing the channel between the riverbank and Doty Island. The park is named for Franklyn Shattuck, a founder of Kimberly-Clark, the industrial giant that switched from flour milling to paper milling in 1872.

Every time you visit, there's something new to experience. On the mainland side of the channel, **Shattuck Park** has gained a concert lawn, a water fountain, a pier extending 250 feet into the harbor, and a pavilion for outdoor concerts and theater. Owners of the former Valley Inn have converted the property into the Holiday Inn-Neenah Riverwalk overlooking Shattuck Park and the Fox. When you visit, be sure to view the Oak Street bridge after dark. New LED lighting accentuates the architecture of the bridge, creating a silhouette on the water.

Riverside Park is already a showplace. A favorite of photographers, the sculpture, "Playing in the Rain" by Dallas J. Anderson, depicts children playing in a fountain that sometimes creates clouds of mist and a rainbow. The park provides a seawall and mooring for sailboats. Since 1955, the Riverside Players have staged outdoor performances in the park, usually a play in late June and a musical in late July or early August.

Just east of the park, the **Bergstrom-Mahler Museum** offers a peek at the home life of a leading paper manufacturing family and its stunning collection of paperweights. John N. Bergstrom and his father, Dedrick Waldemar Bergstrom, formed the Bergstrom Paper Company in 1904. The family later deeded to the city its Tudor revival mansion, containing, in addition to paperweights, changing exhibitions and collections of paintings and glassware. For more information on this fully accessible, glass-filled jewelry box located at 165 North Park Avenue, call (920) 751-4658. Website: www. paperweightmuseum.com.

On the northern side of Doty Island and the river, Menasha offers its own attractions. The **Menasha Marina** provides safe harbor on the canal that runs parallel to the river channel between the Racine Street bridge to the east and the Tayco Street bridge to the west. The Marina, 140 Main Street, has 87 boat slips and the Harborhouse Gift Shop with its nautically themed finds. Phone: (920) 967-5193 in season. Nearby Naut's Landing offers high-topped pizzas and other homemade fare on the site of the former city hall and fire station. Phone: (920) 725-7777. After a hiatus of a few years, Captain Tim Paegelow, Lake Winnebago Sailing Charters, plans to reopen for business in 2008. Phone: (920) 540-3536.

Beginning in 2008, the Tayco Street bridge will be raised and lowered remotely during the navigation season by the bridge tender at Racine Street. Yet, the city plans to keep the **Tayco Street Bridge Museum,** containing photos and artifacts related to historic navigation of the Fox, open to visitors. Phone: (920) 967-5155.

From the marina, boaters can head either upstream beneath the Racine Street bridge and into Lake Winnebago or downstream toward Little Lake Butte des Morts.

Boaters heading upstream soon come to Smith Park on the Menasha side of Doty Island. Along with a boat launch, the park provides temporary docking, fishing access, picnicking, tennis and volleyball courts, softball diamond, and football/soccer field. The combination of a large pavilion with kitchen and semiformal flower gardens featuring a Victorian gazebo, a historic fountain, and latticework arbors make Smith a sought-after spot for weddings. A Memorial Building houses the Menasha Historical Society and serves as the site for various special events. The society also displays an antique Wisconsin Central caboose in a nearby park shelter.

Downstream from the marina, boaters pass under the Tayco Street bridge, through the Menasha Lock, and into Little Lake Butte des Morts. Completed in the 1850s, the hand-cranked lock is one of 17 that enabled river travel on the lower Fox, along with nine on the upper river, including the two at Portage.

Pulp, Paper, and Pollution

The paper mills that have fueled the Fox Valley economy for more than a century have also brought the challenge of water pollution. With about 20 mills operating currently, the lower Fox remains one of the nation's most industrialized rivers. Since the 1970s, paper companies have worked to reduce their dispersal of pollutants into the river, and some contaminants have been cleaned from it. But recently scientists have reported that the lower Fox is more contaminated than previously believed.

The big problem is cancer-causing polychlorinated biphenyl concentrations, or PCBs, once used in the production and recycling of carbonless copy paper. Approximately 64,000 pounds of PCBs remain in the river's sediments, according to Wisconsin Department of Natural Resources (DNR) estimates.

The **Fox River/Green Bay Natural Resource Trustee Council** (composed of the DNR, U.S. Environmental Protection Agency, U.S. Fish and Wildlife Service, Menominee and Oneida tribes of Wisconsin, and the State of Michigan) has documented injuries to the region's natural resources from PCBs. The council has requested federal Superfund support to clean up the Fox.

The council has allocated more than $35 million from settlements with paper manufacturers and council members have provided an additional $14 million in one of the nation's largest clean-up efforts. To learn more, visit the DNR website and search for "Fox River clean-up" or go to http://dnr.wi.gov/org/aw/rr/cleanup/superfund.htm. Or, visit the U.S. Fish and Wildlife website: www.fws.gov/midwest/nrda/.

Near the **Menasha Lock**, the Trestle Trail spans Little Lake Butte des Morts to form the longest (1,600 feet) pedestrian path crossing a body of water in the state. Opened in 2005, the lighted trail features a lift bridge over the Menasha Lock, a center pavilion with seating, and observation and fishing platforms. It connects the City of Menasha with the Town of Menasha's Fritse Park over an abandoned railroad line.

Near shore on the town side of the trail, Mike pointed out an egret, two great blue herons, ducks, and geese. Fritse Park provides a boat landing and access to the Friendship Trail, slated to eventually link Manitowoc, on Lake Michigan, with Stevens Point. Currently, the Friendship Trail leads as far west as the Wiouwash Trail, which runs north and south between Hortonville and Oshkosh.

The Menasha lock

If you're still boating downstream, the next park to provide a boat launch, rest rooms, and picnic area is **Lutz Park** on Appleton's west side. The 2.7-acre park also offers a pavilion, fishing pier, drinking water, grills, playground, and lighted walkway along the Fox River. The **Appleton Yacht Club,** 1200 South Lutz Drive, has served area boaters since the Great Depression.

Additional Appleton parks also draw both locals and visitors to the riverfront. Peabody Park and Telulah Park face each other across the Fox downstream from Lawrence University. The 16.2-acre **Peabody Park,** 601 North Green Bay Road, has a good view of the river from the west bank, plus a pavilion, grills, rest rooms, playground, and basketball court. **Telulah Park,** 1300 East Newberry Street, features a multitude of recreational options, with newly redesigned 18-hole disc golf course, pavilions, ball fields, playground, and rest rooms.

Telulah also contains a trailhead for the **Newberry Trail,** which winds along the river in the Appleton Flats area and connects to the CE Trail. This trail follows County Road CE through Kimberly and Combined Locks to Kaukauna.

The **Appleton Flats** contain several canals and locks that once powered the city's mills and economic growth. Originally called Grand Chute, Appleton once laid claim to sizeable rapids along the Fox. A few mills, a brewery, and other industrial buildings in the Flats have been refurbished into condos, offices, and retail businesses. Another factor in this river renaissance, the Appleton Locks reopened amid much fanfare, music, and a paddle wheeler full of dignitaries in 2007. Soon the lower Fox will be as welcoming to navigation as it was a century ago.

Across the Fox from the Flats, **Lawrence University** is one of two higher education institutions situated on the lower river (the other being St. Norbert College in De Pere). Lawrence began as one of the nation's first coeducational institutions in 1847, more than 20 years before the University of Wisconsin fully accepted women students. The historic private institution is widely recognized for its Conservatory of Music, as well as undergraduate arts and sciences programs. To reach the campus, follow the College Avenue exit off State 441. Website: www.lawrence.edu.

Near the northeast corner of campus, the **Outagamie Museum**, 330 East College Avenue, preserves the history of the lower river valley. Ongoing exhibits explore the lives of magician Houdini and author Edna Ferber, and include such artifacts as a Model T Ford in a vintage gas station. The Museum is open Tuesday through Saturday, 10:00 a.m. to 4:00 p.m., and Sunday, 12:00 p.m. to 4:00 p.m.

Southwest of Lawrence University, **Historic Hearthstone House Museum** rekindles the excitement of the harnessing of electricity. The house at 625 Prospect Avenue — parallel to Water Street and two blocks from the river — was the first in the world to be lighted by hydroelectricity. The elegant Victorian mansion, built by paper manufacturer Harry Rogers in 1882, features electroliers (electric chandeliers), nine fireplaces, and a dining room view of the Fox River. The basement Hydro-Adventure Center enables you to generate electricity from a water wheel and use a Thomas Edison-designed light switch. Phone: (920) 730-8204. Website: www.focol.org/hearthstone.

Rogers also installed an electric generator in one of his paper mills that year, and Appleton plans to move its replica of the world's first hydroelectric station, known as the Vulcan Street Plant, to the new **Vulcan Heritage Park** on the river near Jackman and Prospect streets. The park is southwest of the Paper Discovery Center and near another Fratellos Restaurant on the Fox, this one with a waterfall in addition to riverfront dining.

You can take the equivalent of a semester course in papermaking at the **Paper Discovery Center,** 425 West Water Street, learning tree identification in an outdoor learning center and walking through a replica paper-making machine. The **Paper Industry International Hall of Fame** received the building, the 1878 Atlas Mill, from the Kimberly-Clark Corporation in 1999 and opened this attraction in 2005. It's open Monday through Saturday, 10:00 a.m. to 4:00 p.m. For a more detailed introduction, phone the center at (920) 380-7491. Website: www.paperdiscoverycenter.org.

Sunset Point Park in Kimberly was another Kimberly-Clark gift: The company gave the riverbank property to the village following World War II. In addition to views of the Fox, park highlights include an amphitheater, trails, and softball fields.

Downstream, the Village of Little Chute aims for its own large-scale attraction. **Little Chute Windmill, Inc.** is a nonprofit agency planning to construct a functioning Dutch windmill and visitor center north of the river. The windmill, visitor center, and grounds landscaped with tulips and other flowers will celebrate the area's Dutch heritage and history. Website: www.littlechutewindmill.org.

Little Chute is also known for a historical event predating Dutch immigration. The Menominee Indians ceded much of their land to the United States in the Treaty of the Cedars, signed here in 1837. A Wisconsin State Historical marker on State Highway 96 on the west side of the village notes that the ceded area contains modern-day Marinette, Appleton, Oshkosh, Wausau, Stevens Point, and Wisconsin Rapids. The Menominee received $700,000 for about four million acres. After the signing, the Menominee relocated west of the Wolf River.

About 5 miles down the Fox at Kaukauna, an Indian village stood along a mile-long series of churning rapids, where the Fox dropped 50 feet in a mile. The French called this spot the Grand Kakalin, or "long portage." Sometime before 1760, Pierre Grignon, Sr., and Charles de Langlade of Green Bay established a trading post here. Grignon's son Augustin built a gristmill and sawmill and also traded furs, farmed, and helped travelers portage the rapids. He then moved to Butte des Morts in 1830 and 13 years later built a Greek revival inn, today the privately owned Augustin Grignon Hotel on the National Register of Historic Places.

His son, Charles Augustin Grignon, built a Greek revival house at the Kaukauna rapids in 1837. Owned today by the Outagamie Historical Society, the **Charles A. Grignon Mansion** is open for group tours. The property includes an orchard and gardens and provides access to several of the Kaukauna Locks. The historical society offers a paperback walking tour guide for $5, and thumbnail photos are available online. Phone: (920) 733-8445 ext. 104. Website: www.foxvalleyhistory.org.

Across the canal from the Grignon Mansion, Oscar Thilmany founded the Thilmany Paper Company in 1883.

South of Thilmany, **1000 Islands Environmental Center** traces its history to the late 1960s, when Kaukauna set aside several hundred acres, including several islands and a tract on the southeast bank of the river. The center's first building went up as a U.S. Bicentennial project in 1976. A generation later, thousands of hours of volunteer time — and public and private funding efforts — show in a canoe landing, fishing pier, an eagle observation deck, butterfly garden, and more than 7 miles of trails and boardwalk. Indoors, look for the museum-quality wild animal mounts and the live specimens — parrot, crow, zebra finches, cockatiel, chinchilla, turtle, snakes, and a hedgehog at last count. Phone: (920) 766-6321. Website: www.1000islandsenvironmentalcenter.

South of De Pere, two roads, one on either side of the Fox, invite exploration. Wisconsin Rustic Road 46 follows Old Plank Road to the eastern bank of the river. It features wooded ravines and travels off State Highway 32/57 south of County Road PP. On the west bank, County Road D (Lost Dauphin Road) edges the river all the way from Wrightstown to West De Pere. County Road D leads to a legend and the former site of Lost Dauphin State Park, about 5 miles south of De Pere.

The former park name recalls Eleazer Williams, an Episcopal missionary who eventually built a home here after coming west from New York with a delegation of Oneida Indians and other tribes seeking a place to resettle. Later in his life, Williams claimed to be the Lost Dauphin (royal title of the king's heir), the son of Louis XVI who was imprisoned as a boy after his father died on the guillotine in 1795 during the French Revolution.

At the time, many people believed rumors that the boy had escaped to the American colonies. Scores of men, including naturalist John James Audubon, claimed to be the missing child. Of the many pretenders to the royal heritage, Williams certainly ranks near the top of the list. Prince de Joinville even traveled to Green Bay in 1841 to meet with Williams. Afterward, Williams reported that the prince requested he sign away any rights to the French throne. At least, that's what Williams claimed.

Two Roman Catholic missionaries, Fathers Claude Allouez and Louis André, built the mission of St. Francis Xavier at the rapides des pères near the modern city of De Pere in 1672. You can read a Wisconsin Historical Society marker about these rapids in Voyageur Park, just north of the Claude Allouez Bridge on State Highway 32. In 1687 the Fox Indians burned the mission, but the Jesuits rebuilt it before eventually moving nearer the safety of Fort La Baye.

Voyageur Park offers a boat dock, picnic areas, and playground, and is the site of the annual Celebrate De Pere Festival (www.celebratedepere.com) featuring entertainment, a family fishing tournament, children's area, carnival rides, parade, food vendors, and fireworks. Created in 1990 to celebrate the centennial of the consolidation of the City of West De Pere and the City of De Pere, the celebration has continued annually over Memorial Day weekend; proceeds benefit a number of area veterans and other nonprofit organizations.

At the entrance to Voyageur Park on William Street, a restored 1925 Sinclair gas station — complete with two pumps out front — provides a rest stop for users of the park and the Fox River Trail. Thanks to the efforts of 210 businesses and individuals, the De Pere Historical Society moved the station to the park in 2006 after planned development threatened demolition. Called the C-Hall 4 Service Station by original owner Charles Hall, the 11-by-16-foot building later became known as the Polo Resto Service Station and associated with an adjacent polo field on the river.

The historical society is based east of Voyageur Park at **White Pillars Museum**, 403 North Broadway, and is open from 12:00 p.m. to 4:00 p.m., Monday through Friday. Phone: (920) 336-3877. Website: http://deperehistoricalsociety.org. The Greek revival museum, originally the office of the De Pere Hydraulic Company, served as one of the state's first de facto banks when its notes circulated as currency.

South of the Claude Allouez Bridge on the river's west bank, Abbot Bernard Pennings, a Dutch immigrant priest, founded **Saint Norbert College,** 100 Grant Street, in 1898. He soon expanded the curriculum to include an academic program for lay students, and oversaw its conversion to a coeducational institution in 1952. The private liberal arts college, which contains several historic buildings near the river, currently provides 40 academic programs to more than 2,000 undergraduate students and a few score of graduate students.

A new Claude Allouez Bridge, extending almost two-thirds of a mile over the Fox, replaced the former bridge in 2007, completing another project in a long line of downtown De Pere redevelopment plans. Over the past 20 years, the city has renewed green space and added condos and business developments to the area. Near the bridge, look for the operational De Pere Lock and Dam.

On the west bank of the Fox near De Pere's northern boundary, the Brown County Fairgrounds rocks with crowds, sounds, animals, a midway, and more during the annual fair, held each August. The rest of the year, a

Unlock the Fox

Fourteen years after the Pilgrims landed at Plymouth Rock in 1620, Jean Nicolet landed at Red Banks near Green Bay, and 39 years later Father Pierre Marquette and Louis Jolliet began their trans-Wisconsin journey up the Fox and down the Wisconsin rivers. The Fox-Wisconsin route opened the middle of the continent to explorers, then to fur traders, lumbermen, and settlers.

By the 1800s, the Fox River's 170-foot drop between Lake Winnebago and Green Bay attracted entrepreneurs who saw the river's waterpower potential. Canals, locks, and dams could both control the flow to facilitate boat traffic and provide water power to flour and lumber mills. By the 1850s, this waterway system was largely in place, serving the new State of Wisconsin and its burgeoning lumber industry. Later, the harnessed river supplied hydroelectric power to manufacturing plants and local communities.

Yet with the coming of the railroads and navigational challenges on the Wisconsin, the waterway served only a portion of the region's transportation needs. As the railroads linked more cities and towns, commercial river navigation waned. When the Fox grew increasingly polluted with industrial wastes in the twentieth century, even recreational use of the waterway began to decline.

The Clean Water Act of the 1970s brought some environmental improvements, but river traffic remained light. The U.S. Army Corps of Engineers, facing budget constraints, stopped operating the locks in 1984. Six years later, the Heritage Corridor was established as a pilot project and tourism initiative, with support from the National Trust for Historic Preservation and the Wisconsin Department of Tourism. The Wisconsin Fox River Navigational System Authority was created in 2001 as the entity responsible for maintaining and restoring the 150-year-old locks system. In 2004, the Department of the Army turned over to the state ownership of 17 locks and 140 acres along 39 miles of the lower river. The Friends of the Fox (www.friendsofthefox.org) continue to raise funds to augment $23 million in federal, state, and local support and shorten the time needed to completely "unlock the Fox."

variety of organizations hold events here, and the park is open to urban campers when no events are scheduled. Phone: (920) 448-4466 and press option 2. Website: www.co.brown.wi.us/Parks/parks/brown-county-fairgrounds.

The next stretch of the Fox downstream features three Green Bay museums — the **National Railroad Museum, Heritage Hill State Park,** and **Hazelwood Historic Home Museum.**

Downtown, the **Neville Public Museum** is situated on the west bank of the Fox at 210 Museum Place. One of five permanent exhibitions, On the Edge of the Inland Sea, has led thousands of school children on a walk through time from the Ice Age to the present. Other popular permanent exhibitions focus on the Green Bay Packers football team and provide space for artists to work and interact with museum visitors. The museum is open daily year-round (except for Thanksgiving, Christmas, and New Year's Day) including Wednesday and Thursday evenings to 8:00 p.m. Phone: (920) 448-4460. Website: www.nevillepublicmuseum.org.

Green Bay has experienced much redevelopment in the past 15 years. In the 1990s, the Brown County Courthouse, a Beaux Arts style building constructed in 1911, received a $10-million facelift. If you visit the building, 100 South Jefferson Street, look for the mural depicting Jean Nicolet landing at Red Banks. Also note the increasing decoration as you climb from

Almost directly across the Fox from the National Railroad Museum, Heritage Hill State Park, at the intersection of State 57 and State 172, contains four areas, each focusing on a different time in Green Bay history:

- **La Baye** depicts the fur trade era, featuring a replica bark chapel of the type built by the Menominee for Jesuit priests, an authentic fur trader's cabin, and a maple sugaring house.
- The **Growing Community** section of the park includes an 1803 cottage, the 1912 Allouez Town Hall, the 1835 Baird Law Office, a replica of the 1871 De Pere News Office and Printshop, and an 1872 library.
- The **Fort Howard** section features the original 1834 fort hospital, a replica of a frontier school, the company kitchen, and a reconstructed officers' quarters.
- The **Ethnic Agriculture** section contains a 1904 cheese factory from Kewaunee County, the 1840's home of Captain John Cotton and his wife Mary Arndt, and a windmill and log barn from an early Belgian homestead. This log home appears to be brick because it's covered by a brick façade: One theory is that after the 1871 Peshtigo Fire many people added this type of fire protection to their homes.

the first to the second and third floors and the varying styles of the rotunda columns: Doric on the first floor, Ionic on the second, and Corinthian on the third.

On the river's east bank, several new developments are bringing more people downtown. An increasing number of young professionals and empty-nesters are moving into Riverfront Lofts and other condos.

The 25-mile **Fox River State Trail** follows the river's east bank from downtown Green Bay south to St. Norbert's College and then pulls away to the east as it heads toward its terminus at Holland. The trail swings past the Hazelwood Historic House Museum, Heritage Hill State Park, and Voyageur Park.

Downstream of Hazelwood near Porlier Street, the trail connects to the Porlier Fishing Pier, where a former railroad trestle has been transformed into a pier and observation area over the river. Green Bay created the pier with $200,000 from the Superfund's Natural Resource Damage Assessment and Restoration process (NRDAR).

Although the north end of the trail officially ends (or begins) at Adams and Porlier streets, south of State Highway 32/54, it really does continue downtown. The trail for a time transforms into the riverfront walkway and then continues, approaching the confluence of the Fox and East rivers between downtown and the bay.

What the city may lack in green space along the Fox, it makes up for along the East River, where a series of parks, including **Joannes Park and Family Aquatic Center, Anne Sullivan Park, East River Park, East Lawn Park,** and more combine into one long parkway. A couple of miles farther east, Baird Creek Parkway surrounds an East River tributary. And to the north of Baird's Creek about 2 miles east of the mouth of the Fox, Bay Beach Amusement Park and Bay Beach Wildlife Sanctuary provide additional recreational opportunities.

Green Bay Harbor supports a different resource. The harbor showcases the sights and sounds of a generally healthy regional economy. A total of 213 ships used the port in 2006, carrying over 2.5 million metric tons of cargo, including coal, limestone, cement, salt, and fuel oil.

The Port of Green Bay consists of a collection of 13 terminal operators, including the lime plant, along a 3-mile stretch of riverfront, and supports about 725 jobs. To increase awareness of the port's economic impact, signs identifying each terminal went up in 2007. The signs face the river and feature such messages as "The Port reduces the need for 40,000 rail cars each year." Part of a marketing effort termed Harbor Prosperity (www. harborprosperity.com), the messages have also appeared on area billboards.

Jean Nicolet, the first European to arrive in the bay, expected to meet Asiatics. When he landed in 1634, probably at Red Banks, Nicolet wore a silk embroidered robe and fired a pistol with each hand to impress the "Asians." You can find a statue of Nicolet and read a Wisconsin Historic Society marker about him at the State Highway 57 wayside northeast of Green Bay.

Four centuries ago, most explorers cared little about the continent they were crossing. Their goal was a route to the riches of the Orient. After almost four hundred years — encompassing the eras of the fur trade, the southwestern Wisconsin lead rush, the northern lumber rush, the railroad heyday, the growth of modern manufacturing, and today's technology and communications revolutions — it's clear Nicolet did indeed find a land of vast treasures, as a trip on the Fox attests.

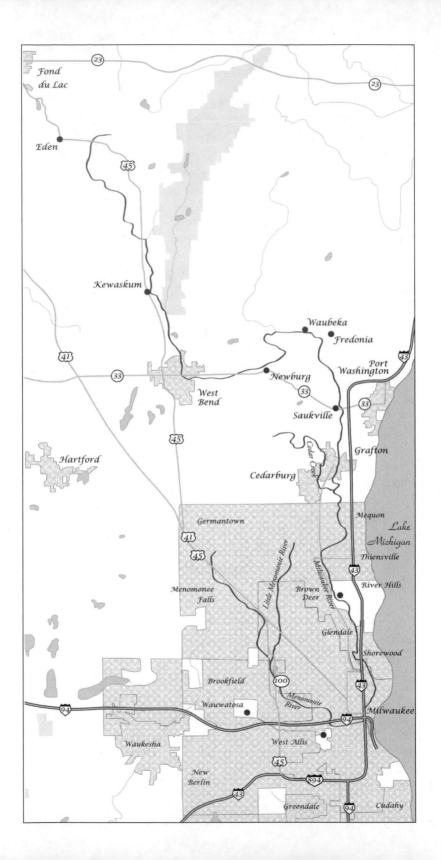

CHAPTER 10

Milwaukee

The Main Branch of the Milwaukee River rises east of Eden (really) in Fond du Lac County. It flows generally southeast for about 100 miles, emptying into Milwaukee Bay on Lake Michigan. Three other branches (West, East, and North) join the Main Branch in northern Washington and Ozaukee counties. On the lower Milwaukee, downstream from Fredonia in Ozaukee County, the main tributaries are Cedar Creek (namesake of Cedarburg), and the Menomonee and Kinnickinnic rivers, which join the Milwaukee just upstream from Milwaukee Bay. The Main Branch of the upper river together with the lower river is often referred to as the "mainstem."

The Milwaukee and its tributaries drain a basin of nearly 900 square miles on the east-facing slope of the Niagara cuesta, the backside of the limestone Niagara escarpment. Many of these streams support warm-water sport and forage fish communities, and there are even some cold-water trout streams, such as the upper 4 miles of the North Branch (formerly known as Nichols Creek) and the Watercress Creek headwaters of the East Branch.

From a high point on the East Branch in the Kettle Moraine to Milwaukee Harbor, the river falls 780 feet. Nearly half of this fall, 370 feet, occurs on the mainstem between Campbellsport and Milwaukee. Numerous falls and rapids on this stretch provided waterpower for nineteenth-century industries. Woodlands provided easily accessible raw materials, as did the very limestone over which the river fell.

Contrary to popular legend, "Milwaukee" does not mean "gathering of waters" or "gathering place by the waters." The name connotes "good place," referring to the ancient intertribal village site or sites around the confluence of the Milwaukee and Menomonee rivers.

The Milwaukee is a portal through time, offering glimpses of regional history. It's a window on contemporary issues, as well: industrial pollution, agricultural runoff, loss of stream-corridor habitat, and controversies over aging dams.

The upper Milwaukee, with its West and East Branches, flows through the glacial landscape of the Kettle Moraine. These moraines, drumlins, kames, eskers, kettles, lakes, and outwash plains developed in an ancient valley of ice that formed between the Green Bay and Lake Michigan glacial lobes. Kettles, which give the region its name, are ponds, small lakes, or even dry holes that resulted from isolated blocks of buried ice melting away as the glaciers retreated. A good place to learn about all this is the **Henry S. Reuss Ice Age Visitor Center,** a half mile west of Dundee on State Highway 67 in the Northern Unit of the Kettle Moraine State Forest. Phone: (920) 533-8322.

Dundee lies on the East Branch, just below an impoundment called Long Lake. The **Long Lake Recreation Area** and, downstream, the **Mauthe Lake Recreation Area,** offer recreational activities on land and water, winter and summer. Unlike the Long Lake impoundment, Mauthe Lake is a natural lake — a kettle, in fact — through which the East Branch runs. There is a spillway dam at its mouth, constructed in the 1950s to raise the water level to make a safer swimming beach. **Parkview General Store,** on County Road GGG near the entrance to the Mauthe Lake State Recreation Area, offers boat, canoe, and paddle boat rentals; snowshoe and cross-country ski rentals; mini golf; fishing gear, licenses and bait; groceries, hand-dipped ice cream, and homemade fudge. Phone: (262) 626-8287. Website: www.parkview-store.com.

For information on trails and three state natural areas, stop at the forest headquarters, off County Road G about 3 miles south of the Ice Age Visitor Center. You can pick up trail maps and directions to the **Milwaukee River Floodplain Forest, Milwaukee River Tamarack Lowlands,** and **Milwaukee River and Swamp** natural areas. They showcase the forest types that once dominated the basin and a variety of wildlife. The heart of the Milwaukee River and Swamp State Natural Area is accessible only by canoe, via the landing on Mauthe Lake.

Southwest of Dundee on State Highway 67, Campbellsport grew from the union of an "old village" established on the river in 1845, and a "new village" about a mile to the west, established in 1873 as the Chicago and Northwestern Railway (CNW) built its line from Milwaukee to Fond du Lac. Ludlin Crouch began the old village, Crouchville, by establishing a dam and mill.

The Campbellsport dam, in what is now a park at the intersection of Highway 67 (Main Street) and County Road Y (New Cassel Street), marks the uppermost waterpower on the Milwaukee River. South of Main Street, off New Cassel Street, Columbus Parc Court leads into **Columbus PARC** (Pleasure, Activites, Recreation, and Community). The park features ball diamonds, volleyball and basketball courts, concession stand, picnic shelter, and playground. **Whispering Trail** runs through a restored prairie along the river. Campbellsport Area Chamber of Commerce phone: 920-979-0080. Website: www.campbell sport.org.

Downstream lies Kewaskum, named after a Potawatomi chief whose village reportedly occupied a nearby hilltop. The modern village dates from 1852, when Jesse H. Myers settled on the riverbank, built a log cabin and water-powered sawmill, and soon added a gristmill. Kewaskum advertises itself as the "Gateway to the Kettle Moraine State Forest." Several trailheads east and south of town give access to the Milwaukee River Segment of the **Ice Age National Scenic Trail,** which parallels the East Branch from Washington County Road H north to Mauthe Lake. Southward, the trail heads toward West Bend. Phone: (800) 227-0046. Website: www.iceagetrail.org.

Where Kewaskum's Main Street (State Highway 28) crosses the river, a dam and millpond once stood, marking the village's historic center. The dam washed out in 1911 and was never rebuilt.

County Road S (Riverview Drive) runs north along the east side of a horseshoe bend. If, instead, you drive south, you will soon reach **River Hill Park,** which straddles the Milwaukee. A dam constructed in 1932 for flood control by the Works Progress Administration links the park's two halves, and a lit pedestrian walkway crosses the dam. The park provides fishing access above and below the dam. At the top of the hill are picnic areas with reservable shelters and kitchen facilities, playgrounds, concession stands, and a bandstand. Just below the dam, downstream-right, a canoe landing marks the beginning of the first canoeable stretch of the mainstem.

The west side of the park contains additional picnic facilities and another playground, as well as a historic log house, moved here by the **Kewaskum Historical Society** from its original location in Sheboygan County. Now the society's headquarters and museum, it is open on Sunday afternoons, 2:00 p.m. to 4:00 p.m., from Memorial Day to Labor Day. Check with the Kewaskum Area Chamber of Commerce for the schedule of the annual Independence Day Fireworks in the park. Phone: (262) 626-3336. Website: www.kewaskum.org.

A short asphalt path at the end of Parkview Drive links the park to the **Eisenbahn State Trail,** and across the trail lies **Kewaskum Creek Park,** near the creek's mouth. The 25-mile, gravel-surfaced trail runs from Eden to

West Bend, crossing or paralleling the Milwaukee River at several points. Just south of Kewaskum, the Eisenbahn intersects the Ice Age Trail. **Washington County Parks** phone: (262) 335-4445. Website: www.co.washington.wi.us. Fond Du Lac County Parks phone: (920) 929-3135. Website: www.co.fond-du-lac.wi.us.

The CNW railroad line roughly paralleled a primitive road laid out in 1845, at the direction of the Wisconsin Territorial Legislature, by highway commissioner Byron Kilbourn (one of the founders of the city of Milwaukee) and surveyor Jasper Vliet. The legislature ordered Kilbourn and Vliet to identify the halfway point of the Milwaukee-to-Fond du Lac road as a rest stop, which they found at the future site of West Bend — named for the westernmost of two sharp curves in the river.

A partnership headed by Kilbourn erected a dam, sawmill, and gristmill at the West Bend falls and rapids. The Fond du Lac Road became Main Street and today North Main Street parallels the central portion of the city's **Riverfront Parkway**, a string of city parks and green space that stretches around the river's bend. This corridor features everything from sports facilities to prairie restorations, with boardwalks over wetlands, canoe landings, and a 3.1-mile Riverwalk. Large maps at information kiosks help you find your way. West Bend Park, Recreation and Forestry Department phone: (262) 335-5080. Website: www.ci.west-bend.wi.us/Departments/PRF/ParkandRec.htm.

Barton Roller Mills stands adjacent to the Barton Dam and millpond (not to be confused with the downstream impoundment called Barton Pond). This sole remaining intact dam and mill complex on the Milwaukee dates to 1845 when Barton Salisbury built a water-powered sawmill on the river. After the sawmill burned, he rebuilt it as a gristmill. Both the dam and the mill went through more re-buildings and changes in ownership until Wilhelm Gadow bought it in 1905. (The mill building as it stands dates from 1865, and the concrete dam, rebuilt by Gadow, from 1918.) For many years Gadow and his sons, William Jr. and Walter, produced the variety of wheat and rye flours listed in the painted signage still visible on the front of the building.

The mill closed down in 1964 after Walter's death, and fell into disrepair. Family members rescued the structure in 1989. Still owned by Walter's granddaughter, Rhea Dricken, her daughter, Kay, and son, Mike, the building is now Roller Mill Suites, a complex of 22 offices at 1784 Barton Avenue. The original water turbine produces electricity under a co-generation agreement with We Energies.

Standing on the sidewalk on the Barton Avenue bridge below the dam, you can see the millrace flowing out from under the building where the tur-

Looking for Young America

North of Barton there used to be another small community by a dam, Young America. Though the dam was removed in 1992, the town still appears on some maps where Woodford Drive crosses the river, just outside the West Bend city limit. Having nothing but curiosity and those maps to go on, Mike and I went looking for Young America one late December evening.

The hamlet never incorporated and remains one of the most tranquil urban spots we encountered on many a whirlwind river exploration. The **Woodford Drive Bridge**, an aged steel truss affair, closed to motorized traffic and on River Drive a one-lane, arched, wooden bridge crosses the Eisenbahn Trail.

bine lies. Milling machinery and some other equipment remains visible inside the Roller Mill complex, which is open Monday through Friday, 8:00 a.m. to 5:00 p.m. Look up after you enter, and you'll see some of the diagonal wooden chutes that once fed grain from enormous hoppers into the roller mills on the main floor. (Roller mills grind grain between steel rollers rather than between millstones.)

The CNW laid its tracks in front of the Barton mill in 1872, giving the mill wider access to both raw materials and markets, and allowing it to remain in operation all those years. Nowadays, of course, that's the Eisenbahn State Trail right out front. The city's historic CNW depot, on Veterans Avenue between Water and Washington streets, is slated for restoration as a welcome center and trailhead.

Near the intersection of State 33 (East Washington Street) and County G (South River Road), the historic Wollen Mills Dam had deteriorated and became a hazard by 1980. West Bend removed the dam in 1988, added 61 acres to Riverside Park, and began its Riverwalk from trails in the expanded park. Riverside has become one of the city's most heavily used parks, with ball fields, and basketball, tennis, and volleyball courts, as well as horseshoe pits and picnic areas. A rentable pavilion overlooks the river and includes a kitchen, gas fireplace, rest rooms, and outside deck.

Wisconsin has removed about 100 dams since 1988, resulting in habitat restoration, improved recerational facilities, and economic development. Of course, not all dams are candidates for removal. Some provide flood control and electric power, while others block invasions of exotic species, agricultural run-off, and the release of pollutants downstream.

From West Bend, the river flows generally eastward to Fredonia, where it turns south for its final plunge to Milwaukee Bay. About 2 miles east of the West Bend airport, at the intersection of State Highway 33 and County Road M, **Goeden County Park** features handicapped-accessible fishing, a boat launch, a picnic area with grills and shelter, a playground, and vault toilets. A scenic nature trail winds along the river and through a wetland.

Head east on Highway 33 to Newburg, where **Fireman's Park** on Main Street lies within a bend in the river. The ball field and picnic shelter come alive on the first weekend in June for the annual firemen's picnic, a fundraiser for the Newburg Fire Department, which has been held annually for nearly 120 years. Website: www.newburgfirerescue.com.

Just upstream and visible from the park are the Newburg Dam and the raging outflow from a millrace that Mike Svob warns canoeists to avoid in *Paddling Southern Wisconsin*. The grassy banks of Fireman's Park, below the dam, are the put-in for canoeing the attractive stretch down to Grafton.

Just over the Ozaukee County line, **Riveredge Nature Center** is located on County Road Y off County Road MY. Established on 72 acres in 1968 by the Whitefish Bay Garden Club, Riveredge now covers 350 acres of restored prairies, forest, and wetland along the Milwaukee River and a tributary, Riveredge Creek. Included in the property, the Ephemeral Pond State Natural Area features 10 miles of hiking trails, 1.5 miles of river frontage, seven types of deciduous forests, nearly 600 species of plants, and a host of wildlife. The Riveredge Visitor Center offers a gift shop, a renovated nineteenth-century barn, and The Coop, a renovated chicken coop providing views of a bird feeding station.

The center offers a multitude of educational programs and recreational activities for all ages, year round. Birders flock to the annual Christmas Bird Count and the spring Birdathon/Bandathon, and gourmands gather for the spring maple sugarin', even if they do learn about enzymes and dissolved carbon dioxide before the sugarin' becomes the eatin'. In pursuit of its primary mission, Riveredge offers curriculum development assistance to schools, continuing education for teachers, and programs for school children and the general public. Daily trail fees apply for nonmembers. Phone: (800) 287-8098. Website: www.riveredge.us.

Riveredge also undertakes research and restoration projects like the Milwaukee River Lake Sturgeon Streamside Rearing Facility. Begun in 2006, this 25-year program aims to restore lake sturgeon to their ancestral home in Lake Michigan and their spawning grounds in its tributaries. Populations of these ancient, giant fish declined in the nineteenth and early twentieth centuries due to habitat loss, over-fishing, degraded water quality, migration-blocking dams, and deliberate destruction because they damaged fisherman's nets. Today 2,000 to 5,000 sturgeon survive in Lake Michigan, perhaps one percent of their population before settlement. None have spawned in the Milwaukee since the 1890s.

The DNR began stocking the Milwaukee with thousands of sturgeon raised at the Wild Rose Fish Hatchery in 2003, releasing them below the dam at Lime Kiln Park in Grafton. This new effort, though, seeks to raise fingerlings in mobile, streamside hatcheries on the Milwaukee and Manitowoc Rivers in Wisconsin and the Cedar and Whitefish Rivers in Michigan. The idea is to let the fish become imprinted with the unique signature of their home river, in hopes that they will someday return to it to spawn. The fish are also implanted with miniature tracking devices.

Want to see the river's past and future at the same time? Find Waubeka, a quaintly fascinating unincorporated village off the beaten track, west of Fredonia and 2 miles downstream from the mouth of the North Branch. Named, like Kewaskum, after a prominent Potawatomi chief whose village stood on the site, Waubeka lies on the wide bend where the Milwaukee turns south. It's where Flag Day originated at Stony Hill School, still standing east of town on County Road Z, and is home to the **National Flag Day Foundation Americanism Center** and museum. Website: www.nationalflagday.com.

From Newburg and the Riveredge Nature Center, follow County Road Y northwesterly across the land within the bend, until County Road Y ends at County Road A. Go east on County Road A about a half mile, then north on County Road H (Cigrand Avenue) across the river and into Waubeka. Note the **Glory Days Sports Bar and Grill** on the left, just over the bridge. This tavern dates to 1880. Phone: (262) 692-9592. Website: www.glory-dayswaubeka.com. Also note the many buildings marked with descriptive signage by the National Flag Day Foundation along the self-guided Chief Waubeka Historical Trail.

The dam that once stretched across the river here was originally built of wood and stone soon after the Potawatomi moved out in 1850. It provided waterpower for a sawmill and a gristmill on the north bank (now the site of the Flag Day VFW Park) and on the south bank for another gristmill (later the Waubeka Feed Mill) and a mother-of-pearl button factory. Look upstream from the County Road H bridge on a gray, misty winter day, and you'll see those two mills still standing on the left — two pale bluish-gray buildings peeking through bare trees, ghosts of Waubeka's past.

Singing for the Sturgeon

One gorgeous October Saturday on the Milwaukee River, about 275 people of all ages gathered near the Thiensville Dam to view 158 primeval fish, six months old and six to eight inches long. Cute little guys. Hard to believe they'll grow to be six to nine feet long, weigh as much as 200 pounds, and live 50 to 100 years — if they survive.

Mike and I gathered by the river for **Riveredge Nature Center's** second annual release of sturgeon fingerlings. Fertilized eggs from Lake Winnebago sturgeon spawning in the lower Wolf River had hatched and grown in Milwaukee River water at the center's Streamside Rearing Facility near Newburg, in hopes they will imprint this river and return here to spawn. A corps of 31 dedicated volunteers has fed them, monitored their growth, cleaned their tanks, tracked water quality, and kept the facility running.

It's hard to let them go, according to volunteer Marilyn John. "Are they strong enough to survive on their own? Will they hold their own against predators? Will they figure it out? It's like watching your kids going to school for the first time, hoping they don't get picked on."

Forest County Potawatomi holy man Billy Daniels and his assistant, Brian Franz, offered prayers in Potawatomi and then sang for the sturgeon. They had the honor of releasing the first fish into the river. Then sponsors who had donated money for the privilege of releasing a sturgeon lined up at the mobile hatchery. Each carried a fish to the river in a small plastic bucket, and, one by one, 158 Milwaukee River sturgeon swam free. If all goes well, in 20 or 25 years, many of the females will return to the Milwaukee to spawn.

Between Waubeka and Fredonia, the Milwaukee turns south for the final 40-mile run to its mouth. Here the river parallels the lakeshore, its course largely determined by the north-south orientation of glacial moraines.

Between Fredonia and Saukville, four Ozaukee County parks (Waubedonia, Hawthorne Hills, Tendick, and Ehlers) offer a variety of riverside activities and facilities. **Hawthorne Hills,** on County Road I south of Waubeka, includes the Hawthorne Hills County Golf Course and the Ozaukee County Historical Society's Pioneer Village. Look for canoe landings at Waubedonia, Tendick, and Ehlers. **Waubedonia,** south of County Road A near its intersection with County Road I, provides six campsites near the canoe landing and is a popular fishing spot for smallmouth bass. It's also the put-in for the 14-mile Grafton Downriver Canoe Race, held each year on the last Sunday in April. Website: www.graftonjaycees.org/Canoe _ Race.html. **Ehlers,** on County Road W, just north of Saukville, is a small park offering fishing and picnicking, besides its canoe landing. **Tendick** is a relatively new park and nature preserve. Most of it is off the river, but its riverside portion includes the canoe landing and a wetland boardwalk. Access is on County Road O, which parallels the river for 4.5 miles north of Saukville's village center.

Saukville has been a historic crossroads village since before European settlement. Two major trails intersected here at a ford in the Milwaukee River. The north-south **Green Bay Trail** linked the Lake Michigan-Des Plaines River portage at Chicago to Green Bay. The east-west **DeKorra** (or Decorah) **Trail** ran from Sauk Creek on Lake Michigan (Port Washington) to the Fox-Wisconsin portage (see Fox Chapter 9). At the Saukville crossroads grew one of the prominent intertribal trading villages in the area, housing at various times representatives of the Ojibwe, Ottawa, Potawatomi, Menominee, Osaki (Sauk), and Mesquaki (Fox). Immigrants flooded in as the tribes vacated the area after 1830, and by the 1850s, they

Releasing sturgeon to repopulate the Milwaukee

had remade the crossroads village in their own image. By then the trails had become government roads that later became segments of the state and federal highway systems. The Dekorra Trail became Highway 33.

The Green Bay Trail was reportedly a segment of a much longer overland route, from Hudson Bay to the Gulf of Mexico. It followed the ridge tops of the lake-border glacial moraines, which stayed relatively dry even in the wet seasons. As with most trails, there were forks and alternate routes along the way, including a western route via Fond du Lac and Lake Winnebago. The mainstem (to borrow a river word) became the Green Bay Road, for some time the only north-south road in eastern Wisconsin.

Federal legislation in 1832 authorized construction of a military road and mail route (a "post road") from Fort Dearborn at Chicago to Fort Howard at Green Bay, and in March 1835 the U.S. Army Corps of Topographical Engineers surveyed and officially marked the route. Eventually sections were "paved" with planking. It took a month for the mail carriers to go each way, on foot.

The Green Bay Road still exists along most of its length, often still with that name, although some urban stretches have been renamed and some stretches became numbered or lettered highways. Since 1993, it has also been marked by the state as the Green Bay Ethnic Trail, highlighting the numerous and distinctive immigrant settlements along it. Between Saukville and downtown Milwaukee the road largely parallels the Milwaukee River, and we followed it to explore that stretch, thankful that the road is now surfaced with asphalt and concrete rather than oak planks!

Our starting point was the State Highway 33 (Green Bay Avenue) bridge over the Milwaukee at Saukville. Built in 1928, this is one of the few steel truss bridges still in service in the area, and the only one we know of still open to vehicular traffic. A block west of the river, Green Bay Avenue forms one side of a triangular village "square," where you'll find a historic marker about the crossroads, a veterans' memorial, and a reconstructed nineteenth-century bandstand.

At this crossroads, the Green Bay and DeKorra trails diverged after meeting about a mile east of the river. Across the road, at the corner of Green Bay Avenue and Ulao Road, stands the Payne Hotel, Saukville's first commercial building. Built in 1847, it is one of the stops on Saukville's self-guided historic walking tour. One block southeast is **Peninsula Park,** a municipal park enclosed within a bend in the river that offers baseball fields, fishing, picnicking, and the annual July Fourth fireworks.

From the triangular square, State Highway 33 (DeKorra Road) runs northwesterly, while the Green Bay Road continues south as County Road

O (Main Street). Follow County Road O to Grafton, where you'll find your-self on Green Bay Road again, until it becomes 12th Avenue for a while. One block east of the intersection of 12th Avenue and Washington State Highway 60 (Street), between 13th Avenue and the river, is **Veterans Memorial Park** on Grafton Millpond. Along the grassy banks of the millpond, the park offers picnicking, fishing, a boat launch, a bandstand, basketball courts, and a play-ground, as well as a shelter with electricity and plumbing.

Across Bridge Street, below the dam, the stone buildings of the **Grafton Mills** complex, dating from the 1880s, have been redeveloped as offices, stu-dios, galleries, and retail shops. The north building, originally a gristmill producing "White Lily" flour, houses the Grafton Yarn Store. The south building, with a distinctive six-story tower, was a branch of the Cedarburg Woolen Mill. Later the Badger Worsted Mills occupied the complex, until that company closed in 1980. The tower originally supported a wooden water tank.

Two blocks west, at the intersection of Bridge Street and 12th Avenue, look for **Paramount Plaza** and the Paramount Restaurant. These celebrate Grafton's role in the early recording industry, and a brief moment in time, from 1929 to 1932, when blues greats Charley Patton, Son House, Skip

Grafton Dam

James, and many others came here to record some of their greatest work in a chair factory on the Green Bay Road.

The story takes us a few blocks south to the intersection of 12th Avenue and Falls Road, near the Falls Road bridge over the Milwaukee. The rapids here, known as Milwaukee Falls, were dammed in 1847. Located in the upper reaches of the **Grafton Dells** where the river cuts through the dolomitic limestone of the Niagara cuesta, the impoundment became known as Chair Factory Millpond after the Milwaukee Falls Chair Company, which operated here from 1848 to 1873. You can still see the foundations along the river at 12th and Falls. Eventually, the factory became a subsidiary of the **Wisconsin Chair Company** of Port Washington. Concrete replaced or reinforced the original dam in 1914.

Wisconsin Chair, established in 1888, was one of a handful of furniture manufacturers in the Lake Michigan basin that pioneered the use of molded plywood in commercial and domestic seating and made cabinets on contract for the Edison Phonograph Company. In 1916, the company launched its own line of phonographs and, like the big three (Edison, Victor, and Columbia) also began producing recordings to sell with them. In 1917, it converted part of the Grafton factory into a record pressing plant for its Paramount Records label.

The growth market for phonographs and recordings in the 1910s and 1920s was in the burgeoning immigrant neighborhoods of burgeoning industrial cities. Wisconsin Chair went after that market, at first focusing on German, Scandinavian, and "Spanish" (Latino) music, recorded in studios in New York City and Chicago, and in Richmond, Indiana. During the 1920s, the company entered the increasing market in the southern states for "race" and "hillbilly" recordings aimed at African- and Anglo-Americans and particularly made a name for itself in the blues and jazz market. Some of those records are now potentially worth thousands on the collector's market.

With the onset of the Great Depression in 1929, the company retrenched, giving up its leased recording studios and creating its own in an outbuilding at the Grafton factory. Hundreds of artists, both local and out-of-state, recorded there. By 1932, however, with the economy bottoming out, Wisconsin Chair closed the Grafton plant and got out of the recording and phonograph business. The company itself survived another two decades.

The chair factory buildings were demolished in 1938, but the dam remained. With no owner of record and no maintenance, the dam deteriorated. In 1985, the DNR classified it as a significant hazard, launching a prolonged debate. The concrete was crumbling, and the spillway had separated from the main structure. The dam had no gates to control high water levels, and a wall of the millrace was in danger of imminent collapse. The DNR declared the dam abandoned, and removed it during December 2000 and January 2001. In September of 2003, an aquatic census at Milwaukee Falls found that the carp and other undesirable species had largely disappeared, and that healthy, breeding populations of smallmouth bass and a dozen other species had become established.

This dam removal may have had one unintended consequence, having nothing to do with river ecology. Rumor had it that when Wisconsin Chair shut down the Grafton plant in 1932, workers dumped boxes of unsold records into the millpond. Other rumors say that records, then made of shellac, were burned for fuel or used to patch holes in walls, and that the metal master discs were sold for scrap. But logic never stopped a good treasure hunt. In 2006, the PBS television program History Detectives picked up the story and came to Grafton to film it. They brought with them a dive team to search the river bottom. The divers found nothing, of course, but the crew learned of the dam removal and the washing away of 159 years' worth of accumulated sediment and debris. Did some undiscovered treasure by Son House go the way of the carp? We'll never know.

Maybe they should have gone diving about a quarter of a mile downstream, at the lower end of Milwaukee Falls, where sediment and debris collect behind the **Lime Kiln Dam** at Lime Kiln Park. To drive to this dam, stay on 12th Avenue, which once again becomes Green Bay Road south of Falls Road, and look for the park entrance on your left. If you continue south on Green Bay Road past the park entrance, you'll climb a substantial hill that was once a coral reef in a tropical sea between 415 and 430 million years ago, when what is now North America was on the equator. Now it's a massive deposit of the magnesium-rich form of limestone known as dolomite. (The Milwaukee Public Museum provides a web page with an interesting exploration of this and other reefs in the Milwaukee area: www.mpm. edu/collections/learn/reef/intro.html.)

This 28-acre park is both a recreation area and a historic site. Three large lime kilns from the late nineteenth century, with explanatory signage, give a glimpse of one of Wisconsin's most important early industries. Watch for the distinctive piles of white "lime spoils," a waste product. Also look for the steel truss bridge that used to be the Bridge Street bridge by Grafton Dam, moved here in 1996 to continue in service as a pedestrian crossing over a small creek. The park boasts picnic areas with grills, a pavilion, disc golf, a boat launch below the dam, and volleyball courts. Follow the asphalt drive into the southeast end of the park to find the picnic area in the old quarry. Against the back wall of the quarry, a huge pile of lime spoils, obviously dumped from the top of the quarry, stands out in bold relief.

Lime Kiln Park hosts two noteworthy annual events. The Holidaze July Fourth Celebration is a three-day festival featuring live bands, carnival rides, bingo and fireworks. In September, the **Grafton Blues Association** sponsors the **Paramount Blues Festival.** Phone: (262) 208-6288. Website: www.graftonblues.org.

Grafton has one other park of special note: **River Island Park,** 1650 Nancy Lynn Court, features a three-hole golf course on an island in the river. Grafton Area Chamber of Commerce phone: (262) 377-1650. Website: www.grafton-wi.org.

South of Grafton, Green Bay Road and the river diverge for a time, the road angling southwesterly to Hamilton, Mequon, and Thiensville.

The road crosses Cedar Creek at Hamilton, site of the first stagecoach stop on the road. **Hamilton Park,** just off Green Bay Road on Hamilton Road, displays several historical markers. A rapids near the Green Bay Road bridge marks the place where a dam was removed in 1996. Upstream is the historic mill town of Cedarburg, now a popular tourist destination, and

Lime Kiln Park in Grafton

Limestone Roasting on an Open Fire

One of the largest yet least known of Wisconsin's early industries was the manufacture of high-grade lime for use in cement, mortar, plaster, whitewash, soil conditioning, and leather tanning. The manufacture of lime is not complex, and many early settlers made their own or manufactured it for sale on a small scale. The ruins of small, individual kilns for "roasting" limestone, as it was called, dot the landscape wherever limestone was easily accessible.

The quarries in **Grafton's Lime Kiln Park** opened in the 1870s after the Wisconsin Central Railway (later absorbed by the Milwaukee Road) laid a track along the Milwaukee River on its way from Milwaukee to Green Bay. Water power from the falls drove air compressors for the pneumatic drills used in the quarry. There were once five large kilns in a row here, operated by the Milwaukee Falls Lime Company, incorporated in 1890. The kilns operated until about 1930, when the depression, changing markets, and new technologies put many Wisconsin lime producers out of business.

Three of the kilns have been restored. At the end of the row you'll also see the foundation of a head frame that housed a large winch. Horse- or mule-drawn dump cars on rails carried the quarried stone to the kilns. Then the winch pulled the cars up onto a trestle running above the top of the kilns, where they dumped their loads into the central shafts.

Several white piles of lime spoils are visible in Grafton's Lime Kiln Park. They are also visible in another Lime Kiln Park, this one a wooded oasis along the Menomonee River in downtown Menomonee Falls, just south of the Main Street Bridge. This is one of a long, intermittent string of parks and greenspace forming the Menomonee River Parkway through Milwaukee and Waukesha Counties. A lighted asphalt path takes you along the river and through the woods, where the river plunges through a gorge cut through Silurian reef. The rapids here, including one modest waterfall, are the Menomonee Falls from which the village takes its name.

The two surviving kilns date from 1891. You'll find them, and a spoils pile, next to the waterfall. Across the river is the quarry that fed them, now overgrown but accessible via a path that descends from a footbridge over a small tributary. The site has recently been designated the Lime Kiln Natural Area, and plans are afoot to restore and maintain it.

farther upstream in **Covered Bridge County Park** is the sole surviving original covered bridge in the state, built in 1876, spanning Cedar Creek.

Downstream, the river meanders into Mequon, a township that incorporated as a city in 1957. The shoreline is mostly wooded, but increasingly developed as the river approaches Thiensville, a historic village now surrounded by the City of Mequon. Despite development, Mequon does have several small parks and a nature preserve along the river. **City of Mequon Parks Department** phone: (262) 236-2945. Website: www.mequon. govoffice.com.

Jochim Heinrich Thien, an immigrant from Saxony, built the first dam and mill at Thiensville in 1842–43. Today, **Village Park** on the Thiensville Dam millpond provides a paved boat launch, picnic area and shelter, playground, ball field, and the Rotary Riverwalk between the river and the former millrace. From Green Bay Road in Thiensville, turn east (left) on Elm Street and drive one block to the park.

Return to Green Bay Road, which curves west to intersect with Main Street/Cedarburg Road. Turn left and continue south. Though the name has changed, you're still on the old Green Bay Road. Soon you'll see Remington's

Thiensville Rotary Riverwalk, between river and a former mill race

River Inn, which provides a deck overlooking the river, and Fiddleheads Espresso Bar and Café, which features a dining room with river views.

Division Street marks the southern boundary of Thiensville; across it, to the south, are **Mequon Community Park** and City Hall. On your left, between Cedarburg Road and the river, you'll see **Old Settlers Park,** tiny, and without facilities. What is there, however, is an old house, the Yankee Settler's Cottage. Built in 1839 by Isham Day, the cottage is reportedly the oldest building in Ozaukee County still standing on its original foundation.

The intersection just ahead, Mequon Road, is where State Highway 57 turns east toward I-43. South of the intersection, Cedarburg Road/Green Bay Road remains Highway 57. On the southeast corner of the intersection, with its back to the river, is the Riversite Building, a strip mall built in 1988. According to a plaque in the foyer, the building "reflects the forms, proportion, materials, and lighting common to Ozaukee County's mill and river edge buildings of the early nineteenth century." The Riversite Restaurant, in the south end of the building, offers a full bar, outdoor patio, and dining room with a full view of the river.

Continue south on Highway 57 into Milwaukee County, and you'll see the highway become Green Bay Road again. About 5 miles into Milwaukee County, you'll come to **Kletzsch County Park** in Glendale, and then **Lincoln Park** at the intersection of Green Bay and Hampton Roads. On the northeast corner of the intersection, look for a concrete obelisk bearing a bronze plaque commemorating the pioneer road from Chicago to Green Bay. The Wisconsin Society of Chicago began erecting these markers along the Green Bay Road in the fall of 1927, with a goal of placing one every mile, all the way from Chicago to Green Bay. We don't know how far they got before the Great Depression closed in, or how many markers have survived.

South of **Lincoln Park,** Green Bay Avenue no longer closely follows the river, which curves sharply east. The highway transforms into Martin Luther King Drive, which becomes Old World Third Street, meeting the river again at **Pere Marquette Park** downtown. Eventually, to the south in Racine County, Green Bay Road resurfaces as State Highway 31, continuing on toward Chicago.

We returned to Kletzsch Park to follow the thread of parks along the river between the Milwaukee County line and North Avenue (the foremost being Kletzsch, Lincoln, Estabrook, Kern, Gordon, and Riverside). All offer a variety of picnicking, sports, fishing, and other recreational amenities, including access to the **Milwaukee Urban Water Trail** and the **Oak Leaf Recreational Trail.** The Friends of Milwaukee's Rivers created the water

Fishermen at Kletzsch Park Falls

trail, a 25-mile paddling route on portions of the Milwaukee, Menomonee, and Kinnickinnic rivers, in 2005. For maps and detailed information on the parks and bike trail, contact the Milwaukee County Parks System. Phone: (414) 257-7275. Website: www.countyparks.com. For maps and information about the urban water trail, contact Friends of Milwaukee's Rivers. Phone: (414) 287-0207. Website: www.mkeriverkeeper.org.

The parks are virtually contiguous, linked by greenspace that forms a parkway with few interruptions. Milwaukee River Parkway from the north end of Kletzsch Park to Hampton Road in Lincoln Park, Hampton to Estabrook Parkway, and Estabrook Parkway to the south end of Estabrook Park at Capitol Drive, combine to present a seamless drive along the river.

Kletzsch Park Falls is a bit deceiving at first glance — it's actually a dam, built for flood control by the Civilian Conservation Corps in the 1930s, but done in serpentine shape with limestone facing to make it look like a natural falls.

Estabrook Falls, in the northern part of Estabrook Park, is a natural drop over a dolomite ledge, and the park also boasts a unique flood control dam built by the Public Works Administration in 1940. Its 10 floodgates are generally open from May to October and closed during the winter. Just upstream from the dam, a line of concrete "dragon's teeth" deflect ice floes and other debris during spring floods, preventing them from crashing into the flood gates.

On the northern edge of Estabrook, the **Hilton Milwaukee River Hotel,** 4700 North Port Washington Road, offers guests many river-facing rooms, and diners in The Anchorage Restaurant have their pick of tables along a wall of riverfront windows. Phone: (414) 962-6040. Website: www.milwaukeeriver.hilton.com.

Just inside the southern end of Estabrook Park, across from picnic area number seven, the Benjamin Church house, also known as **Kilbourntown House,** dates to 1844. Church, a pioneer carpenter and builder, built this Greek revival house at Fourth and Court streets in Byron Kilbourn's section of pioneer Milwaukee, across the river from the settlement established by Kilbourn's arch rival, Solomon Juneau. Church built the house of hand-hewn oak and elm timbers, lining the exterior walls with brick for insulation and strength. Moved to the park in 1938, the house is open from July 1 to Labor Day, 9:00 a.m. to 5:00 p.m. Tuesdays, Thursdays, and Saturdays, and 1:00 to 5:00 p.m. Sundays.

Estabrook Falls

The dragon's teeth at the north end of Estabrook Park

Downstream, across from Kern Park, **Hubbard Park** was once called, in turn, Leuddemann's-on-the-River, Zwietusch's Mineral Springs Park, Wonderland, Coney Island, and Ravenna. In the early 1900s, the area boomed with music and bustled with activities including a huge water slide and Ferris wheel, and, later, a roller coaster. Wisconsin poet Ella Wheeler Wilcox even wrote a poem, "Luedemann's-on-the-River," a happy memory of carefree times at the park. The village of Shorewood purchased the property in 1920. The roller coaster is long gone, but the park provides access to the Oak Leaf Trail along the river, and you can walk through a double-stone arch underpass beneath the former Chicago and Northwestern Railroad tracks. CNW built the underpass to enable ice-cutters to drive their horse-drawn wagons to the river.

In case you spot the boat-shaped house, 3138 North Cambridge Avenue, and wonder, it is indeed a permanently grounded ship. "Captain" Gustafson built this small home facing the river in 1923 — with help from his friends and parts from a Sturgeon Bay shipyard, according to Professor

Frederick I. Olson and Virginia A. Palmer, authors of the University of Wisconsin–Extension *Guide to the Milwaukee River.*

The **Oak Leaf Trail** continues along the former CNW railroad bed along the east bank through **Riverside Park,** home to the Urban Ecology Center. This nonprofit organization promotes environmental awareness, presents educational programs, and helps preserve the Milwaukee River. From Owl Prowls to snowshoe treks and an annual Halloween costume canoe trip, the center organizes imaginative experiences to link urban children and adults with the river that runs through their city. Phone: (414) 964-8505. Website: www.UrbanEcologyCenter.org.

The first dam at North Avenue was made of timber and constructed in 1835 to control flows in both the river and the Rock River Canal. In the aftermath of the huge success of the Erie Canal, the Milwaukee and Rock River Canal Company concocted an unrealistic plan (at any rate unrealistic in twenty-first-century hindsight) to dig a channel from the Milwaukee and Menomonee rivers to the Rock River and from there establish a shipping route through Madison's four lakes to the Mississippi.

The company completed only about a 1-mile section before going bankrupt in 1866, but not before a number of water-powered mills had been established on the canal.

South of North Avenue on the east bank of the river, the River Boat Restaurant operated for years on River Boat Road off Commerce Street before becoming Melanec's Wheelhouse Dinner Theatre, which subsequently also closed. We hope that the distinctive building with old street lamps topping an iron fence will reopen in the future. South of River Boat Road, segments of the completed RiverWalk line both sides of the Milwaukee, offering river access, recreational opportunities, and even commuting options.

Pere Marquette Park, west of the river between State Street and Kilbourn Avenue, provides a hub for many RiverWalk activities. A water taxi, operated by Inner Harbor Marine, docks at the park; and the Westown Association sponsors free Wednesday evening concerts, River Rhythms, from June through Labor Day. Special events — like RiverSplash! at the beginning of June and the Milwaukee River Challenge, a September rowing competition — enliven the 1.9-acre park. This central public space contains a gazebo on the river and a bronze statue of Father Jacques Marquette, who reportedly once camped in the vicinity in 1673.

The Father Marquette statue is one of a series of sculptures in varied metals, neon, and other materials, that have been positioned along the river

Milwaukee's RiverWalk

or nearby. The walk itself features 18 bronze medallions embedded in the pathway. Designed by elementary school children, the medallions were cast by artist Peter Flanary.

On the west side of Pere Marquette Park, the Milwaukee County Historical Museum offers permanent and changing exhibitions about area history, including local parks and other urban natural areas. Phone: (414) 273-8288. Website: www.milwaukeecountyhistsoc.org.

Across the river from Pere Marquette Park, the **Marcus Center for the Performing Arts** makes a home for the Milwaukee Symphony Orchestra, Florentine Opera Company, Milwaukee Ballet Company, First Stage Milwaukee, Milwaukee Youth Symphony Orchestra, Martin Luther King Day Celebration, United Performing Arts Fund, Ethnic and Cultural Festivals, and scores of special events each year. Phone: (414) 273-7121. Website: www.marcuscenter.org.

In addition to the water taxi, two other boats offer river cruises. **The Iroquois** provides narrated tours of the river and harbor, operating a regular daily schedule from Memorial Day through Labor Day. Phone: (414) 294-9450. Website: www.mkeboat.com. The *Brew City Queen II* offers RiverWalk cocktail and dinner tours plus weekend brewery tours from May through October. Pontoon and paddleboat rentals are also available. Phone: (414) 283-9999. Website: www.riverwalkboats.com.

If you'd prefer to stroll, **Historic Milwaukee, Inc.,** 828 North Broadway, Suite 110, offers walking tours, special events, and presentations, all with a historical focus. Phone: (414) 277-7795. Website: www.historicmilwaukee.org.

The revitalized **Historic Third Ward** fronts the east bank of the Milwaukee south of I-794. The nineteenth-century industrial and warehouse district now displays galleries, theaters, eateries, shops, condos, and apartments. Several businesses are located directly on the RiverWalk. The Milwaukee Institute of Art and Design (MIAD) presents twin galleries downriver from the confluence with the Menomonee: The Brooks Stevens Gallery of Industrial Design and the Frederick Layton Gallery, which showcases contemporary fine art. Phone: (414) 847-3200. Website: www.miad.edu.

In the Third Ward, businesses not on the riverfront are no more than a short saunter from it, and a parking ramp at the corner of Chicago and Water streets is little more than a block from the RiverWalk. **Historic Third Ward Association** phone: (414) 273-1173. Website: www.historicthirdward.org.

When visiting the Third Ward, we're always drawn to the **Milwaukee Public Market,** where we find fresh ethnic foods to try and ingredients to take home. The second floor offers seating to enjoy your finds, along with river vistas. The market also provides cooking classes and events like arts and gift shows. Phone: (414) 336-1111. Website: www.milwaukeepublicmarket.org.

From the RiverWalk you can see the mouth of the Menomonee, with an old Soo (Minneapolis, St. Paul, and Sault Ste. Marie) Line swing bridge spanning the big tributary just east of Plankinton Avenue. Like the Milwaukee, the Menomonee — not to mention the Kinnickinnic and the Little Menomonee rivers, plus Honey and Underwood creeks — is surrounded by parks, golf courses, and other greenspace in its journey through this urban area. The **Hank Aaron State Trail** roughly parallels the Menomonee, connecting Miller Park Stadium to downtown trails and Lake Michigan. North of Canal Street, a trail loop directly flanks the river's south bank.

Before settlement, the Milwaukee River entered Lake Michigan more than a half mile south of the current location, in a low delta of wild rice and grass fields. Indian villages occupied the conjunction of rivers and lake. A sandbar had built up across the natural mouth, obstructing the entrance of ships into the river. In 1857, a straight cut from the lake to the river provided a shipping entrance and a secure inner harbor.

The straight cut created **Jones Island,** surrounded by the channel, Lake Michigan, and the Kinnickinnic and Milwaukee rivers. Named for James Monroe Jones, who had a shipbuilding business here, the island became a peninsula as sediment filled in the original mouth.

In the 1870s, the island attracted Kashubes, Polish immigrants from the Baltic Seacoast, who brought with them a strong fishing culture and built homes, taverns, stores, and a post office. Within a few years they had established a vibrant, bustling seafaring community. Scandinavian and German fishermen and their families also settled on the island.

The first Kashube settler, Jacob Muza, bought a house from a German owner but never received a deed. As more people moved onto the island, lands were divided and sold, often without official registration. In the 1890s, the Illinois Steel Mills challenged the ownership of many properties in court, and many island homes were removed to make way for the steel plant.

In 1915 the city condemned Jones Island, first, to make way for a sewage treatment plant. Later, outer harbor facilities replaced the remains of the fishing settlement, as well as the Illinois Steel Mills.

You can take a fishing boat tour of the area with a stop for lunch at a restaurant overlooking the island, through the nonprofit organization, **Urban Anthropology, Inc.** It also offers a cruise up the Milwaukee and Menomonee rivers led by an anthropologist who discusses the communities of Indians, Irish, Italians, and other ethnic groups who settled the area. An optional 30-minute add-on walking tour explores the Third Ward, its history and renaissance. Phone: (414) 271-9417. Website: www. urbananthropology.org.

Another historic location, the **Milwaukee River Flushing Station/ Alterra Coffee,** 1701 Lincoln Memorial Drive, serves hot coffee to patrons streaming by on their way to offices, condos, or apartments. The coffee shop and interpretive center, a partnership between Alterra Coffee Roasters and the Metropolitan Milwaukee Sewerage District, commemorates the history of the flushing station. Built in 1888, the station could pump 500 million gallons of lake water into the lower Milwaukee River to flush out pollution and waste. The interpretive center also provides information on energy conservation, environmental protection, and sustainability. Alterra Coffee Roaster phone: (414) 273-3747.

From source to mouth, the Milwaukee River cuts a channel through silt, gravel, rock, and time. Like the layers of rock exposed in a road cut, the river tells the stories of the plants, wildlife, and peoples who have lived along it. From Indian to fur trader, fisherman to boat captain, German to Italian settler, the river leads to them all. Who knows what ghost will arise around the next river bend? Each twist and turn reveals a new perspective on the multi-layered past of Southeast Wisconsin.

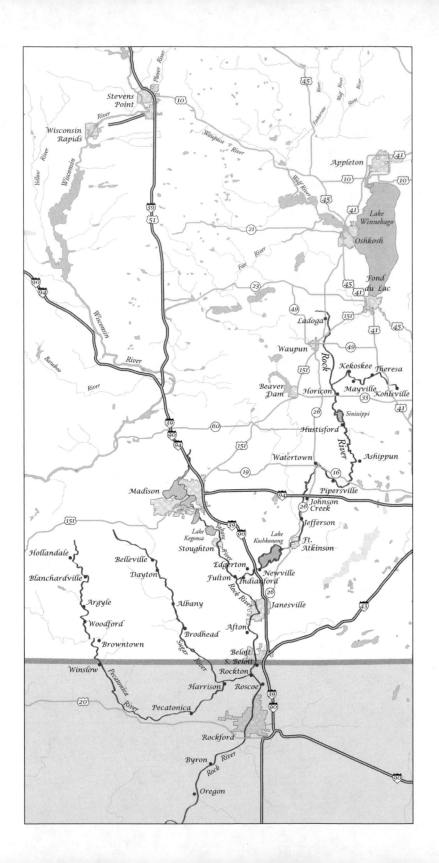

CHAPTER 11

Rock

ompared to the Fox and the Wisconsin, the Rock River is flatter with a lower gradient, dropping, for example, only 34 feet over the 58 miles between Horicon Marsh and the Watertown Dam. The East, South, and West branches of the Rock meet in **Horicon Marsh,** and the full river leaves the marsh from its southern edge at the city of Horicon. From there, the Rock flows about 130 miles to the Wisconsin-Illinois border and another 160 miles across Illinois.

If you've never been in Horicon Marsh (I hadn't until we visited in the late spring of 2007), your first visit might surprise you. The wildlife area southwest of Lake Winnebago is perhaps one fourth as large as the lake.

Blue Heron Landing, Horicon

While I'd driven west of Horicon on more than one fall day and seen the huge numbers of Canada geese, I'd never actually set foot in the marsh. Up close, it appeared as big and complex as the swirling swarms of geese, which can number up to 250,000 in October and November.

Mike and I took a pontoon boat tour from **Blue Heron Landing** near the State Highway 33 bridge in downtown Horicon. Horicon Marsh Boat Tours also offers historical displays including a mounted heron and its nest of twigs, a gift shop, and canoe and kayak rentals. Phone: (920) 485-4663. Website: www.horiconmarsh.com.

Our tour began with two boats lashed side-to-side, piloted by one captain. I picked a seat on the outer edge of one boat in hopes of scoping more birds. More than any other wildlife, this marsh is about the birds, though mink, muskrat, beaver, deer, red fox, turtles, and frogs live here too.

We slid away from the landing and headed upriver, running beneath the Highway 33 Bridge and past a city park where geese grazed on the grass. Our captain noted that there are 11 sub-species of wild geese, all similar in appearance but of different sizes. Soon, we were motoring under a second bridge where barn swallows nested on horizontal girders beneath the deck. After we passed the extensive John Deere Horicon Works along the right bank, we found ourselves on the broad sweep of Horicon Marsh.

Before us, flat, watery fields of cattails, areas of open water, and occasional wooded islands and dikes stretched as far as I could see. Our captain explained that Horicon is the largest freshwater cattail marsh in the nation, containing 32,000 acres in a 3- to 5-mile-wide band extending over 13 miles. Eons ago, Horicon was a glacial lake, hemmed on the east by the Niagara Escarpment, the limestone and dolomite ledge that extends from Wisconsin to New York, where it forms the base of Niagara Falls. Now fed by branches of the Rock, other streams, and groundwater springs, the waters of Horicon Marsh are generally less than two feet deep, except in river channels and the dredged Main Ditch, which bisects the marsh from north to south.

We headed into the straight 5.5-foot deep ditch, while the river channel continued northwest toward Mieske Bay. We waved to a family in kayaks, who slowly poked along the shore, casting a line into the water every now and then. While the marsh contains a large number of carp, it also offers up panfish and other more desirable species.

The **Main Ditch** was dredged from 1910 to 1914 in an attempt to drain the land and promote agriculture. But the plan failed when the marsh's exposed peat burned, leaving a wasteland behind.

Earlier efforts to tame the marsh had proved equally unsuccessful. In 1846, early entrepreneurs built a dam to power a sawmill, holding back the water and flooding the marsh to create a 51-square-mile Lake Horicon, devastating the wetland habitat in the process. It's hard to picture now, but in 1860 five steamboats plied the lake carrying farmers' produce to Horicon for shipment by rail. Farming in the peaty soil, however, proved unproductive in the long run. The dam was removed in 1869, and the habitat and wildlife returned — along with unregulated hunting that resulted in the loss of duck populations by 1900.

Citizen interest revived in restoring the marsh. Louis "Curly" Radke led a seven-year campaign lobbying the Wisconsin legislature to support restoration. The Horicon Marsh Wildlife Refuge Bill, passed in 1927, mandated a dam at Horicon to restore water levels appropriate to the marsh. The U.S. Fish and Wildlife Service purchased the northern section of the marsh in the 1940s, designating it a National Wildlife Refuge. Today, the federally maintained section encompasses about 21,000 acres, with the state retaining and managing about 11,000 acres of the southern marsh.

This cooperative effort has bequeathed to us a wetland world rich in wildlife. Though managed primarily for geese and ducks, the marsh attracts more than 260 kinds of birds, including several species an amateur birder like me had never heard of: the black-necked stilt, marbled gotwit, black-crowned night heron, and red-necked phalarope.

Mike and I did not see any of these uncommon species on our trip through the state-managed portion of the marsh, but we did see an abundance of birds — great blue herons, egrets, double-crested cormorants, black terns, swamp sparrows, and red-winged blackbirds. We also saw a few of the several thousand white pelicans that live in the marsh. Had one flown directly over us, its nine-foot wing span would have cast a big shadow on our eight-foot-wide boat.

Of all these birds, the most impressive were the great blue herons. Never before had we seen so many in one place. Paddle the Wisconsin, Mississippi, or many other of the state's rivers, and you might catch sight of one along a swampy shore. But there are few other places where you might spot a double handful or more of these regal birds.

Not so long ago, herons numbered 4,000 in the marsh, before habitat overcrowding, a fierce storm in 1998, and other factors caused their population to dwindle. The Wisconsin Department of Natural Resources is working to restore Horicon's great blue herons, and, as part of this effort, two nesting sites, Fourmile Island and Cotton Island, are closed to visitors from April 1 to September 15.

Along with the richness of bird life, we noted a turtle on a log and signs of beaver. In fact, beaver signs were difficult to ignore. We noted three large beaver houses on the dikes bordering the Main Ditch, and spotted gnawed-

Horicon goslings

off stumps, as well as several girdled cottonwoods destined to soon die and topple into the water. The largest of the cottonwood stumps measured perhaps two feet in diameter. How big was the beaver that took it down?

The hour-long boat tour ended all too soon, but at least it provided a flavor of the marsh and a sense of its size and diverse wildlife. "You've got to get out of your car to understand the marsh," our captain said in parting.

We drove north to the DNR Field Office (follow Palmatory Street north in the city of Horicon), to hike up and down the drumlins and onto dikes into the marsh. On the drumlin walk along the edge of the woods, we spotted a bird perched on the front of a bluebird house poking food inside. "Look, there's a bluebird feeding its young," I said. But I was wrong. It wasn't a bluebird. A tree swallow had taken over the house for the season.

On the dike portion of our hike, we walked more slowly, so as not to frighten the geese and goslings hanging out on the path and stepped gingerly around the goose poop! We squinted through binoculars to make out black terns swooping over water, more tree swallows, and swamp sparrows.

Bicycles are not permitted on these trails in the marsh, but the Wild Goose Trail provides access along the western edge of Horicon. This smooth trail of compacted limestone screenings runs 34 miles on a former railroad grade from Fond du Lac southwest to Juneau.

We stopped briefly at the DNR Service Center, located off State Highway 28, before continuing north along the eastern edge of the marsh. Both DNR offices provide observation platforms, picnic tables, and rest rooms, as well as colorful butterfly gardens; however, they are open only weekdays, except during October and November when they welcome visitors seven days a week.

Following County Road Z, we drove north toward State Highway 49, which crosses the northern section of the marsh. Just before we reached the highway, we noted the sign on our right, marking several effigy mounds on private property. Wisconsin's first geologist, Increase Lapham, mapped 500 mounds around Horicon Marsh in the 1850s. The mounds, built by Indians between AD 700 and AD 1200, represented various animal and geometric shapes. Most of the mounds have disappeared, destroyed by lumbering or farming.

Trucks barreled east and west through the marsh on Highway 49, and Mike carefully turned left onto the hectic highway. Later we learned that this highway poses a serious death zone for the wildlife, with traffic killing many birds, amphibians, and small mammals each year.

A few cars had pulled off onto the broad shoulder and we joined them, using our Forester as a blind to edge close to a covey of coots diving unconcernedly into the shallow water near the busy road. We spotted a few egrets, but they were too far away for me to get a decent picture. Mike eased the car forward, trying to get near the egret closest to the highway, but whenever we got almost within camera range, the bird moved away — almost but never quite close enough to photograph. Eventually, we tired of this game and moved on.

We spied the sign for the entrance to the TernPike Auto Tour Route and turned onto a paved loop circling a wilderness of marsh, upland fields, and scattered woodland. Almost immediately we saw another sign: "Please to not drive over snakes basking on road." Clearly, we were in an unusual, special place.

Ready for a black-crowned night heron, or, at least, a least bittern, we actually saw few birds along the TernPike, even though it was now late afternoon. But, then, Mike suddenly spotted a beaver! At least he thought it was a beaver disappearing off the pull-out where we had paused.

We parked near the National Wildlife Refuge Visitor Center and joined other birders on the Egret Trail and Floating Boardwalk. The bouncy boardwalk carried us over the water and among the cattails, offering several observation areas. We walked slowly, and without effort spotted multiple sandhill cranes, egrets, and great blue herons. Still, we heard more birds than we saw, not to mention bullfrogs. The marsh was peaceful, but not quiet.

Located on the north side of Highway 49 not far from the entrance to the TernPike, the **Marsh Haven Nature Center** complements the educational work of the federal and state agencies. Marsh Haven is the largest volunteer-run nature center in the Midwest. Founded by Larry Vine in 1984, the complex contains a lodge, picnic shelter, and visitor center with museum exhibits, wildlife gallery, and even live bobwhite quails. Trails and an observation tower invite exploration of the center's 47 acres of wetland, prairie, and woodland. Phone: (920) 324-5818. Website: www.MarshHaven.com.

In cooperation with the DNR, the Friends of **Horicon Marsh International Education Center** raised sufficient funds by early 2007 to solicit bids for another center to be built on Highway 28 between Horicon and Mayville. It will serve as a learning hub with auditorium, exhibits, conference space, dining facilities, and library. Website: www.horiconmarsh.org.

Other visitor attractions include a number of annual special events. The Horicon Marsh Bird Festival, held around the second weekend in May, features boat and bus tours, kids' activities, bird banding demonstrations, night hikes, and the Big Sit, in which birders patiently see how many species they can observe from the deck at the DNR Field Office at the end of Palmatory Street in Horicon. Website: www.horiconmarshbirdclub.com.

Both birders and photographers can also observe birds from two blinds set up near the DNR Service Center on Highway 28. There is no charge for their use, and you can reserve a blind. Phone: (920) 387-7860.

On the south edge of Horicon, the river flows past the city's largest park, **River Bend,** which offers a boat launch on the west bank. In addition to picnic and playground areas, community residents come to use the tennis courts and ball fields.

The boardwalk at Horicon

Below the park, the Rock slowly drifts through marshy areas before widening out into Sinissippi Lake, formed by the Hustisford Dam. Sinissippi's elongated islands are the tops of drumlins that mark the direction of ancient glacial flows. Lined with trees, homes, and lawns, the 2,800-acre lake benefits from the conservation efforts of both the Lake Sinissippi Association, Inc., an association of local citizens and businesses, and the Lake Sinissippi Improvement District. Website: www.lakesinissippi.org.

In Hustisford, **Riverside Park** provides an opportunity for a satisfying stroll along the Rock's west bank down from the dam. A walk through downtown reveals several old storefronts, historic churches, and other signs of an earlier era. The **John Hustis House and Museum,** 134 North Ridge Street in Memorial Park, preserves the story of the man who founded the village and built a log dam and sawmill in the 1840s, followed by a grist mill in 1850. The museum is open from June through September, 1:00 p.m. to 3:00 p.m., or by appointment. Phone: (920) 349-3501.

Downstream, the river runs through farmland and more wetlands before reaching **Harnischfeger County Park.** Roughly 8 miles east of Watertown and west of Ashippun off County Road O, Dodge County's newest park takes in almost a mile of Rock River shoreline. Until a few years ago, the park was owned by an employee benefits association of the Harnischfeger Corporation, Milwaukee. The company bought the parcel in 1969 as a park for its workers, and then transferred ownership to the workers association. In 2004, the company decided to cease maintaining the park since few workers used it, so the benefits association sold the parcel to the county.

The 132-acre park offers a long list of facilities and amenities — a clubhouse, two shelters, canoe and kayak rentals, miniature and disc golf, and hiking and horse trails, to name a few. Among the latest additions are nine campsites, several with electricity. The Friends of Dodge County Parks, Inc. has spearheaded a fundraising campaign to restore two barns, part of two separate former family farms within the park. Once restored, they might be available for barn dances, weddings, and other events.

Continuing downriver, the twisty Rubicon and Ashippun rivers enter the Rock from the east, and not far past State Highway 16, the larger but equally twisty Oconomowoc joins the Rock from the same direction.

The Oconomowoc rises in southern Washington County and runs through the Loew Lake Unit of the Kettle Moraine State Forest before heading into a series of lakes — North, Okauchee, Oconomowoc, and Lac La Belle on the western edge of the City of Oconomowoc. The **Ice Age National Scenic Trail** also runs through this section of the state forest, crossing the

Oconomowoc south of the unit and flanking it before turning east toward Bark River, another Rock River tributary. Many sections of the Oconomowoc can be paddled, and Marsh-N-Stream Kayak Outings, Milwaukee, offers guided trips to Loew Lake, as well as trips on the Milwaukee River. Phone: (414) 688-2378. Website: www.marshnstream.com.

Off Highway 16 to the north on Rock River Road, **Kanow County Park** offers a canoe launch, fishing, picnicking, a shelter, toilets, and playground. The 47-acre Jefferson County park also provides benches and a short trail along the river.

Just south of Rock River Road on Highway 16, watch for the wayside and Wisconsin Historical Society marker noting the numbered designation of highways. Until Wisconsin created the numbered highway system in 1917, motorists often lost their way, especially on long trips when they ventured far from local streams, churches, and other landmarks. The first designated route, Highway 19, today is State Highway 16.

Watertown occupies and surrounds the crook of the Rock, where, like an inverted V, it changes course from northwest to southwest. Each side of this V has its own dam.

On the eastern side of the V, **Riverside Park,** established in 1910, is the city's oldest, and, some visitors would say, its best. In only 29 acres, the park manages to find room for an aquatic center (1009 Perry Street), and provides access to the riverbank. The aquatic center features shallow areas, lap lanes, a one-meter diving board, and an area set aside for water basketball, in addition to a 216-foot waterslide. Phone: (920) 262-8085. Riverside Park is also the setting for many community events, such as one of the oldest farm markets in Wisconsin, an annual art fair in mid-June, Fourth of July celebration, and Riverfest, an early August extravaganza of music, carnival, and A Taste of Watertown.

South and east of Riverside Park on the corner of Tivoli Drive and East Main Street (Highway 16), **Tivoli Island Natural Park,** a project of the Izaak Walton League, is a popular spot to feed the ducks, and provides a bridge over the river.

To the west, Watertown's historic downtown flourishes with retail shops, pubs, Mullen's Dairy Bar, 212 West Main Street (phone: (920) 261-4278), and other restaurants. A Riverwalk lines the Rock here, as the city's Main Street program continues to create more reasons for folks to come downtown.

While the I-94 corridor between Madison and Milwaukee has experienced considerable development in recent decades as more and more people seek to live close to both cities but in neither of them, the Rock River south of Watertown still flows largely through wooded and marshy areas. Hahn's Lake and several sloughs still provide wildlife habitat within a half dozen miles of the Interstate. **Rock River County Park,** on the west side of the County Road B Bridge about a half mile west of Johnson Creek, provides the first boat landing downstream from Watertown. The small Jefferson County park also features a shelter, toilet, grills, and picnic tables. Bring a jug to fill from the artesian springs.

Approximately 3 miles south of the park — and 2 miles north of Jefferson — the **Glacial Drumlin State Trail** crosses the river. The 52-mile recreational trail stretches along former railroad tracks from Cottage Grove east of Madison to the Fox River Sanctuary in Waukesha. A couple of miles west of the Rock, the trail crosses its Crawfish River tributary.

The Crawfish begins north of Sun Prairie in Columbia County and wends northeast through Columbus, then east and south into the Waterloo and Mud Lake state wildlife areas in Dodge County. From Mud Lake it meanders south to meet the Rock at Jefferson.

Southeast of Columbus, the Crawfish bends back on itself, surrounding three sides of **Astico County Park** at the point where the river widens above the Danville dam. A flourmill operated here into the 1960s. On warm weekends, campers fill the riverside sites, and anglers fish from spots along the bank. This 100-acre Dodge County Park offers two artesian wells, the Astico Castle Playground for the kids, and pedestrian bridges connecting trails on both sides of the river.

Just north of the Glacial Drumlin State Trail, the Crawfish runs through Aztalan State Park, an archaeological site at the location of a twelfth-century Indian village. The park offers fishing, hiking, and picnicking. Two sections of the stockade surrounding the Middle-Mississippian village and ceremonial complex have been reconstructed, and you can walk up short staircases to the top of a restored mound. Park sticker required.

On the north end of the property at the intersection of County Road B and County Road Q, the **Lake Mills Aztalan Historical Society** operates a museum complex featuring a Mamre Moravian log church, an 1852 Baptist church, and a granary with an old tool collection once owned by former Wisconsin Supreme Court Justice Connor T. Hansen. The historical society opens the museum to visitors from May 15 through September, Thursday through Sunday, 12:00 p.m. to 4:00 p.m.

At the juncture of the Crawfish and Rock rivers, Jefferson has joined other river cities in planning redevelopment along historic downtown waterfronts. The city already displays a riverwalk along the Rock's east bank,

> **Downtown Fort Atkinson offers a reiverwalk and the Barrie Park Bandshell, where the Fort City Band performs summer concerts. Though I'm tempted to mention a long list of downtown businesses, here are a few faves:**
>
> - On the riverwalk, **Café Carpe,** 18 South Water Street W, has been offering food, drinks, and music (generally folk) with an attitude since 1985. Smoke-free throughout, Café Carpe is open for brunch on Sunday, lunch Tuesday through Friday, and dinner Tuesday through Saturday. Phone: (920) 563-9391. Website: www.cafecarpe.com.
> - Next to Café Carpe, 90 South Main Street, **I Love Funky's** and the **Velvet Lips Lounge** offer offbeat antiques, collectibles, and gifts with refreshments downstairs.
> - **Soap and Pepper,** also directly on the river at 91 South Main Street, features specialty foods, wines, spices, cookbooks, bath and body products, and other gifts.
> - **Bienfangs Bar,** 28 North Water Street E, has been in the Bienfang family since 1906, when Charlie Bienfang bought the former Eagles Inn. Phone: (920) 563-8046.
> - The **Rock River Canoe Company, LLC,** 99 North Main Street, rents canoes and builds wooden boats to sell along with paddling and outdoor gear. Phone: (920) 563-1075. Website: www.rockrivercanoe.com.

pedestrian bridges over the river, and several parks. **Rotary and Tensfeldt parks** border the Rock, and **Riverfront Park** lies on the south bank of the Crawfish. Plans under consideration call for expanding the riverwalk and recreational trails to connect with the Glacial Drumlin State Trail. The city is also looking at adding residential options and encouraging more people to live downtown, while over time relocating industry outside of the downtown area to facilitate modernization and expansion.

One Jefferson business that's found its niche and place on the Rock is the Rivers Edge Farm Market, 843 South Whitewater Street (County Road N). Located on the first floor of a restored barn, the market began selling meat and processing venison almost a decade ago. Owner Scott Fischer runs the business with his wife, three daughters, a son-in-law, and several employees. They sell local produce, provide custom butchering, and smoke their own sausage including 25 kinds of brats — with flavors like horseradish cheddar and apple. This Wisconsin market also features squeaky cheese curds, and recently added catering to its mix of customized services. Phone: (920) 674-6466.

Six miles south off State Highway 26, Fort Atkinson is booming, too, especially its downtown riverfront, which features a variety of businesses and the **Allan Haukom RiverWalk,** named for the man who suggested it, the retired president of Nasco, International, Inc., the Fort-Atkinson-based producer of educational supplies. Also downtown is the trailhead for the 7-mile **Glacial River Trail** that runs south to Milton and will eventually link to the Glacial Drumlin State Trail.

This short, flat, paved regional trail is long on amenities and a good choice for a family outing. An archway topped by Brady Lueck's sculpture of a bike and grasses marks a trail entry point on West Sherman Avenue. Bronze statues, including several of children at play, line the former Union Pacific route, and an open-sided shelter resembling an old depot provides a rest stop at the corner of Janesville Avenue and South Third Street West. South of the city, a 51-foot covered bridge offers another port in a storm.

Fort Atkinson has also paid attention to amenities in its parks, and, like Watertown, offers an aquatic center. The Fort Atkinson Family Aquatic Center features a 175-foot waterslide and takes up a section of the city's largest park, Rock River, at 1300 Lillian Street. In addition, the park contains a clubhouse, lighted tennis and basketball courts, lighted sports fields, an archery range, and a wooded walking trail.

Rock River Park also displays a replica of Fort Koshkonong, once located east of the park near the river. General Henry Atkinson served as commander at the fort during the Black Hawk War of 1832, and later lent his name to the modern city. Today, a reproduction stockade comes alive on Memorial Day weekend, when it is the setting of the annual Buckskinners Rendezvous.

State Highway 106 (Riverside Street) edges both the park and the river. Not far from the park on Highway 106, the **Panther Intaglio** offers a rare example of an Indian intaglio — like a mound in shape but scooped out rather than built up — dating to about AD 1000. Increase A. Lapham discovered the Panther in 1850, one of only a dozen or so ever documented in Wisconsin and the only one remaining. The highway also offers river views and connects the park to downtown.

Downriver from "Fort," the Rock flows alongside the **Lake Koshkonong Marsh State Wildlife Area,** which features two boat landings, and offers snowmobiling and cross-country skiing in winter.

Nearby on Blackhawk Island Road off Highway 26, Lorine Niedecker's cabin still stands. Perhaps Wisconsin's most overlooked poet, Niedecker wrote clear-cut descriptions of the sights and sounds of the Rock River area.

> **Sections of a large wetland are preserved by the state, Dane County, and City of Madison:**
>
> - The **Cherokee Marsh State Fishery Area** consists of 948 acres of the upper marsh, with some open water, cattails, and wooded wetlands.
> - **Cherokee Marsh State Natural Area** access from Buckley Road, west of Daenti Road, off U.S. Highway 51 just south of I-90/94.
> - The City of Madison's **Cherokee Marsh Conservation Park** offers more than 7 miles of boardwalk and trails in three separate units. The North Unit at the end of Sherman Avenue features two observation decks and rest rooms. When I worked on Madison's north side for a number of years, this was an occasional lunch escape for my coworkers and me.
> - Dane County's **Yahara Heights/Cherokee Marsh Natural Resource Site** lies near the intersection of State Highway 113 and County Road M. The 325-acre parcel contains a 20-acre pet exercise area along the river. A 400-foot trail off the end of the parking lot leads to a canoe launch.

Among her collections of poetry are *New Goose,* her first book, and *My Life by Water,* her last. Born in 1903, she attended Beloit College for two years and worked as a library assistant and proofreader at Hoard's Dairyman, and, when finances were tight, as a cleaning woman at a local hospital. In 1963, Niedecker married her second husband and moved to Milwaukee, where she had more time to write.

Blackhawk Island Road also leads to the Blackhawk Club, which offers camping and canoeing on the lake, and to the Riverfront Resort, offering wayfarers food and other restoratives year-round.

A few miles to the east, Norm's Hideaway Bar & Grill resembles a log and stone haunt on a Northwoods lake, except it's closer to home for many Wisconsinites. Open daily, the Hideaway offers a seasonal campground, outdoor seating, and boat launch, in addition to nightly dinner specials and Sunday brunch. It's located at N2150 Danielson Road, Edgerton. From State Highway 106 north of Lake Koshkonong, drive south on County Road A and turn left at Carcajou Road. Phone: (608) 884-4823. Website: www.normshideawaybarandgrill.com.

Lake Koshkonong draws thousands of anglers annually, who, in turn, lure fish — walleyes, catfish, muskie, northern, bluegill, bass, and more. Fishing continues year-round, with ice fishers often dotting the 10,500-acre lake in winter.

The shallow lake also attracts birds and bird-watchers. The Lake Koshkonong Wetland Association invites you to report your sightings of

Dark clouds gather over the Yahara bridge and underpass at Washington Avenue in Madison

osprey, white pelicans, sandhill cranes, and other species at its website: www.koshwetlands.org.

On the eastern shore, south of **Lake Koshkonong State Wildlife Area,** the **Jefferson County Indian Mounds and Trail Park and Golf Course** overlook the lake, and you can follow an old Indian trail to eleven mounds abutting the golf course. These linear, conical, and effigy mounds are all that's left of a collection of 72, the General Atkinson Mound Group. To get there from Fort Atkinson, drive south on Highway 26 to Old State Highway 26 and turn west (right). Drive to Koshkonong Mounds Road, turn right again, and follow this road to the park.

The **Indianford Dam,** 4 miles downstream on County Road M, deepens Lake Koshkonong, which in the early nineteenth century was a wetland. The first dam here, built in the mid-1800s, powered a sawmill. A concrete hydropower dam replaced it in 1917, was remodeled in 1931, and produced hydroelectric power for several more decades.

Less than 2 miles downstream, a major tributary joins the Rock. The Yahara River drains the four lakes (Mendota, Monona, Waubesa, and Kegonsa) of the Madison area and provides the largest wetland areas remaining in

Dane County. Rising in southern Columbia County, the Yahara flows south through De Forest and into **Cherokee Marsh** on Madison's north side.

The Yahara helps define the City of Madison. The river runs into Lake Mendota west of Highway 113 and exits at the Tenney Locks a little more than a mile from the State Capitol. Controlled by the locks and straightened, the Yahara then runs arrowlike into Lake Monona on the other side of the city's downtown isthmus.

Lake Mendota's depth (up to 84 feet) and breadth (9,842 acres) bring boaters and anglers whenever the weather permits. Yet the lake's best charms surround its shoreline. Near the inlet of the Yahara, the Von Rutenberg family has created an array of dining possibilities, from the traditional Mariner's Inn to the more relaxed Nau-ti-gal and Captain Bill's seafood restaurant, as well as a marina. To the east, you can tour the **Governor's Mansion** or walk to Governor's Island, now connected to the shore by a narrow causeway. To the west, **Governor Nelson State Park** features a boat launch, swimming areas for both people and dogs, and views of the Capitol across the lake. On the southern shore, visitors and residents flock each summer to the **University of Wisconsin–Madison Memorial Union Terrace** for ice cream, or just to watch the sailboats drift before the wind. Also on campus, **Picnic Point** is a popular destination for walkers and joggers.

With help from many volunteers and the Friends of the Yahara Parkway, the channel between Lake Mendota and Lake Monona has become as friendly to pedestrians and bicyclists as to boaters. The mile-long parkway, established in the early 1900s, had been neglected and restrained by busy highway bridges. Restored in 2007, the parkway now circumnavigates heavy city traffic via a tunnel under East Johnson Street and an underpass on both sides of the river beneath the Halle Steensland Bridge on East Washington Avenue. Benches and plantings enhance the parkway that can now be used by people trying to get from one side of the isthmus to the other without driving a car.

You could easily spend a weekend touring Monona's shoreline, and you wouldn't go wrong to begin a tour at the **Olbrich Botanical Gardens.** The gardens connect to Monona's north shore via Olbrich City Park, and connect to the world via a Thai Pavilion crafted in Thailand, then transported and reassembled here. Sixteen acres of outdoor gardens and the Bolz Conservatory, filled with orchids, more exotic plants, birds, and a waterfall, are like a massage for a weary soul.

The lakeshore's standout attraction, the **Monona Terrace Community and Convention Center,** in **Law Park** at One John Nolen Drive, opened in 1997, almost 90 years after landscape architect John Nolen envisioned a mall and esplanade connecting the Capitol Square to the lake. In the mid-1900s Frank Lloyd Wright designed three plans for implementing Nolen's vision, but all were rejected. Long after Wright's death, architects at his Taliesin Studio in Spring Green revised his plans in 1990, and the city accepted them. The center juts dramatically over the lake and ties the high ground of the isthmus and State Capitol with the Lake Monona shoreline. Phone: (608) 261-4000. Website: www.mononaterrace.com.

Law Park also serves as the stage for the MadCity Ski Team, which performs at 6:00 p.m. Sunday from Memorial Day to Labor Day. Website: www.madcityskiteam.com.

Another John Nolen design, the 1910 Brittingham Boat House, 617 North Shore Drive, has been recently restored. This National Historic Landmark is home to the Camp Randall Rowing Club.

On the lakeshore south of the boathouse, **Olin Park** became the city's first park in 1912, but by then the site had already been a gathering spot for many years. In 1854 it held a sanitarium and hospital that was renovated to create a resort hotel, the Lakeside House, in 1866. Years after the hotel was destroyed by fire in 1877, the property became the site of the Monona Lake Assembly Chautauqua, hosting a variety of lectures and musical events.

Not far from Olin Park, Wingra Creek empties into Lake Monona. At the head of the creek, small Lake Wingra offers a full palette of outdoor opportunities. I've rented a canoe at Wingra Park on the northwest shore and one day will take out a paddleboat. To the east, **Edgewood College,** once the home of Wisconsin Governor Cadwallader Washburn, provides a Catholic liberal arts education with a service-oriented emphasis. Phone: (800) 444-4861. Website: www.edgewood.edu. The **Henry Vilas Zoo,** 702 South Randall Avenue, offers free admission and year-round exhibits. The newest residents are three giraffes, "megavertebrates." Phone: (608) 266-4733. Website: www.vilaszoo.com. On the south and east shore, you can hike through some of the oldest restored prairies in the nation at the **University of Wisconsin–Madison Arboretum.** Watch for special events like guided hikes and free trolley tours. Phone: (608) 263-7888. Website: www.uwarboretum.org.

To the east, the city of Monona encircles the southeastern shoreline of Lake Monona. Off a lobe of the lake, the Yahara River exits to the southeast.

Downstream, the Yahara widens into Upper Mud Lake before flowing into Lake Waubesa. Lovely Lake Waubesa has experienced increasing pressure from development, thanks to its proximity to Madison. Yet, the pressure of development has sparked efforts to preserve areas around this 2,080-acre lake.

Eventually, **Capital Springs State Park** will join Dane County's **Lake Farm Park** with recently acquired property in a cooperatively managed park along the northwest shore. The park currently offers picnic shelters, a boat launch, and campground. A highlight is a 1.5-mile archaeological trail describing Indian history and artifacts identified in the area. For camping or shelter reservations, contact Dane County Parks. Phone: (608) 246-3896. Website: www.co.dane.wi.us/lwrd/parks. Recreational trails connect to the **Capital City State Trail,** which traverses the area adjacent to Nine Springs Creek. It also links to the Military Ridge State Trail heading southwest, and will one day link to the Glacial Drumlin State Trail that crosses the Rock to the east.

The Yahara leaves Lake Waubesa at the **Babcock County Park Lock and Dam,** McFarland, which helps regulate water levels to support fish spawning upstream. Park facilities include a boat launch, fish-cleaning facility, handicapped-accessible pier, rest rooms, and campground containing 25 sites, all with electricity.

Not far downriver, a trail at the Jaeger Canoe Landing leads northwest through the McFarland School Forest to **Indian Mound Park.** The park contains conical, linear, and effigy mounds, as well as a restored oak savannah.

Beyond the landing, the Yahara soon flows into Lower Mud Lake, which has a maximum depth of 15 feet and is largely surrounded by marsh.

About a mile below Mud Lake, Wisconsin Rustic Road 20 crosses the Yahara on the wood-decked **Dyreson Bridge.** The 1897 iron truss bridge was rehabilitated in 1983 and is again scheduled for restoration work. Fair warning: there have been reports of ghostly sights and sounds on this historic bridge! Rustic Road 20 runs 2.9 miles from County Road AB north of Lake Kegonsa crossing U.S. Highway 51 to Schneider Drive on the lake's western shore.

Lake Kegonsa, the most southerly of the four lakes, has attracted anglers for many years. In 1895 George Barber and Anton Anderson set up a saloon on a sandbar in the southwestern section of the lake to serve alcohol to boaters, avoiding the ordinances of dry towns to either side. Buoys mark the spot. At the inlet of the Yahara, **Fish Camp County Park** on County Road AB east of Highway 51 provides accessible piers, a fish-cleaning area, canoe launch, rest rooms, and picnicking. Across the Yahara on its south bank, Kegonsa Cove offers gas service, boat slips, and canoe and pontoon boat rentals. Phone: (608) 838-6494.

At the northeast shore, **Lake Kegonsa State Park** was developed with families in mind. A playground overlooks the lake, and a swimming beach provides a way to cool down on hot days. On the other hand, a sledding hill offers a cure for cabin fever in the winter. Most of the three group campsites and 80 individual sites offer shady shelter among the park's mighty oaks. The park's 0.75-mile long shoreline holds a boat launch and fishing pier. There's a wetland boardwalk, and a pet hiking trail and swimming area. From I-90, exit on County Road N and drive west to Koshkonong Road. Turn north and at the T-intersection with Door Creek Road, take a left to head south to the park entrance.

Vermont Yankee Luke Stoughton founded the city that bears his name in a bend of the Yahara in the late 1840s. The railroad arrived in the following decade, guaranteeing the town's rising success. Following the Civil War, T. G. Mandt started a wagon factory, recruiting workers from his native Norway. Slowly Norwegian immigrants began to influence the culture, arts, and customs of Stoughton. The coffee break was one Scandinavian practice that caught on here and spread. Norwegian women reportedly agreed to work in the town's 17 tobacco warehouses providing they received a break at mid-morning and another mid-afternoon to go home, check on the children, and start dinner. Naturally, they also took the time to have a cup of coffee.

You can also view the city's history along Main Street, and the Stoughton Landmarks Commission has identified walking tours of four historic districts. Printed guides are available free at the city hall, the Chamber of Commerce office, and the public library. Or, request the guides from the Stoughton City Hall (fee for postage and handling). Phone: (608) 873-6677. Website: www.stoughtonlandmarks.com.

Stoughton Historical Society Museum, 324 South Page Street, offers many local history exhibits in a former church on Sundays, from 1:00 p.m. to 4:00 p.m. during the summer and for special events, as well as virtual tours anytime. Phone: (608) 873-8005. Website: http://expressiveimage.com/historical_museum/historical_museum.html.

Downriver from the museum, Stoughton offers two parks on the Yahara. **Riverside,** at the Fourth Street Dam, hosts the conclusion of the Syttende Mai canoe race. Adjacent to the east, **Mandt Park** is home to the Stoughton Junior Fair, held in July. It also holds a swimming pool, bathhouse, shelter, skateboard ramp, a lighted softball diamond, and basketball courts.

Below Stoughton, the Yahara runs about 9 miles southeast to join the Rock downstream of Indianford. Dams at Dunkirk and Stebbinsville mean portages for paddlers, but the 9-mile stretch from the Stebbinsville dam to the Yahara's mouth provides an easy, meandering journey through generally wooded terrain.

Wisconsin's Park Place, Janesville, comes by its nickname honestly, and several of the city's outstanding parks extend along the Rock. **Riverside Park,** on the west bank of the river and north side of town off Business 14 (North Washington Street), encompasses an 18-hole golf course. It provides a boat launch, nature trail, picnicking, shelters, rest rooms, sports fields, playground, and wading pool. When Mike and I wandered the riverfront, a number of geese were in comfortable residence. An artesian well pumps water from 1,000 feet underground.

An 8.5-mile section of the **Ice Age National Scenic Trail** begins in Riverside Park and continues along the Rock south all the way downtown, where it crosses the river south of the mouth of Blackhawk Creek. From here, the trail soon turns east for a time, following the course of Black Hawk Creek and the green space around it, including Rotary Gardens and Lions Beach. The trail then turns northeast, passes through Palmer Park, and eventually shares the city's Spring Brook Trail. In some sections the trail is on sidewalks, as opposed to paved recreational paths. Trivial tidbit of the chapter: More than one-fifth of Wisconsinites live within 10 miles of the Ice Age Trail, according to the *Ice Age Trail Companion Guide 2006.*

Several parks in the town of Beloit encourage river exploration and enjoyment.

- **Big Hill Community Park** tops a wooded hill overlooking the Rock. The 190-acre park boasts an environmental education center, picnic shelter, rest rooms, and play equipment, as well as cross-country ski, nature, and hiking trails on the river's west bank. The park is situated at the intersection of County Road D (Afton Road) and Big Hill Road.

- Busy all summer with boaters and picnickers, **Preservation Park** continues full of activity into the fall. The Festival on the Rock, usually the second Saturday of September, means pontoon boat rides, train rides, a horseshoe tournament, and kids chalk art contest, along with music and food (free admission). Later in the month, the Autorama Car Show presents more than 1,000 cars on display, a swap meet, arts and crafts, food, and music. Mike and I visited in May, when four families of geese and goslings swam about, unperturbed by the powerboats and jet skis. Preservation Park is located at 3444 South Riverside Drive (Highway 51) about 3 miles north of Beloit.

- **Armstrong Eddy Park** entices visitors with a fishing pier, boat launch (fee), picnic area, play equipments, rest rooms, and walking path. It's located right on Highway 51 north of the Henry Avenue bridge.

If you follow the river downstream, the next park to appear is **Traxler** on the east bank on Highway 51 (Parker Drive). In addition to boat launches, an outdoor hockey and ice rink, and the usual park facilities, Traxler displays a fountain in the river and a Medal of Honor Veterans Walkway. The park is home base for the **Rock Aqua Jays Water Ski Show Team.** The team performs Sunday and Wednesday evenings from Memorial Day to Labor Day. Website: www.rockaquajays.org. In the winter, come for the holiday light display. Traxler's annual Parade of Lights, sponsored by the South Central Wisconsin Builders Association, is designed to be viewed from your car. Donations are accepted for the Rock County Habitat for Humanity.

Downtown, the Ice Age Trail continues along the west bank of the river. While several cities upriver are endeavoring to encourage more people to live downtown, Janesville has already done so, with condominiums and apartment buildings affording Rock River views. Curious about **The Cotton Mills,** we learned that the city had helped develop this apartment complex, transforming an early water-powered plant into modern housing. The earliest mills on the Rock in the 1840s were flour and lumber mills, followed in the 1850s by woolen and paper mills, and, later, by cotton mills.

The **Janesville Performing Arts Center,** which opened in 2004 at 408 South Main Street, brings together Rock County's performing arts

Goslings at Beloit Preservation Park

groups — including the Beloit Janesville Symphony Orchestra, Badger Chordhawks, and Spotlight on Kids — in a section of a renovated high school. Leaded glass, carved wood, and ornate plaster molding created in the 1920s have been restored. The old school auditorium is the new 650-seat theater with balcony, extended stage, and upgraded light and sound systems. The rest of the building has been converted into 55 apartments. Phone: (608) 758-0297. Website: www.janesvillepac.org.

Monterey Park and Stadium lies nestled in a bump in the river south of downtown. Located on the west bank and Rockport Road, this park offers fishing access and a paved trail in addition to team sports facilities.

To the west, Janesville's biggest park, **Rockport,** is not quite on the river, but separated from it by Afton Road and the recreational path, the **Rock River Parkway Trail.** We saw wild phlox edging this trail in late spring, and short side trails led to fishing spots on the riverbank. The park features an outdoor swimming pool with diving well, a wading pool, and six miles of hiking trails. Another attraction is the Peace Park Playground, containing a two-story teepee with peace paintings, a peace pole, roller slide, and spring teeter-totter. The Indian-themed playground gives children a chance to learn about cultural diversity as they play.

For a very different kind of experience, adults and older children can tour Janesville's **North American Hydro** plant, spring through fall. Tours can be arranged by calling the operations manager of the hydroelectric company's southern region in Maquoketa, Iowa: (563) 652-0044. Website: www.nahydro.com.

Below Janesville, the Rock River Parkway and green space on the west bank extend as far as the Rock County Airport. South of the airport on the east bank, **Happy Hollow County Park** provides boaters with a concrete ramp (donation requested), picnic tables, rest rooms, drinking water, and hiking trails through the 206-acre park. Driving access is from Highway 51; turn west on Happy Hollow Road (misnamed Happy Valley Road on a recent official Wisconsin State Highway map).

Rock River Prairie State Natural Area preserves many uncommon dry prairie plants. Look for pasque flowers in early spring, cream wild indigo and rock sandwort in May, and prairie gentian in September. You can also find the state-endangered wild petunia, as well as woolly milkweed and prairie false dandelion. From Happy Hollow County Park, follow Highway 51 south to West Town Line Road. Turn west, cross the Rock, and drive to Walters Road. Turn south on Walters Road and drive 1 mile to the parking area on the east side of the road.

The city of **Beloit's Riverside Park** brims with activity much of the year. There's the annual July Fourth celebration and, later in July, RiverFest, a four-day event with over 50 bands performing blues, jazz, rock and roll, and country. Website: www.beloitriverfest.com.

Riverside Park is also all about turtles. A turtle welcomes children to the playground on Turtle Island, and the Turtle Geoglyph sculpture allows people to walk into the Geoglyph and sit at a council ring to enjoy the park and the river. At a Turtles in the Park event in August, hundreds of decorated turtles are auctioned to support the arts. Turtle races and turtle sundaes also play a role in this family-oriented event.

Turtles link Beloit to its past. Effigy mounds, including several in the shape of a turtle, were built roughly 1,000 years ago on the bluffs above the river. You can still find 23 mounds, including a restored turtle effigy, on the **Beloit College** campus, above the river's east bank.

The Ho-Chunk maintained a village at the confluence of Turtle Creek and the Rock River until 1832. That year, the Ho-Chunk for a time sheltered the Sac leader Black Hawk and his followers during the Black Hawk War. After Black Hawk left, the Ho-Chunk abandoned Turtle Village, fearing retribution from General Henry Atkinson and his troops. When Atkinson arrived, he found only the deserted village and gardens. Today, the **Turtle Creek Greenway Recreation Area,** with a hiking trail and fishing spots, lines much of the creek east of Riverside Park.

The works of sculptor O. V. "Verne" Shaffer, Princeton, Illinois, also mark the town where he lived while attending Beloit College. His curving metal structures often seem to be reaching ever onward, outward, or skyward. Shaffer installed Celebration in Riverside Park in 1977. The Landing, an undulating flame to the stars, has loomed 60 feet overhead near the Grand Avenue bridge since 2004. Incorporating more than five tons of steel, scratched to reflect the light, the piece gleams when lit at night. At its base, steel silhouettes honor the workers who built this manufacturing city.

Nearby, the **Beloit Ironworks** complex contains offices and other commercial spaces. It's lined with a mural, a series of historic photos of workers. The Beloit Corporation operated its plant along the riverfront from 1858 to 1999.

An example of earlier industry, the restored **Beckman Mill** still operates on Raccoon Creek (a.k.a. Coon Creek) in Beckman Mill County Park, 6 miles west of Beloit. A mill has stood on this site since the 1840s; however, the first mill was destroyed by fire in 1853. William Howe purchased the property from original owner Charles F. H. Goodhue, Jr., in 1868 and constructed a new gristmill. In 1882 Catherine Beckman, wife of Hanover miller August Beckman, bought the mill, which remained in the family until 1978, when it was sold to Rock County.

The Friends of the Beckman Mill, Inc., restored the building in 1998, rebuilt the dam in 2001, and added a fish passage to the dam in 2002. The organization offers guided tours from May through October on Saturdays and Sundays, 1:00 p.m. to 4:00 p.m. (fee). The 50-acre park also contains a shelter, picnic tables, rest rooms, an 1848 cooperage, a nature trail and foot-bridge, and a gift shop where you can buy corn ground at the mill. To get there, drive west of Beloit on State Highway 81 to County Road H. Turn south on County Road H and drive about a mile to the park. To schedule a tour, phone: (608) 751-1551 or email: beckmanmill@yahoo.com. Website: www.beckmanmill.org.

Raccoon Creek flows into the Sugar River, which in turn runs into the Pecatonica River, which enters the Rock near Rockton, Illinois. The Sugar begins east of Mount Horeb in southwestern Dane County and flows through Belleville, Albany, and Brodhead before crossing into Illinois.

The Little Sugar flows by New Glarus and into the main stream near Albany. From New Glarus to Brodhead, the **Sugar River State Trail,** also a designated National Recreation Trail, generally follows the Little and Sugar

Belleville Dam on the Sugar River

rivers along the abandoned Chicago, Milwaukee, St. Paul railroad line. If you like bridges, this is the trail to explore: Fourteen trestle bridges, including a replica covered bridge, cross the Sugar along the way. A restored 1887 depot in New Glarus serves as trail headquarters and is home to the local welcome center, where you can pick up information about this town that celebrates its Swiss heritage with events, architecture, shops, and restaurants reflecting the Old Country. Website: www.swisstown.com.

A section of the trail, from Exeter Crossing Road north of Monticello to Albany, is another segment of the Ice Age National Scenic Trail. This section travels through the 1,928-acre **Albany State Wildlife Area** where you might catch sight of deer, turkeys, pheasants, quail, or woodcock.

Above the confluence of the Little Sugar and Sugar rivers at Albany, the Village of Belleville overlooks Lake Belle View, where the West Branch of the Sugar River joins the main channel.

Below the picturesque dam at Albany, which bills itself as "the pearl of the Sugar River," paddlers encounter additional dams at Decatur Lake and Brodhead, though this is still a popular paddling stream. You can rent canoes and tubes at Crazy Horse Campground, N3201 Crazy Horse Lane, Brodhead. Phone: (800) 897-3611. Website: www.crazyhorsewi.com.

Downstream from Brodhead, the Sugar flows through the **Avon Bottoms State Wildlife Area,** featuring a lowland hardwood forest with many maples, swamp white oaks, and green ash. Over the Illinois line, the river runs through the Colored Sands Forest Preserve before joining the Pecatonica west of Rockton.

Like the Sugar, the Pecatonica begins south of U.S. Highway 18, which runs between Madison and Prairie du Chien generally along the Old Military Road and the divide marking the Lower Wisconsin watershed. Streams to the north of Highway 18 flow into the Wisconsin, while those to the south flow either directly into the Mississippi (for instance, the Grant River) or indirectly by way of the Rock and other streams.

The Pecatonica begins near Cobb in Iowa County and flows southeast to Darlington and near Gratiot and Browntown before dropping south into Illinois. Darlington, county seat of Lafayette County, presents a historic downtown and courthouse with a Tiffany glass rotunda, and copper and marble decoration. The city makes paddlers happy by maintaining a campground, **Pecatonica River Trails Park,** with 24 sites on the river (18 with electricity), fishing pier, rest rooms, and showers. No reservations required; first come, first served (fee). Darlington, the "pearl of the Pecatonica," hosts a Canoe Festival every year in June. Phone: (608) 776-3067. Website: www.darlingtonwi.org.

The Pecatonica River Trail runs adjacent to the city campground and through town. The Cheese Country ATV Trail runs 47 miles from Mineral Point to Monroe, crossing the river several times.

Downstream, the East Branch of the Pecatonica enters the main channel between South Wayne and Browntown. On its journey south, it runs through Hollandale, Blanchardville, Argyle, and Woodford. The Blanchardville Historical Society Museum, 101 South Main Street, is located at the bridge. The Village of Argyle continues to receive about four percent of its power needs from the Pecatonica River, with the remainder coming from Dairyland Power in La Crosse. When a lightning strike took the plant out of operation in 2007, the village opted to repair it. Parts of this water-powered plant date to 1928.

Less than 10 miles to the east, Yellowstone Lake flows into Yellowstone River, a short tributary of the East Branch of the Pecatonica. **Yellowstone State Park** is the place to camp in the area, with 128 individual sites; 36 are open year-round. Yellowstone has very few mosquitoes, thanks to about 4,000 little brown bats that roost in 31 houses throughout the park during the summer.

By the time the Pecatonica reaches its mouth in Illinois, the Rock River has grown wide and mighty. The river that once powered the nineteenth-century furniture factories of Rockford is today more appreciated for other qualities. Parks and paths line much of the city's riverfront, and the Rock is a place to unwind after a long day.

Below Rockford, state parks and lands trail beside the river as it heads southwest toward its rendezvous with the Mississippi. And all along the way, people look to the river to define their days, a centering force connecting them to this precious planet.

CHAPTER 12

Upper Wisconsin

The Wisconsin runs like a lifeline through the state. Like Wisconsin's lifeblood, the river carries away sediments and some pollutants, ferries oxygen to fish, and sustains thousands of other animals and plants, both endangered and common. A river of sand and 100-foot bluffs, coniferous and deciduous forests, prairies and wetlands, droughts and floods, wind and calm, the Wisconsin is like a kaleidoscope of the past, revealing, in twist after turn, scenes from old centuries of human history and long-ended epochs of geologic upheaval. Looking through this prism, it doesn't seem so long ago, really, that hunters clutched their spears and edged the retreating glaciers to follow the mastodons. Whatever else it is, the river encourages the long view, the patient wait, and the rejuvenation of spirit that comes from forever meandering through wild places.

For more than three centuries, scholars have debated the derivation of "Wisconsin," the name of first a river, and then a state. According to a State Historical Marker erected in 1954 on State Highway 45, 1.5 miles south of Land O' Lakes, "wees-konsan" meant "the gathering of the waters" in the Algonquian tongue, while various writers reported the meaning as "stream of a thousand isles," and "grassy place," among other definitions listed on the Wisconsin Historical Society website: www.wisconsinhistory.org.

The name can be traced to 1673, when Miami guides brought Jacques Marquette and Louis Joliet to the Fox-Wisconsin portage and the mixed Miami-Kickapoo-Mascouten village (Fox Chapter 9). There, Marquette first wrote down the Miami name for the river, rendered in French as Meskousing.

Although the last native speakers of Miami as it was spoken in the 17th century died long ago, scholars have been able to resurrect the language. Linguist Michael McCafferty of Indiana University determined that Meskousing rendered a Miami term meaning "it lies red" — connoting that the river runs through something red. Reddish sandstone is evident along the river at Wisconsin Dells, and at other points from its headwaters to Prairie du Sac.

Unfortunately, Jolliet lost the original copy of Marquette's report when his canoe overturned near Montreal while returning to New France in 1674. Marquette's duplicate copy did not reach the French authorities until 1675. By then, the name had been garbled by copying errors into Ouisconsing, which later became Wisconsing and other variants. Territorial governor James Duane Doty preferred the spelling Wiskonsan, but Wisconsin eventually won out, after first appearing in an 1830 U.S. House of Representative report about laying out the town of Helena on the Wisconsin River.

Though the origin of its name has been long obscured, there's no question about the river's source. The Wisconsin flows about 420 miles from Lac Vieux Desert, on the state's border with Upper Michigan, generally south and then southwest to join the Mississippi near Prairie du Chien at

Near the headwaters of the Wisconsin

Wyalusing State Park. It drains more than 12,000 square miles, almost a quarter of the state, and has a vertical drop of more than 1,050 feet. The average flow at the mouth is about 12,000 cubic feet per second, though this amount varies widely. Roughly 400 streams drain into the Wisconsin, with the largest including the Tomahawk, Rib, Eau Claire, Yellow, Lemonweir, Baraboo, and Kickapoo rivers.

Twenty-six dams control the river's flow, and 25 hydroelectric plants generate power for the customers of public utilities and industries including paper production. The majority of these are located in the river's central section, though the greatest vertical drop occurs in the upper section near Grandfather Falls Dam. The proliferation of dams once gave the Wisconsin the title of "the hardest working river in America," according to the historical marker at its headwaters near Land O' Lakes. Scores of cities and villages line the river, with Eagle River, Rhinelander, Tomahawk, Merrill, Wausau, Mosinee, Stevens Point, Wisconsin Rapids, Wisconsin Dells, Portage, Prairie du Sac, and Prairie du Chien being among the most notable.

The Wisconsin Department of Natural Resources long ago divided the Wisconsin River basin into three sections: roughly from its headwaters to the Merrill dam, from Merrill to Castle Rock Dam, and from Castle Rock to the Mississippi River. Pleading poetic license for this book, I've adopted a different three-section division:

1. From the headwaters to Stevens Point
2. From Stevens Point to the Prairie du Sac Dam
3. From the Prairie du Sac Dam to the Mississippi

While the upper section covers more river miles, the central section contains larger cities and more complex urban development for travelers to explore. The lower section corresponds to the Lower Wisconsin State Riverway, created in 1989 to preserve the 92 miles of the river from its last dam at Prairie du Sac to its mouth at the Mississippi.

Though not especially well marked, the source of the Wisconsin is easy to find. From State Highway 32/U.S. Highway 45 south of Land O' Lakes, turn east on County Road E and drive to West Shore Road. Turn onto West Shore Road, following the sign to the **Lac Vieux Desert Campground** in the Nicolet National Forest. Drive 0.3 mile and turn into an inconsequential looking parking lot on your right that has room for perhaps half a dozen cars.

The parking area fronts marshy lowland flanked by northern forests. I'd been here before, but it still took me a moment to realize that the beautiful brook beyond the guardrail launches the state's home river.

Dells of the Eau Claire County Park

Mike and I followed the trail (no dogs allowed) to the point where the Wisconsin flows over a dam from the lake, finding a picnic area and a Wisconsin Historical Society marker. It noted that the name of the lake derives from the French for "old planting ground," a reference to the gardens established by Indians on one of three islands. In 1791, Jean Baptiste Perrault wintered here, and in the 1850s, white settlers built the first cabin on this site. Before the Civil War, the Wausau to Ontonagon, Michigan, road crossed here, and later the military road from Green Bay. Leonard Thomas built a summer resort here in 1884.

Watching the steady flow from the lake, I'm glad that all the frontier activity is history and that today the only building is an inconspicuous pit toilet stuck behind me in the woods. If I face the river, all I can see is the heart of Wisconsin, beating down through forests and towns, farms and cities, to eventually join the Mississippi and run to the sea.

Two miles downriver on Highway 32/45, a Wisconsin welcome center introduces visitors to the amenities of the Badger State, providing a boat landing, picnic areas, and toilets, plus two Wisconsin Historical Society markers. One recognizes the Wisconsin headwaters and the importance of the river to the state; the other honors the 32nd Division, a National Guard unit of soldiers from Wisconsin and Michigan who vanquished 23 German

Wisconsin Valley Improvement Company

The Wisconsin Valley Improvement Company (WVIC) coordinates the operation of the 25 hydroelectric plants on the river and 21 reservoirs to provide a uniform flow down the river. Created by state legislation in 1907 to coordinate the operation of a dozen timber-and-earth logging dams, the private corporation is the only entity in the nation to control the flow of an entire river system. The 10 utility and paper company owners of the river's 25 hydro plants pay for the work of the WVIC.

The company's goals are to maximize hydroelectric generation while controlling flooding, conserving water, and enhancing recreation. For example, the WVIC sends a portion of the river's flow down a kayak course in Wausau, making world-class kayak races possible (see Middle Wisconsin Chapter 13).

divisions in World War I. This "Red Arrow" Division was reactivated in World War II, serving with gallantry in the Pacific Theater.

Following the Red Arrow highway south, Mike, Rumpus, and I headed into Eagle River. The city provides a wayside at State Highway 17 and State Highway 70 near the confluence of the Eagle and Wisconsin rivers. Here, you can grill, picnic, launch a boat, and dream of paddling the length of the Wisconsin and down the Mississippi to New Orleans, where you'd change your canoe for a yacht and head into the Gulf of Mexico and beyond. And why not dream big? Rivers, above all, carry us to our dreams, just as they carried the Indians, explorers, and voyageurs.

Not far from town, a historic marine railway and the **Burnt Rollways Boat Hoist** add excitement for boaters jaded by ordinary running about on northern lakes. Operated by Wisconsin Valley Improvement Company, the hoist will haul your boat over the Burnt Rollways Dam between the Eagle River and Three Lakes chains of lakes. Part of the Wisconsin River Reservoir System, the Three Lakes chain is regulated by Burnt Rollways Dam at the lower end of Long Lake.

The dam takes its name from a lumbermen's protest in the late nineteenth century. When a jobber was unable to pay the lumberjacks for stacking his timber on a rollway at the edge of Ninemile Creek, they set fire to the logs, figuring that if they weren't going to be paid, neither was the jobber.

The Wisconsin Valley Improvement Company (WVIC) built the first steam-powered boat hoist here in 1911. Since 1952, an electric gantry hoist runs on a 165-foot-long trestle to haul vessels over the dam. The hoist operates Friday through Wednesday, 10:00 a.m. to 6:00 p.m., from late May through September. To reach the hoist, drive south of Eagle River, on Highway 45, about 4.5 miles to Oneida Farms Road. Turn left onto Oneida Farms Road and follow it to Van Bussum Road. Turn right on Van Bussum Road and drive to Dam Road, turning right again and following Dam Road to the boat hoist.

West of Eagle River, **Rainbow Flowage** gathers the waters of a wide area of Oneida and Vilas counties into the Wisconsin. In 2004, the state purchased more than 10,000 acres of the flowage and Pickerel Lake from the WVIC. Contained largely within the Northern Highland American Legion State Forest, the flowage is likely to remain a haven for anglers, birders, and hikers for many generations to come.

The flowage was not its usual sparkly self when we checked it out in August 2007. The reservoir, dependent on rainfall from Vilas County, was more than nine feet below average levels, with piers riding high and dry above the water. This resulted in a broader beach, which Rumpus eagerly explored, and larger islands. Maybe the shallower waters are what attracted a flock of floating Canadian geese that, despite my patient stalking, stayed out of camera range.

Old memories surfaced as we drove south into Rhinelander on Highway 47. I came of age during two summers working at Miller's Shorewood Vista on nearby Lake George. Tucked between memories of bins of laundry and buckets of carrot salads, images of sophisticated Chicagoland guests, a tribe of medical-student waiters, and grinning college women sprang to mind.

Lake George is where I first heard of the hodag, a grisly, ferocious, mythical beast I had no intention of mentioning in this serious book. But the 1896 invention of Gene Shepard won't leave my mind. Shepard "captured" the seven-foot-long creature in the woods near Rhinelander and later exhibited it like a sideshow sensation. Truthfully, it was a phenomenon, with black fur, a bull-shaped head, horns, and dragonlike spines down its back. You've probably already heard of the hodag, but in case you haven't, this beast still promotes the city of Rhinelander, serves as the mascot of the local high school, and lends its name to the local country music event, the Hodag Country Festival.

The Wisconsin Speleological Society hosts an annual Hodag Hunt, where the search for a cave hodag is part of the program. When the hunt took place at Governor Dodge State Park, the search was for the Maddag (as in Madtown), a close relative of the original hodag living in southern Wisconsin. From Lake George to Madison, the mythical beast still lurks.

Hodag Park, along the east shore of Boom Lake in Rhinelander, provides a canoe landing, beach, and areas to play baseball, basketball, and tennis. It's also home to **Hodag Waterski Shows** at 7:30 p.m. every Thursday and Sunday during the summer. Website: www.rhinelanderchamber.com/waterski.html.

Pioneer Park also fronts the water near Business U.S. Highway 8 and Oneida Avenue. The star of the park, the **Rhinelander Logging Museum Complex,** contains a collection of museums, such as the Duke Montgomery Antique Outboard and Fishing Museum, the Soo Line Depot, and the Rhinelander School Museum, as well as outdoor exhibits of railroad and logging equipment. The Logging Museum, an 1870s lumber camp replica, features a cook shanty, bunkhouse, and blacksmith shop that could be put to work tomorrow, were there lumbermen to man it. The complex is open daily, 10:00 a.m. to 5:00 p.m., from Memorial Day to Labor Day. Free, but donations accepted. If you go, look for the replica of Shepard's hodag, carved from wood in 1951.

On the south edge of Rhinelander, the *Wilderness Queen* began offering Wisconsin River cruises from below the mouth of the Pelican River to Hat Rapids Dam and back. The 76-foot boat operates from May into October. Reservations are required for afternoon sightseeing, sunset dinner, TGIF pizza, and autumn brunch cruises. Phone: (715) 369-7500. Website: www.WisconsinRiverCruises.com. The *Wilderness Queen* previously offered cruises from Willow Flowage, but moved to be nearer to a major highway and greater numbers of North Woods visitors.

Willow Flowage State Scenic Waters Area lies west of Rhinelander and U.S. Highway 51 and north of Tomahawk, and is listed on the Wisconsin Department of Natural Resources' website as one of its top 10 acquisitions since 1990. Now containing more than 16,000 acres, the original parcel comprised 8,720 acres of mainland and 106 islands that included 64 miles of shoreline at the meeting of the Willow and Squirrel and Tomahawk rivers. Only 12 miles from Tomahawk, the reservoir is largely undeveloped.

Tomahawk offers tourists seeking scenic areas whatever they need — food, supplies, information, and more. I had not visited Tomahawk on Old U.S. Highway 51 for many years, so when Mike, Rumpus, and I drove through the downtown, it was an upbeat surprise. Some sights, like a reliable old friend, remained unchanged: We drove over the Veterans Memorial Bridge near the location where you can still catch free water ski shows at 7:30 p.m. on Tuesday, Thursday, and Saturday from Memorial Day to Labor

Day. The Kwahamot (Tomahawk spelled backward) Water Ski Club has provided shows on Lake Alice above King's Dam for more than 60 years. Website: www.kwahamot.org.

This pinery town has two additional dams. Jersey City Dam, near the mouth of the Tomahawk River, provides power for the Wisconsin Service Corporation, as does the larger Tomahawk Dam, located on the Wisconsin above the mouth of the Spirit River.

The best surprise of this visit was on the town's main street, where things had definitely changed. In the 1960s, when my family vacationed here, the street would be jumping, especially with the big parade held every Fourth of July. But when I'd last traveled these short blocks, they had seemed less vibrant and emptier. But not, storefronts had been spruced up, their banners waving in the breeze, and most overflowed with sounds and activity.

Lumberman William Bradley would have rejoiced at the sight. He played a large role in establishing the town in 1886 on the Wisconsin near the confluence of the Somo and Tomahawk rivers, close above the mouth of the Spirit River. As Tomahawk's first mayor, Bradley was involved in many of the town's early businesses, from its bank to its newspaper, hotel, and even an opera house, as well as a dam and sawmill. He played with equal gusto. Bradley had a string of houseboats, built to resemble railroad cars and pulled by a towboat, that he used to entertain guests on Lake Mohawksin (the name a combination of Somo, Tomahawk, and Wisconsin), the flowage above the Tomahawk Dam.

We left Tomahawk on County Road S to pick up State Highway 107 south of town, which borders the east bank of the river south to Merrill. Large homes had begun to fill in the woodlands a point made by nothern rivers advocate Gail Gilson Pierce: "The number one challenge is to hand forward what we have been given, without a patchwork of development. Rivers are the next frontier, because the desirable lake fronts have been developed."

Such changes touch all Wisconsinites — both humans and wildlife. Years ago when my mother and I drove along this stretch of Highway 107, a bear crossed the highway ahead of us, but I no longer keep my eyes peeled for a bear here. Bears, wolves, and bobcats prefer large wild tracts in which to roam, and the fragmentation of wild lands reduces valuable habitat.

About 15 miles south of Tomahawk on Highway 107 (once also known as Grandfather Road), **Grandfather Falls Dam** has controlled the waters of the Wisconsin River since 1938. Owned by the Wisconsin Public Service Corporation, the dam has a generation capacity of 17,240 kilowatts and annually produces about 101,700 megawatts. At 200 acres, the reservoir

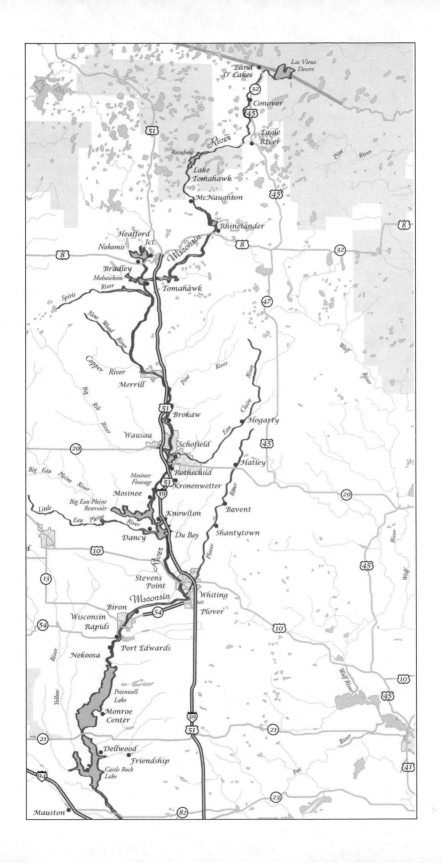

formed above this dam is the smallest on the Wisconsin River. Except for periods of high water in spring, the dam diverts most of the water to a reach that lies just east of the riverbed and from there to two wooden penstocks, or large pipes, that carry the flow to the turbines in the powerhouse. A leg of the **Ice Age National Scenic Trail** runs from below the dam along the spit of land between the reach and the river.

Paddlers can stay in their canoes until the impoundment ends above the penstocks. The take-out point is on the east bank, and the portage trail runs along the penstocks.

Downriver, at the point where the water enters the 1,315-foot-long penstocks, a short drive leads to a parking and fishing access area. You can also access the Ice Age Trail from here and get a close-up view of the penstocks. These two giant tubes run above the ground and resemble elongated barrels, with narrow wooden staves held together by steel rings.

The trail took Mike, Rumpus, and I above the northern end of the penstocks and over a footbridge to the river, a section of rapids, and what is left of **Grandfather Falls.** The moonscape of hundreds of rounded, basaltic rocks would certainly give a paddler pause in high water. This rock, dated at about 1.8 billion years, is approximately the same age as that exposed at the Dells of the Eau Claire, the tributary that runs into the Wisconsin near Wausau. The bedrock at these two sites is the oldest along the Ice Age Trail.

On the west side of the river, you can hike along the rapids to locate a large boulder considered a Manitou, by the Indians, who placed offerings on it when they passed. Like many other sacred spots, **Turtle Rock** has a position of significance, near a waterway and on a trail.

Not far to the south of the portage take-out, another short driveway off Highway 107 leads to the powerhouse at the end of the penstocks. As we stood in the parking area facing the red brick plant, we noticed an old staircase heading to the top of a steep hill to the north. It appeared to be a former section of the old portage trail, now replaced by a sweeping path around the knoll.

A future issue for the Wisconsin Public Service's Grandfather Station might be permitting periodic releases into the old riverbed to enable whitewater enthusiasts to try the mile-long series of serious rapids. The dam's Federal Energy Regulatory Commission license expires in 2018.

South of Grandfather Falls and just north of Bill Cross State Wildlife Area, **Camp New Wood County Park** was established in 1935 on the site of a U.S. Civilian Conservation Corps (CCC) camp. The 16-acre park on the Wisconsin River offers a canoe landing, beach, seven primitive campsites, picnic area, water, and toilets. The Grandfather Falls segment of the Ice Age National Scenic Trail runs through the park and north toward the hydro plant.

Bill Cross Rapids was named for an early settler of the area who was a skilled interpreter in several European and Indian languages, and who operated a trading post on the Wisconsin downriver of the mouth of the New Wood River, reported Richard Durbin, author of *The Wisconsin River: An Odyssey Through Time and Space.* The rapids mark the point where powerboats venturing upriver from Lake Alexander must turn around.

The pioneer also gave his name to **Bill Cross State Wildlife Area,** a 1,485-acre parcel stretching along the river and both sides of Highway 107 about 5 miles northwest of Merrill. If you walk its trails, be on the alert for deer, snowshoe hares, bald eagles, ruffed grouse, and other wildlife.

In the southern section of the wildlife area and just south of Big Hill Drive on Highway 107, a granite monument to Father René Ménard stands on the east side of the road at the top of Ninemile Hill. Placed by Merrill's Knights of Columbus, the monument honors the man who disappeared — presumed either lost or attacked — while on a mission to assist Huron refugees near the headwaters of the Black River. The Hurons had fled west from Ontario, Canada, following the destruction of their homeland by the

Grandfather Falls Moonscape

Iroquois in 1648–49. While some historians believe Ménard disappeared while portaging the Wisconsin's Bill Cross Rapids, others think his disappearance and death more likely took place on the Rib River in Taylor County, or possibly on a tributary of the Chippewa. What's not disputed is the year of his death, 1661, or the fact that he followed after his Huron converts in 1660 and spent the winter on Keweenaw Bay before striking overland across Upper Michigan.

Nestled in a curve of the river at the south end of Lake Alexander, **Council Grounds State Park** takes its name from stories about Indians using the site for an annual gathering place as they canoed between summer and winter camps. The 508-acre park began as Merrill's Wildwood City Park, and in 1938 the original 278 acres were given to the state and designated Council Grounds State Forest. Federal Works Progress Administration (WPA) crews developed the park and planted many trees. Today, you'll see 35 species of deciduous and coniferous trees, including hemlock and white and Norway pines. After a term as a roadside park, Council Grounds became a state park in 1978.

We drove along the river, stopping to get out of the car and explore the boat landing, handicapped-accessible fishing pier, water ski dock, and the **Alexander Dam.** Built in 1925, the dam created the 803-acre Lake Alexander, a 30-foot-deep fishing hole, where anglers find northern pike, smallmouth bass, muskie, walleye, and several varieties of panfish.

With few other state parks in the vicinity (the closest being Rib Mountain in Wausau), Council Grounds is a popular camping destination. Its wooded campground offers 55 sites, 19 with electricity. As is the case for all state park and forest campgrounds, you can make reservations online. Website: www.dnr.state.wi.us. Or, take your chances and arrive in the afternoon to reserve a site for the night.

Trails lead from the campground to the river road through the park, the Big Pines Nature Trail, and the River Run Hiking Trail. In addition to visitors, many local residents use these trails, which connect to paths in the adjacent **Merrill Area Recreation Complex.** This facility offers sport fields, an outdoor ice-skating rink, and the Smith Multi-Purpose Center with an indoor skating/walking rink, weight room, and community room.

Merrill presented a welcoming green retreat of parkland along the Prairie River just above its confluence with the Wisconsin. Two city parks face each other across State Highway 64/107: **Stange's Kitchenette Park** offers the usual park amenities with a volleyball court thrown in for good measure, and **Stange's Park** features a flower garden and historical signage.

While I ambled about Stange's Kitchenette Park with a camera, Mike and Rumpus explored its edges, eventually calling me over to the bank above the river. Rumpus had nosed out a turtle nesting area, where the enlarged holes into the gravelly earth and scattered, broken shells gave witness to an annihilation, with raccoons being the likely marauders.

Stange's Park overlooks a picturesque, three-arch, granite bridge, built in 1904 to replace a wooden truss bridge. The park also contains foot-bridges, an outdoor pool, lighted basketball and tennis courts, and the River Rat statue, commemorating logging in the area around Jenny Bull Falls.

Jenny Bull Falls was only one of Merrill's former names, according to Richard Durbin. Originally called Virginia Falls, the name evolved next to Warren Falls, and eventually to Jenny Bull Falls and then simply Jenny, before being rechristened Merrill in 1881. The term "jenny" generally denoted "small" and described the nearby rapids, which were smaller than the Big Bull Rapids downriver at Wausau, and needed also to be distinguished from Little Bull Rapids (now Mosinee). The word "Bull" referred to the fact that from a distance these rapids sounded like the lowing of a bull. All three communities opted to be called something other than "bull" well before the end of the nineteenth century. Sherburn S. Merrill, general manager of the Chicago, Milwaukee, and St. Paul Railroad, lent his name to the community following the arrival of the railroad.

Merrill offers other inviting river parkland, chiefly **Riverside Park** at the end of O'Day Street. It provides a boat landing, picnic areas, shelter, volleyball courts, horseshoes, and rest rooms, plus a nine-hole disc golf course on an island.

Following a short drive on Highway 51 downriver from Merrill, we headed to the **Dells of the Eau Claire County Park** east of Wausau. Like the dells of the St. Croix and the Wolf, the dark palisades of the Eau Claire are basaltic, standing guard over a fast-flowing stream broken by rocks and ledges. The exposed bedrock here and at Grandfather Falls is about 1.8 billion years old. This tributary has a much different appearance from the broad river of the same name that flows into the Chippewa less than a hundred miles to the west.

On sunny days the Eau Claire's ledges, marked by occasional potholes, attract waders and photographers. On rainy days they still lure hikers and wildlife. Despite the wet weather, we met a number of people on the park trails. Some hikers no doubt came from the campgrounds, either from one of the 28 family sites (17 with electricity) or from the large group campground that can accommodate up to 300. I wondered whether any were strays from a gathering of square dancers whom we had noticed treading the boards of a park shelter.

In search of a trail map, we walked along the gorge and over a bridge to reach the ranger's cabin. She was out, but in another of the happy coincidences that marked the research of this book, another park worker arrived on the scene, radioed the ranger, and located maps and brochures in the cabin.

Trails on both sides of the river and two footbridges — one running along the top of the dam — provided excellent access to the damp, dripping gorge. Cliffs of tilted rhyolite schist gave silent, solid witness to earlier epochs. The river's present course was set near the end of the glacial age. Originally a tributary of the Plover River, the Eau Claire once drained a glacial lake, but was diverted by a plug of glacial debris.

A link to the **Ice Age National Scenic Trail** runs from the park's River Trail. The Ice Age Trail enters the southwest corner of the park and exits on the north edge at County Y. Along the way it passes through the 40-acre Dells of the Eau Claire River State Natural Area, a designation that further protects this Marathon County public land.

Even if we had not been hiking, deep breaths were in order. The scent of rain mingled with damp earth and last year's leaves. Hemlock, sugar

A test of kayak skills at Wausau

maple, yellow birch, and mountain maple ran to the riverbanks. Patches of yew attested to a low number of deer, since white-tails commonly browse this evergreen shrub. If we had visited later in the year, we might have spotted the bright red berries of three other evergreen plants — bunch berry, partridge berry, and wintergreen.

To reach the park from Wausau, follow County Road Z east 14 miles to County Road Y. Drive north on County Road Y about 1.5 miles to the park.

We arrived in Wausau during one of the city's kayak competitions, held near the Washington Street bridge and **Wausau Whitewater Park.** Wearing colorful helmets and t-shirts, skinny young men spun, rolled, and flipped their snub-nosed, neon-toned kayaks below a short drop. Each had a minute to show off his skills.

The Wausau Kayak/Canoe Corporation coordinates local, national, and international clinics, training, and competitive events. Organized in 1974, the group got the Wisconsin Public Service utility to open dam gates to the east channel and develop it into one of the nation's top slalom courses. The Wausau course hosts competitors from around the world, including Olympic medalists and U.S. Kayak and Canoe Team members, as well as local paddlers. Website: www.wausauwhitewater.org.

Spectators at the competition that we saw lined the riverbank and a railroad trestle. While the former Chicago Northwestern Railroad depot across the street has been converted to house several businesses, the track on which onlookers stood was still in active use. At the sound of a distant whistle, mothers grabbed children and everyone stepped back as an old Illinois Central engine roared into view from the north. When the train receded from view, the crowd climbed back on the trestle.

Wausau Whitewater Park is located on one of several small islands in this stretch of the river, connected to one another by footbridges and the **River Edge Trail.** Adjacent to Whitewater Park, **Woodson Park** features a kayaker statue sculpted by Mike Capser. A path from the statue leads beneath the Scott Street bridge and over a footbridge to **Barker Stewart Island Park,** where you can still see the vestiges of an old sawmill.

South of the downtown you can find two more parks, accessible by either the River Edge Trail or by car from River Drive. **Oak Island and Fern Island** parks survive as valuable community green space, and each August, Fern Island is the site of the Big Bull Falls Blues Festival, a two-day event that draws fans from near and far.

Wausau, established as **Big Bull Falls** in 1845 on the west channel, was located where the Wisconsin dropped more than 20 feet in a third mile, and

Alexander Dam at Council Grounds State Park

Lumberyard Rock and other boulders led to the death of many raftsmen. The town's name was eventually changed to Wausau, because it supposedly sounded like an Ojibwe word meaning "faraway place." Signs along the River Edge Trail shed light on the city's early history.

After Wausau, Mosinee at first appeared insignificant, but the 150-year-old river town still offers plenty of restaurants and shops to explore. **River Park,** the site of various fairs and celebrations throughout the year, provides a gazebo and views of the dam and the Wausau Paper plant.

Located southwest of Mosinee at the intersection of Marathon, Portage, and Wood counties, the **George W. Mead State Wildlife Area** contains more than 28,000 acres of marsh, forest, and frontage along the Little Eau Pleine River, which flows into Lake Du Bay. This teeming refuge once figured in Mead's extravagant plans in the 1930s to construct two reservoirs — one on the Little Eau Pleine and one on the Big Eau Pleine — with a connecting tunnel between them. Mead and others believed that the reservoirs would lessen flooding on the Wisconsin and improve water flow to enable the development of additional power dams downstream. At Portage, an improved canal between the Wisconsin and the Fox could be used to divert water down the Fox and facilitate the development of additional paper mills on that river.

Despite many years of effort and the construction of the Big Eau Pleine Reservoir in 1937 and the Petenwell (1949) and Castle Rock (1950) dams, the ambitious and increasingly expensive dream never materialized. First federal funding was denied, and later environmental and outdoor sports organizations opposed it. Finally in 1959, Mead's Consolidated Paper Company donated the core acreage to the state for the current wildlife area.

Starting from Mosinee, we drove south toward Stevens Point on I-39/U.S. Highway 51 and then got off the freeway at Knowlton to follow State Highway 34 to **Lake Du Bay County Park** on County Road E about a mile south of Dancy. Formed by a dam in 1942, Lake Du Bay covers the site of a ford and a trading post established for the American Fur Company by John Baptiste Du Bay in 1834. The fur trader married Madeline, daughter of Oshkosh, a famed Menominee chief. On the day we visited, the park bristled with activity: Sailboats, powerboats, and water skiers slid over the lake, and children ran about the playground, beach, and spacious, wooded campground. They played on land both loved and preserved by generations of users.

All along the length of the Wisconsin, the past is veiled behind layers of change. Parks cover old trading sites, and dams have buried long-ago villages. The shifting river channel has turned prosperous river hamlets into ghost towns, and modern bridges span old fords. Still, you can push aside these curtains of change to reveal the foundations of modern river life. Wherever you travel along the Wisconsin, remnants of the past may sometimes surprise you.

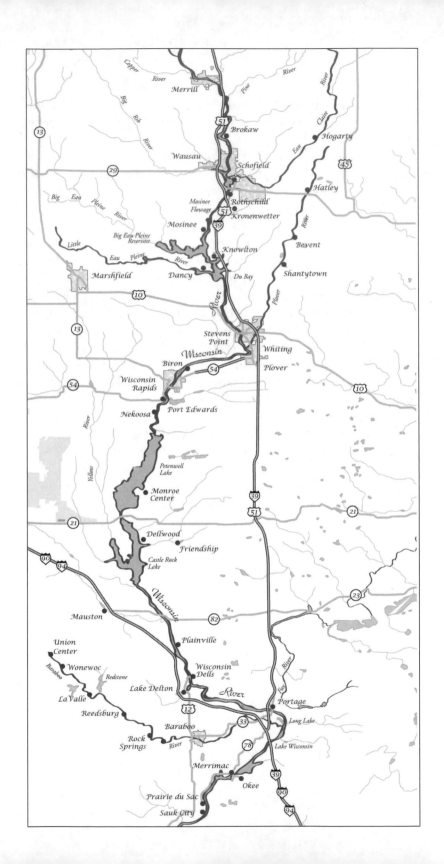

CHAPTER 13

Middle
Wisconsin

With its **Green Circle Trail** following the Wisconsin and Plover rivers on the west and south and encircling its airport on the northeast, Stevens Point has a well-deserved reputation as a recreational haven. It also offers considerable riverfront parkland, most prominently **Whiting Park** along both banks of the Plover, and Mead and **Pfiffner Pioneer parks** on either side of the Wisconsin north of the Clark Street (U.S. Highway 10) bridge downtown. On the west bank, Mead Park provides active youngsters with plenty of space to run, a playground, bathrooms, and picnic areas where their parents can set up snacks or a meal. On the east bank, Pfiffner Park provides equal facilities, along with a fountain, footbridge, boat ramp, band shell, and peaceful shoreline setting for the **Riverfront Arts Center.**

This small arts center features changing exhibitions by local and regional artists. It is open from 11:00 a.m. to 5:00 p.m., Tuesday through Friday, and from 11:00 a.m. to 3:00 p.m. on Saturday and Sunday. Free. Phone: (715) 343-6251. Website: www.uwsp.edu/cofac/rac/index.htm.

In Stevens Point, south of the Clark Street bridge on the east bank, look for the **Riverman Mural** at the corner of Water and Clark streets. The first of a series, this mural commemorates the city's logging heritage. Other local history can be found in Pfiffner Pioneer Park signs marking ice harvesting on the river, the Gateway to the Pineries, and city founder George Stevens. The lumberman arrived here in 1839 and established a trading post. Soon, the post became a staging area for lumbermen, with barns, warehouses, taverns, and inns cropping up around the trading post.

Ferry service, then a bridge across the 800-foot-wide river, dams, and major industry developed at this site in the mid-nineteenth century. William Johnson reportedly built the first dam all the way across the river in conjunction with a sawmill around 1846. A flourmill and other businesses followed, and the Winnebago and Superior Railroad arrived in 1871. Twenty years later, the Wisconsin River Pulp and Paper Company constructed a dam and pulp and paper mills, and soon the firm was producing the first newsprint in the county.

Although the paper industry began in Milwaukee three months before Wisconsin became a state in 1848, it grew to prominence along the Fox and Wisconsin rivers, supported by water power, accessible lumber, and river distribution routes. Papermaking today continues to dominate manufacturing in the central Wisconsin River Valley, with roughly 20 companies operating from Appleton to Wisconsin Rapids.

> **Three companies offer public tours at four plants along the Wisconsin River:**
> - **Domtar Paper Company, LLC,** in Rothschild. Phone: (715) 359-3101.
> - **Wausau Paper** in Mosinee. Phone: (715) 693-2111.
> - **Stora Enso** in Stevens Point and Wisconsin Rapids. Phone: (715) 422-3789.

Stora Enso paper mill at Wisconsin Rapids

Cranberries

Well before the Civil War, pioneers harvested wild cranberries from the marshes west of the Wisconsin River, trading the fruit for flour and other necessities, and by the end of the war farmers were commercially cultivating the native crop in Juneau and Wood counties. Daniel Whitney, the entrepreneur who built a sawmill at Nekoosa and a shot tower at Helena (see Lower Wisconsin Chapter 14), hired Indians to pick cranberries that he then shipped downriver to market in St. Louis.

Today, Wisconsin ranks at the top of the industry, with 110,000 acres of inland marshes producing more than 300 million pounds of cranberries — over half the amount that Americans consume each year.

For marsh harvest tours (October), historical exhibits, recipes, gifts, cranberry ice cream, and cranberry pie, visit the Wisconsin Cranberry Discovery Center located in a former cranberry sorting warehouse at 204 Main Street, Warrens. Phone: (608) 378-4878. Website: www.discovercranberries.com.

To plan your own tour, contact the Wisconsin Rapids Area Visitors and Convention Bureau. Phone: (800) 554-4484. Website: www.visitwisrapids.com. The bureau has developed a 50-mile Cranberry Highway auto tour and a 24-mile bike route through the bogs.

Most plants require visitors to call in advance for an appointment, but individuals and families can show up for Stora Enso's regularly scheduled tours of its Wisconsin Rapids plant without calling ahead.

I arrived at the plant on a gray Saturday morning. Stora Enso also offers free 90-minute tours at 10:00 a.m. on Wednesdays and Thursdays, as well as by appointment. Obediently, I'd worn closed-toe shoes and left my camera in the car. With more than a mile of walking, two staircases, and considerable noise, the tour is moderately challenging.

It began with a video and overview of Stora Enso, which operates six of the state's 46 paper and pulp plants. Headquartered in Helsinki, Finland, Stora Enso incredibly can document its roots back 700 years, to a mining company that may actually have begun operating much earlier. The Finnish firm bought Consolidated Papers and this plant in 2000.

Wisconsin Rapids Paper Mill began operations in 1904, the result of years of planning and a partnership that had created the Consolidated Water Power Company from several water-powered mills. George Mead I, a

Rockford, Illinois, furniture dealer, had married the daughter of one of the original partners, and after this partner's death, Mead was drawn into the project. In the end, he led the firm for 59 years, adding machinery, expanding production, and bringing in new leaders, including his son. Following his death, the Mead family retained ownership until George W. Mead, great grandson of George Mead I, finally sold to Stora Enso.

After the video, our group of 10, including a family with two children and three German tourists, left the visitor center and followed a painted path on the plant's cement floor to the towering No. 16 paper machine. Like a dry-docked battleship, the 520-foot long machine reached close to the ceiling in Stora Enso's Wisconsin Rapids Mill.

Wood chips, together with paper recycled from within the mill, traveled on a belt into the machine's digester, where water was added. A slurry of water, wood fibers, and clay then moved onto a synthetic screen where some of the water was removed. Next, the mix moved onto a fabric or felt, where more water was pressed out of the developing paper. From the felt, the 20-foot wide sheet moved into drums, where it was further dried to a composition of 98 percent paper and only 2 percent water. After the paper received a primer coat, it passed through more drying drums and was wound onto reels.

Forty-nine automated guided vehicles (AGVs), which replaced fork lifts, carry the paper to storage and retrieve it for shipment to customers. The computer-guided, battery-powered AGVs travel at speeds of three miles per hour along more than a mile of pathways throughout the plant. Though they have "eyes" that can sense when a person or other machine is too close, their eyes are not omni-directional and an AGV zipped within an inch or two of hitting our guide.

Our tour ended back in the visitor center, where we wandered among the exhibits of company history and processes, and picked up souvenirs. I passed on the four-color high-gloss sample posters and the tree seedlings but accepted a folder stuffed with the company's centennial publication, sustainability report, notepad, and postcard. I left knowing a great deal more about what's involved in producing immense quantities of high-grade paper. I also learned to respect the attention, skill, and perseverance of all the people who work a swing shift in a high-decibel mill.

Across the river from Stora Enso in Wisconsin Rapids, the **Mead River View Park** provides a stage for the **Clock Tower.** The clock and bell in this tower were originally installed in the city hall at First and Baker Streets in 1892, when the town on this side of the river was known as **Grand Rapids.**

Two other towns, Centralia and South Centralia (also called Hurleytown), stood on the west bank, separated from Grand Rapids by the river, multiple islands, and Sherman Rock, which divided the rapids into two channels. In 1900, the towns united as one city bearing the Grand Rapids name. Grand Rapids, in turn, became Wisconsin Rapids in 1920, following the misdirection of way too much mail to Grand Rapids, Michigan. The old city hall was demolished in 1957 and the clock and bell put into storage until they were restored here.

Park signage tells the story in more detail, and describes the legacy of the first George Mead and his heirs, the history of Wisconsin River logging, and early river traffic. The first bridge to span the river here was a wooden toll bridge constructed in 1867 and washed out in 1888. The last lumber raft came through in 1887; already the sawmill industry was waning along the middle river.

If you have time to stroll about the city, **East River Bank Park** (below the Grand Avenue bridge) and **Legion Park** (downstream from the dam and generally across from Stora Enso) provide more river views. Legion Park also showcases a mural and offers benches. The Wisconsin Rapids Area Visitors and Convention Bureau has developed three **Heritage River Walks** to highlight historic sites, including the Clock Tower, an early brewing company, two churches, and many impressive residences.

You can climb back into your vehicle to continue downriver, or onto your bike to follow the **Wisconsin River Trail,** a 9.5-mile paved path leading from Wisconsin Rapids through Port Edwards to Nekoosa.

Port Edwards is home to the **Alexander House,** a combination historical museum and art gallery located at 1131 Wisconsin River Drive (State Highway 34/54). Hours: 1:00 p.m. to 4:00 p.m., Sunday, Tuesday, and Thursday.

Nekoosa offers its own **Riverside Park,** and just south of town, **Historic Point Basse** provides a window to Wisconsin's pioneer past. The Wisconsin State Historical Society's Point Basse marker is located in Riverside Park on Highway 54. Daniel Whitney built the first sawmill on the Wisconsin River near here at Whitney's Rapids in 1831, about the same time that he contracted with workers to establish a shot tower downriver at Helena.

Below a string of five rapids including Whitney's Rapids, Robert Wakeley (now often spelled "Wakely") built an inn at Point Basse in 1831 to serve the river traveler and lumber raftsmen. Point Basse (meaning "low point" or "shallow place") marks an underwater shelf and the river crossing of an Indian trail that ran from Lake Poygan to Black River Falls. Wakeley Creek ran through

Cabin at Point Basse

the property, and lumbermen regularly tied up near it to refit and lash their rafts together after running the 3-mile series of rapids, according to Richard Durbin. In 1844 the steamboats *Maid of Iowa* and *Enterprise* carried passengers and cargo between Point Basse and Prairie du Chien.

Albert Woodbury purchased Wakeley's tavern in 1871, disassembled it, and rafted the building components downriver to Lone Rock. On October 15, 1925, it was destroyed by fire in a blaze that could have been seen from our house, had we lived above the river then where we do now.

While the tavern is gone, the Wakely Foundation has restored Robert Wakely's house at Point Basse. Constructed around 1842, the Greek Revival white clapboard home is one of the oldest balloon-frame houses in Central Wisconsin. The extensive Historic Point Basse site also features a replica shed/ice house, blacksmith shop, and an 1860s schoolhouse and early 1800s log cabin that were moved to this site. The cabin, which originally stood on land in Wisconsin Rapids owned by Wakely, has been restored as a fur trader's cabin. The interiors of these buildings are open during special events. A signed nature trail and trails to and along the Wisconsin River are open year-round (beware of poison ivy).

Drive to Point Basse from Nekoosa by following State Highway 73 east across the Wisconsin River to County Road Z. Turn south on County Road

Z and drive 0.6 miles to Wakely Road. Turn right on Wakely Road to reach the historic site. To view an events calendar or plan your visit, see www.historicpointbasse.com. Phone: (715) 886-4202 or (715) 423-3120.

Below Point Basse, the river has changed much since the days of the fur traders and lumbermen. Miles of meanders were flooded by the creation of the **Petenwell Dam** and replaced by the second largest inland lake in the state: **Petenwell Flowage** covers 36 square miles and is the largest of the 21 reservoirs on the Wisconsin.

Completed in 1951, the dam was one of the nation's first floating type dams built on sand instead of bedrock. Constructed of concrete, Petenwell Dam featured imbedded cutoff walls that penetrated deeply into the sand of ancient Glacial Lake Wisconsin. The dam was built on land, and dikes were built to both contain the new flowage and redirect the river channel to the dam.

Petenwell County Park provides a variety of year-round recreational options. The Adams County park features 500 campsites, heated shower and rest room facilities, a game room, a swimming area, a boat launch and marina with 90 slips, a playground, and hiking trails. Day-use and campground fees. From Friendship, follow State Highway 13 west for 9 miles. Turn west on County Road C and drive 6.5 miles to County Road Z, following it a quarter mile to Bighorn Drive, which runs a half mile along the lakeshore to the park. On Bighorn Drive, watch for a grave marker on the lakeshore; it marks the 1854 death of an "Indian Baby."

Across the flowage, Juneau County's Wilderness Park offers over 100 campsites, with electricity, grills, and picnic tables, as well as showers, a playground, and concessions. Visitors come to hike, boat, swim, fish, and water ski.

The flowage took its name from **Petenwell Rock,** a 100-foot-high sandstone mound near the State Highway 21 bridge over the Wisconsin. The rock got its name, according to legend, from Peter Wells, a pioneer traveler who fell in love with an Indian maiden. She returned his love but was promised to another man. Wells and his maiden escaped from her village one night. With men from her tribe in hot pursuit, the couple fled to the rock and dove to their death in the river.

A few miles downriver, **Castle Rock Dam** and **Castle Rock Flowage** trace their name to a sandstone outlier located about 5 miles below the dam. How many Castle Rocks are there in Wisconsin? **Castle Rock Wayside** marks the mini mountain on I-90/94 near Camp Douglas. Another wayside offers a trail up Castle Mound east of Black River Falls (see Black Chapter 15).

Like Petenwell Dam, Castle Rock Dam was built to "float" on the deep sands of Glacial Lake Wisconsin. The dam backed up the waters of the Wisconsin at the mouth of the Yellow River, erasing forever the lumber towns of Germantown and Werner. And it created the flowage, countless sloughs, and the peninsula now protected as **Buckhorn State Park.** Trails at both dams provide anglers and hikers public access to the flowages.

Buckhorn preserves a wilderness attractive to wildlife (and hunters and anglers) while providing excellent facilities for people with disabilities and folks who enjoy rustic camping but are not quite ready for — or up to — hiking miles to reach a backpacking site. In addition to 11 drive-in sites and a group camp, the park offers 42 backpack campsites located down a trail from the parking area. The length of these trails range from 40 to 350 yards. Garden carts to transport your gear make many of these doable for even the most laden of family campers. Some of these sites can also be reached by boat. Campers at sites 10–12 can take advantage of a rustic shelter with screened windows in which to cook or just escape the mosquitoes.

A handicapped-accessible cabin features more amenities than many motel rooms: heating and air-conditioning, a bedroom with two hospital beds, a living room with a sofa sleeper, a bathroom with a wheel-in shower, and a kitchen with a low counter, stove, microwave, and refrigerator. That's not all. There's a two-level accessible wildlife blind, two accessible waterfowl hunting blinds, an accessible fishing pier, and a floating, boat boarding pier. A section of the Savanna Nature Trail is also accessible.

Buckhorn State Park offers 4 miles of hiking trails. The Sandblow Walk leads to a vista of a desertlike area. The 0.75-mile Pond Trail leads to a pond with benches where you can stop to observe the wildlife.

If you paddle the flowage, allow an hour or more to check out the 10-station interpretative canoe trail. You can pick up a brochure at the park office describing the wetlands, plants, and wildlife along the 1.8-mile trail.

The park office and nature center building contains animal mounts and artifacts from Indians and early white settlers — not to mention helpful, friendly staff. Buckhorn also offers a children's fishing pond, beach, and changing stalls. In addition to bow and gun hunting, trapping is permitted according to state regulations and seasons. Drive to the park from County Road G southeast of Necedah.

Both Adams and Juneau counties have established **Castle Rock parks** on the east and west shores of the flowage. Adams County's park is open year-round. It offers 200 campsites, hiking trails, picnic tables, a shelter, playground, game room, rest rooms, showers, swimming beach, dressing rooms, and a boat landing. Juneau County's park provides more than 300 campsites on the flowage's western shore, as well as showers, playgrounds, a supervised swimming beach, boat access, fishing, water skiing, grills, shelter, electricity, and concessions. For a camping reservation, call (608) 847-9389 or (608) 847-7089.

More than a third of Juneau County's total land area is dedicated to wildlife preservation and available for public recreation. Some 43,000 acres of this public area comprises the **Necedah National Wildlife Refuge.** Situated a few miles west of the Wisconsin and bordered on the east by State Highway 80, the refuge provides needed habitat for many birds such as trumpeter swans and a migratory flock of whooping cranes, reintroduced here in 2001. The Little Yellow River and other streams run through the refuge, which also plays host to many mammals, amphibians, and insects, including the endangered Karner blue butterfly. Several roads, three trails, and observation decks facilitate wildlife viewing.

If you canoe the Wisconsin below Castle Rock Dam, another bluff rises just downstream from the mouth of the Lemonweir River. It runs about 60 miles southeasterly from Jackson County and flows by New Lisbon and Mauston, with attractive access both from **Riverside Park** in New Lisbon and **Kennedy County Park,** north of town. This Juneau County park provides a dozen rustic campsites in the middle of a 200-acre county forest, along with swimming, picnicking, hiking, and boating. Kennedy Park is located on County Road M about 3 miles north of New Lisbon. As the Lemonweir approaches the Wisconsin, it flows through increasing sloughs, channels, and wetlands. If you continue to paddle on the Wisconsin, you will soon reach Wisconsin Dells.

Mike and I set out to find the old Dells beneath the expanding, shining skyline of water parks, hotels, and condos. While water parks and the Ho-Chunk Casino in Baraboo have transformed the area into a year-round destination, thousands of visitors still seek the old Dells aboard the boats and ducks that ply the river from May through October.

Dells Boat Tours offers hour-long, motor launch trips on the Lower Dells (below the dam) and two-hour trips on the Upper Dells that include landings at **Witches Gulch** and **Stand Rock** to witness the Jumping Dog of Juneau County. Other Lower Dells tour options are via duck and jet boat — a fast, lower-draft launch that can skim into shallow coves and get close to rock formations. We opted to combine an Upper Dells motor launch tour with a duck tour of the Lower Dells, because we've both wanted to ride a duck since about age 8.

Created by General Motors for the U.S. military in World War II, the amphibious ducks transported soldiers and supplies from deep-sea ships to European beaches. From 1943 to the mid 1960s, ducks motored across water, sand, rocks, and woods to inland staging areas. While many ducks were left to continue their work abroad, others once used in training exercises within the United States were sold. Today these same ducks, carefully preserved and maintained, comprise the fleets of several tour companies, including one in Branson, Missouri, and two in Wisconsin Dells: the Dells Army Ducks and the Original Wisconsin Ducks.

The Original Wisconsin Ducks has 92 ducks, the largest fleet in the country. Of these, 45 are used for tours and seven serve as shuttles to and from the major resorts. Our duck was the *Tulagi*, built in 1942. (Most of the company's ducks bear the names of places where ducks served in World War II; a few bear female names, reportedly for the girlfriends of early Dells duck drivers.) Our driver was Alex Moore, a University of Wisconsin–Milwaukee student who grew up in the Dells and began driving ducks the previous summer. After introducing himself, the trip — 8.5 miles, half on land, half on water — and the duck, he noted that its maximum speed is about 50 mph on land and 7 knots in the water. It boasts four- and six-wheel drive (for mud and soft sand), weighs seven tons, and is 31 feet in length.

Moore shifted into gear and we were off with a roar, barreling into a copse of trees behind the parking lot. For a vehicle that's essentially a truck, the *Tulagi* demonstrated excellent acceleration. Soon we were zipping down a path lined with weathered statuary resembling erratics on a terminal moraine. These granite, hand-chiseled figures and columns once graced the Chicago Board of Trade Building. Businessman W. J. Newman moved them here in 1927 to decorate his Dells property.

But the more remarkable sights along our route were natural ones. Fern Dell reminded us of home with its hillsides of tall, small, and interrupted ferns. Before we knew it, we were plunging into the chilly waters of the Wisconsin River off Echo Point. Though our driver had warned us, we were still sitting ducks in the refreshing spray that showered us and our camera, thankfully without harm.

I photographed **Pulpit Rock, Hawk's Beak,** and the **Baby Grand Piano** slipping backward into the river, while Moore explained that the fantastic rock formations were created in Potsdam sandstone, similar to that found in Potsdam, New York; Potsdam, Germany; and Zurich, Switzerland. This stone formed during the end of the Cambrian period over 500 million years ago, when the area was on the sandy shore of an ancient inland sea.

Under slow pressure, the sand compacted into stone, softer in the center but with a hard shell at the top, where it was more firmly cemented by wind and weather. Millions of years later, glaciers missed this area, stopping within miles of the Dells.

When the climate warmed and the glaciers receded, they left glacial Lake Wisconsin, which once covered most of Juneau County and Wisconsin Dells. Then, 14,000 years ago, the lake burst through an ice dam near Cascade Mountain. The resulting flood carved this segment of the Wisconsin River channel, leaving ledges of the harder shells protruding from the bluffs and fanciful formations engraved deeply into the softer underlying layers.

Beyond Hawk's Beak, the river is 65 feet deep, the deepest point reached on this Lower Dells tour. I glanced at the life preservers in the shelves overhead, but there was no time to think about the potential for disaster.

Soon, we were heading up the mouth of Dell Creek. We landed briefly to portage **Newman's Dam** before re-entering the Creek, now Lake Delton. Long before Tommy Bartlett made the lake famous with his water ski shows, W. J. Newman built the 18-foot-high dam to create the lake in 1927.

The *Tulagi* skirted **Dawn Manor,** which still stands as the last building of old Newport. Begun in 1849 near the creek's mouth in anticipation of a

A duck's eye view of the Dells

railroad bridging the Wisconsin at this point, Newport boomed briefly, with hotels, stores, and schools springing up to serve a sudden population of 2,000 in the wilderness. But in June 1856 the rug — or, rather, the track — was pulled out from the town with the decision of the La Crosse and Milwaukee Railroad to locate its bridge upriver at Kilbourn City. That town, named for railroad president Byron Kilbourn, was renamed Wisconsin Dells in 1931.

Dawn Manor's most revered owner was Helen Raab, who purchased the property in 1942 and restored it with help from her friend, Frank Lloyd Wright. She also purchased 600 acres of surrounding land and planted white and jack pines along the riverbank. In 1956, much of this land was transferred to Dells Boat Company, with the stipulation that it be kept in its natural state for the enjoyment of future generations.

Following the forgotten roads of Newport, the *Tulagi* bumped through the pine plantations, up and down **Roller Coaster Hill.** Before my stomach resettled, we were at **Suicide Hill;** at least in summer the leaf-on vegetation gave the appearance of netting, should the *Tulagi* slip over the precipitous edge. Next comes a hairpin curve to the left before our track leveled and the duck entered Lowland Trail. This flat path along the river once formed part of an old stagecoach run.

But this was the Dells, after all, and soon we were climbing again, as our driver swung left toward **Red Bird Gorge.** Ferns and vines lined the narrow canyon, and trees brushed the sides of the eight-foot-wide *Tulagi*. The sheltered ravine is fitting tribute for the peaceable Red Bird, a Ho-Chunk chief who surrendered to the United States in 1827 in an effort to keep his people safe and living in peace (see Fox Chapter 9).

A short distance into the woods, our driver stopped to shift gears before the descent into **Black Hawk Gorge,** a memorial to the chief who led the Sauk during the Black Hawk War of 1832. In April, about 1,700 Sauk followed Black Hawk across the Mississippi River near the mouth of the Des Moines River, continuing north to the mouth of the Rock River, where they had lived in their village of Saukenuk and raised crops for generations. White squatters had taken over the area, and the Sauk, mistakenly believing that the British, Potowatami, and other tribes would help them reclaim their homeland, determined to make a stand. Help, however, never materialized, and U.S. troops and local militia pursued Black Hawk's band north through Illinois and Wisconsin. Fearing extermination, Black Hawk tried to surrender but the soldiers ignored the Sauk's white flag and misunderstood their offer to lay down arms. On July 21, 60 Sauk held off 700 troops in the

Battle of Wisconsin Heights, enabling many women, children, and elderly Sauk to escape across the Wisconsin River. The war came to a brutal end on August 2 at the Battle of Bad Axe, near the mouth of the Bad Axe River on the Mississippi in Crawford County. A few Sauk, including Black Hawk, escaped the massacre. Black Hawk was later captured by two Ho-Chunk at Wisconsin Dells and turned over to authorities. Black Hawk spent time in federal prisons before returning to his tribe in Iowa, where he died in 1838. As we emerged from Black Hawk Gorge, a deer walked slowly through the woods to the right of our trail. Two hundred yards farther, four more deer placidly turned their heads to watch the *Tulagi* roar past. The deer clearly have grown used to the din.

Without warning, our duck broke from the trees and the dock appeared directly ahead. Before we disembarked, we asked final questions and purchased a tour booklet from Moore before reluctantly leaving the *Tulagi* to other lucky passengers. To prolong our experience, we lingered in the gift shop, where Mike viewed a documentary on the ducks during war and we both observed the tools, bilge pump, and other military artifacts on display. We couldn't resist buying a commemorative book, and when we finally left the gift shop, like a kid at the midway, I longed to get in line and go on the ride again. Maybe next year. Phone: (608) 254-8751. Website: www.wisconsinducktours.com.

For lunch and a break between tours, we headed to the Mexicali Rose, offering both indoor and outdoor dining areas overlooking the **Kilbourn Dam.** Later we learned that the first dam built here in 1856 caused a lumber raftsman to drown, and surviving crew members tore out the dam. Eventually, state law mandated that dams be built with chutes at least 60 feet wide, so that strings of rafts could safely shoot through. In the 1890s, 50–100 rafts traveled over the dam daily.

The staff at the Mexicali Rose proved friendly, the chips thick-cut, and our selections ample and well-prepared. We can vouch for the seafood quesadilla and the enchiladas de carne. Mexicali Rose is adjacent to the Lower Dells boat dock. Phone: (608) 354-6036. Website: www.mexical-rose.com.

When we left the restaurant, a blue heron winged by the dam, and suddenly, I longed to be on the river again.

Captain Harlan Feldt, a retired science teacher, and tour guide Meredith Williams, a University of Wisconsin–Platteville student, welcomed us aboard the *Belle Boyd* for our 15-mile Upper Dells trip. Born in Virginia, Belle Boyd worked as a spy for the Confederacy during the Civil War and died in Wisconsin Dells while on a speaking tour.

Our *Belle Boyd* pulled away from the dock and the town built atop the intricately carved bluffs. Our captain pointed to the trees growing from the opposite bluff top; their roots can penetrate many feet into the soft sandstone for anchorage, water, and nutrients. Even swallows can hollow out this stone to create their nests.

The first significant formations rose simultaneously on both sides of the river. The 65-foot **High Rock Cliff** stands on the east bank and the 75-foot **Romance Cliff** towers above the west bank. According to a pseudo Indian legend, before a wedding, the groom would toss a lighted pine bough from Romance Cliff. If it was still alight when it hit the river, the marriage would be long and happy. Romance and High Rock cliffs form the lower jaw or gateway to the Upper Dells' formations. The Wisconsin is about 100 feet deep at this point.

Formations now passed in a steady procession, as if in a parade that we watched from a stationary gallery. **Chimney Rock** appeared and floated away, as did **Black Hawk's profile,** jutting from the face of a bluff. When the river divided around the large **Black Hawk Island,** the *Belle Boyd* followed the main channel, the 52-foot wide **Narrows,** along its eastern shore. The

The river carved beautiful formations at the Dells

rugged island, now owned by the University of Wisconsin–Extension, was once the site of Dell House, where lumbermen gathered to eat and drink.

Before the Wisconsin was dammed, the Narrows was shallower and more treacherous to lumbermen, who sometimes broke their lumber rafts into smaller segments and carefully prodded them through the right-angled **Devil's Elbow** one section at a time. A few lumbermen became skilled at running rafts through the Narrows and stayed in the area to provide their services to rafts as they came downriver.

One of these standing river pilots, Louis Gates, became legendary for running the Narrows in top hat and tails. He also constructed a toll bridge across the river with his father in 1850 and offered rowboat tours of the Dells to visitors, who both paid for his commentary and did the rowing.

We passed Gate's precisely carved inscription beneath a sandstone overhang: "Leroy Gates Dells & River Pilot from 1849 to 1858." The *Belle Boyd* also carried us to and beyond **Grant's Shield,** a vertical slab that served as an unofficial high water marker, and **Steamboat Rock.**

Soon we reached the stop I'd been waiting for and pulled up to the dock at the trailhead to **Witches Gulch.** Like snowdrifts, the chasm walls appeared shorter than I remembered from a childhood trip, but the Gulch remained an amazing, cavelike glacial reminder. We followed the boardwalk into the canyon, at points so narrow that we could only proceed single file. Below us, a trout stream flowed from Monk's Pond. High above us, a thin band of sunshine streamed between the chasm walls.

When the canyon widened, we came out onto a deck with a concession stand, bathrooms, and historical signage. Beyond the deck, a parking lot and drive provided vehicle access to River Road, north of Wisconsin Dells.

One sign described the opening of Witches Gulch to visitors in 1875 by Henry Hamilton Bennett, famed Dells photographer. With help from a local steamboat captain, he cleaned out debris, floated logs into the chasm, and built a walkway.

When it was time to walk back through the gulch to our boat, Mike and I lingered, last in line. I wanted to prolong this experience, to sear this canyon into memory.

Our next and last landing was H. H. Bennett's most famous site where he photographed his son Ashley leaping five feet from a bluff to the top of **Stand Rock,** a 47-foot column a short walk inland from the river. When Bennett photographed Ashley, he not only popularized the Dells, but also demonstrated the efficacy of the stop-action camera shutter he'd invented.

While visitors were once permitted to make the leap themselves, today a trained German shepherd, the "Jumping Dog of Juneau County," and the dog's handler hurdle the distance. I was happy to see the net stretched far below them, even if, from where we stood, it appeared no more substantial than a spider's web.

At the adjacent gift shop, we passed up the postcards and t-shirts but were mesmerized by the extensive display of historical Dells souvenirs and Bennett photographs, including one of the last steamboat on the river, the *Winnebago*, taken in 1942. His work is also preserved at the **H. H. Bennett Studio and History Center,** a Wisconsin Historical Society Historic Site in downtown Wisconsin Dells.

We took a longer walk back to the landing to view **Visor Ledge** and the **Demon's Anvil** formations, noting several shallow rock shelters in the sandstone bordering our trail. We also passed the former **Stand Rock Ceremonial Amphitheater,** site of Ho-Chunk performances from the 1930s to 1995.

Back on board, our guide pointed out **Louis' Bluff,** named for Louis Dupless, an early settler who operated a trading post at its base. This bluff marked the beginning of the Dells.

Our return trip downriver seemed to take no time at all. We quickly passed the **Palisades,** named after New York's Hudson River Palisades, and observed several areas of cross bedding in the bluffs. The cross bedding formed when winds swept across the lee faces of ancient sand dunes.

As we approached downtown, the *Belle Boyd* passed the five-story Riverwalk Hotel and we decided to drive to it. Located on River Road, the hotel includes Andy's Restaurant and Drinker's Landing Bar and features a boat dock and balcony over the river. Phone: (608) 659-5495. Website: www.dells.com.

Drinker's Landing served as the dock for the first Dells steamboat tours. Captain Wood first piloted the *Modocawanda,* a 50-foot side wheeler, upriver and back in June 1873. Unsurprisingly, the first hotel on this site was called the Blackhawk, constructed in 1924. It was renamed the River Inn in 1956 and destroyed by fire in 1984. The current hotel was built in 1985.

We parked at the hotel and followed the sidewalk south toward the downtown. Soon we were strolling along the **Dells Riverwalk,** a pedestrian parkway providing occasional benches, picnic tables, and tables with checkerboard tops. Our path led past the Riverwalk Pub, which offers several decks and live music outdoors from spring through fall. Phone: (608) 254-8215. Website: www.theriverwalkpub.com.

Before leaving the Dells, we wanted to find one more river site: the drive-in access to Witches Gulch. We returned to the car and drove north on River Road. From River Road and Broadway, the drive to the Witches Gulch access road is 3.9 miles. When the River Road curves left (west) at 0.7 miles north of Broadway, continue to follow it; do not head straight north. Continue past Coldwater Canyon Golf Course and the growing resort and condominium complex of Chula Vista until the gated road appears on your left. Follow the short winding road to the parking area and expect to pay $3 to enter Witches Gulch. By now, the light was fading, and we opted to turn around, satisfied by simply finding the gulch's back entrance.

As Mike drove homeward, I skimmed through the stack of brochures we'd picked up and became fascinated by an account of Yellow Thunder (1774–1874). This Ho-Chunk chief became renowned for his refusal to leave the area of the Wisconsin Dells. After the Treaty of 1837, the Ho-Chunk were pushed west of the Mississippi River, but some refused to leave. Between 1844 and 1873, the U.S. government at four different times forcibly rounded up the Ho-Chunk who could be found, including Yellow Thunder, and moved them to Iowa, Minnesota, or Nebraska. And four times, Yellow Thunder walked back, sometimes leading other Ho-Chunk with him.

Yellow Thunder purchased 40 acres of land in the Town of Delton in 1849, figuring that if he were a taxpaying landowner, he would not be sent away. Though his plan failed, Yellow Thunder's homestead became a haven for the Ho-Chunk. Finally in 1873, 24 years after he purchased the parcel, the U.S. government canceled its removal policy. The *Official Guidebook of Dells Boat Tours* quotes Yellow Thunder, who, at age 99, learned that he and his descendents could stay in the land "where wave and rock and tall pine meet."

The Ho-Chunk Nation recently reclaimed part of its old lands when the Wisconsin Department of Transportation returned the **Kingsley Bend Wayside** to the tribe in 2007. Located on State Highway 16 near the Wisconsin River about 3 miles east of the Dells, the wayside contains several conical, linear, and effigy mounds dating as far back as AD 600. The state was unable to maintain the site, and the Ho-Chunk Nation has already begun cleaning it up.

Not far downriver, **Aldo Leopold's shack** overlooks a seemingly different Wisconsin from the river running through the Dells. The cliffs and rocks have been left behind upstream, replaced by sand, prairie, and pine plantations. The shack has become a sacred place for new generations of earth stewards, who undertake the pilgrimage here from many different terrains and climates. Thanks to the efforts of his family, a foundation, and thousands of supporters, Leopold's former chicken coop stands as it did when the University of Wisconsin educator rescued it in the 1930s. He bought the farmed-out land from the county after the house burned and the former owner (a bootlegger, according to Leopold) lost the land due to unpaid property taxes.

Besides preserving the shack, the Aldo Leopold Foundation opened the **Aldo Leopold Legacy Center** in the spring of 2007. It welcomes visitors, and houses exhibits, archives, a small gift shop, and meeting spaces dedicated to connecting people to the land. Built near the spot where Leopold died of a heart attack while fighting a wildfire in 1948, the legacy building is located less than a mile from his beloved shack. When I climbed the hill from the parking lot, the center looked almost as large as a football field.

The green-designed building attracts architects seeking to learn how to create structures that are made of sustainable materials and produce all the energy they need. The center is constructed from pine planted by Leopold and his five children 75 years ago, along with oak, maple, and black cherry from lands owned by The Leopold Foundation and Aldo's oldest daughter, Nina Leopold Bradley, who lives just up the road. Heating and cooling is largely accomplished by temperature exchange through 200-foot-deep pipes sunk into rock measuring a constant 55 degrees Fahrenheit. A window-walled corridor on the building's south side also aids winter warming and summer cooling. The U.S. Green Building Council awarded the center a platinum Leadership in Energy and Environmental Design (LEED) certification in 2007.

But I've mainly come — as most visitors do — to see the shack.

The tour (cost: $15) began in the Legacy Center with a film explaining the basics of Leopold's history and the development of his land ethic. Leopold was not a purist endeavoring to preserve his land as it appeared to original European settlers, but rather a pragmatist seeking to live on the land without ruining it. The problem of an urban landscape, he felt, was that people didn't understand their connection to the land.

Leopold's love for the land is palpable in the center, the simple shack, the restored prairies, and the trees planted. The first year the family planted 3,000 trees, and almost all of them died due to a drought. All told, Leopold, his family, students, and friends, planted more than 30,000 trees, mostly pine, between 1935 and 1948.

Our tour group climbed into our guide's van and drove to a wooded parking area. Guide Phyllis McKenzie led us to the trail that wound along

The Wisconsin as Aldo Leopold saw it

the woods and past a savanna toward the shack. Beginning in 1935, Leopold restored a prairie in front of the shack, she explained, so that he had a clear view of Grand Marsh beyond. The restored prairie is one of the oldest in the United States. We paused to admire low-growing mallow blooms and the pods of butterfly milkweed.

The approach to the shack stirred the memory of an earlier visit. It had not changed: the same two huge elm stumps out front, the water pump, the fire circle, and a bench. Inside, the fireplace and hearth still dominated the small space, with one five-foot wide stone crossing the hearth and topped by a timber mantel.

McKenzie passed around black-and-white photos depicting the family at work and play in and around the shack. In one, Leopold and his sons are standing on the roof adding bricks to the chimney. In another, Nina skis along the road. And, in a third, Leopold, wearing boots and carrying a basket, trudges along the same road, now flooded, a dog prancing ahead of him. McKenzie explained that these photos were taken by Leopold's son Carl and that the Foundation hopes to digitize them and make them available online.

When we rose from the old canvas-slung chairs, I glanced up. On a horizontal rafter, a wooden cylinder approximately the shape of a soup can seemed cemented in place. A rope encircled its top edge. Like the rafter and ceiling, the post was whitewashed. I pointed. "What's that?"

"I'm glad you asked," McKenzie said. "That was a perch for a falcon and a crow that were pets of the Leopold children." Long after the family had cleaned out the former chicken coop, birds apparently still occupied the space.

Our trek to the Wisconsin River was longer than the path taken by the Leopolds in the 1930s. The river has changed course since then, adding an estimated 50 to 100 acres to the Leopold lands.

We followed the trail behind the shack and slogged through deep sand. When we arrived at the riverbank, located between Portage and Wisconsin Dells, McKenzie identified many of the plants bordering the sandy bank. She indicated sneezeweed, the spikes of cardinal flowers, false dragonhead, and, unfortunately, purple loosestrife. McKenzie pulled out all the invasive loosestrife except for one plant, leaving it to point out to other visitors.

A leopard frog hid beneath a chunk of driftwood. Raccoon and deer prints formed intricate patterns in the sand, and at one spot a pile of large fish scales recorded a raccoon family's picnic dinner. To cap our tour, two sandhill cranes flew overhead, calling to each other, and to our souls.

McKenzie led our small group to a plaque in the ground marking the site of **The Good Oak,** hit by lightning and preserved in memory by Leopold in *A Sand County Almanac* and *Sketches from Here and There*. She quoted his description of cutting this oak for firewood and how "fragrant little chips of history" flew from the saw.

The fragrant chips of history still seem to litter this spot of earth, inviting us to collect them and mold them into a bright and balanced future. The Legacy Center now provides a model for nurturing the land that connects and sustains us.

The Aldo Leopold Legacy Center is located on Levee Road. To get there, drive on U.S. Highway 12 north of Baraboo. At the stoplight at the Ho-Chunk Casino, turn east on Reedsburg Road. Follow Reedsburg Road across County Road A and continue to County Road T. Turn left on County Road T and drive over I-90/94. Levee Road is the next right after I-90/94 at a curve. Turn right; the center is located at E13701 Levee Road. Website: www.aldoleopold.org.

At Portage, the Wisconsin River swings sharply east, looping around the Baraboo Hills before cutting southwest through the state's Driftless Region to the Mississippi. About 2 miles to the east, the Fox River abruptly changes its westward course, swinging north and then northeast in its journey to Green Bay and Lake Michigan. The two rivers curve and reach toward one another, finally meeting in the canal completed in 1851. See the Fox River chapter to learn more about this restored historic canal and the city that grew at the center of the Fox-Wisconsin waterway, the first major passage to traverse the state.

More distant from one another than the Fox and Wisconsin rivers at Portage, the upper reaches of two Wisconsin River tributaries nevertheless run close together between Wilton and Elroy. The Kickapoo and, about 5 miles to the west, the Baraboo, are linked by the **Elroy-Sparta State Trail,** so that cyclists who enjoy paddling and paddlers who enjoy biking can find the best of both worlds on one outdoor excursion. The Elroy-Sparta trail runs close to the Baraboo River, occasionally bridging it, through Elroy, where it ends at the **"400" State Trail,** named for the 400-mile stretch of former railroad track between Chicago, Illinois, and Minneapolis, Minnesota. The "400" and the Baraboo River run flirtatiously near one another through Union Center and La Valle into Reedsburg, where the trail ends. Whether on a bike or in a canoe, it's impossible to overlook several sandstone formations, castlelike outliers that once were islands in a glacial lake.

Mike and I canoed a stretch of the Baraboo years ago. The sluggish brown river then meandered slowly through farm fields and woodlots, bordered by muddy banks. Today it runs clearer and faster on its way to the Wisconsin below Portage. Dam removal has made the difference.

Once seven dams interrupted the Baraboo, which rises near Hillsboro and runs about 115 miles to the Wisconsin River, dropping over 150 feet in elevation, including 45 feet in the city of Baraboo. The last five dams (three in Baraboo) were removed between 1997 and 2001. Sturgeon and other fish have returned, and bald eagles have followed them, along with a growing number of canoeists. The city of Baraboo has gained a new Ringling Riverfront, and the elephants at **Circus World Museum** have a new water playground, though they've been too timid to use it the past several years.

Circus World Museum provides excellent river views and a footbridge over the Baraboo. Located on the site of the Ringling Brothers Circus winter quarters, the museum features many year-round attractions including a big-screen video about circus history, exhibits, and the world's largest collection of antique circus wagons. From mid-May through early September, visitors enjoy site tours, clowns, wild animal antics, magic shows, and goodies from the pie (dining) car. Phone: (608) 356-8341 or (800) 693-1500. Website: www.circusworldmuseum.com.

Also in Baraboo, Boo Canoe and Raft/Riverstop offers canoe and raft rentals, as well as sandwiches, salads, ice cream, coffee, and gifts near the Broadway Bridge at 101 South Boulevard. Phone: (608) 356-8856. Website: www.boocanoe.com.

A few blocks to the west, Island Court (north from Shaw Street) bisects an oxbow curve in the river. The city's Riverwalk extends along the east side of the oxbow at Ochsner Park, and Haskins Park offers a view of the restored rapids south of Shaw Street.

Downstream, the river cuts through the Lower Narrows and the Precambrian quartzite cliffs of the **Baraboo Hills.** Created more than 500 million years ago, the gorge was buried by sediments in an ancient sea for 150 million years before wind, water, and glaciers uncovered the vertically tilted pink quartzite. The Baraboo also flows through the Upper Narrows

The Wisconsin River is a wide expanse at Portage

gorge, located upstream near Rock Springs. The third and greatest gorge through the Baraboo Hills is Devil's Lake, formed 15,000 years ago when glacial debris plugged its major outlet.

Beyond the Lower Narrows, the Baraboo River skirts two wild areas. It follows the southern edge of the **Pine Island State Wildlife Area** and then defines the northern boundary of the **Leopold Wetland Management District.**

In the triangle of land bordered by I-33, I90/94, and State Highway 33, the Leopold Wetland Management District is a federal waterfowl production area established in 1993. Waterfowl production areas consist of wetland habitat surrounded by grassland and woodland managed primarily for ducks and geese. They also support other waterfowl, grassland birds like bobolink and dickcissel, and the endangered Blandings turtle. Access from Portage is west on Highway 33 to Cascade Mountain Road; turn south and follow Cascade Mountain Road 2 miles to the district.

Despite its proximity to major highways and the Cascade Mountain Ski Area, the Lower Baraboo remains a rural river, cloistered from the hubbub of cities. It twists and turns through the broad, forested floodplain of the Wisconsin, joining the bigger river just north of Dekorra. This town developed as a convenient stopping point below the Wisconsin-Fox portage in 1836, eight years before the Wisconsin's longest running ferry began operating downriver at Merrimac.

Stand at sunset on the south bank of the Wisconsin at Merrimac, where the river runs generally west, to see the *Colsac III* dramatically dark against an orange and red sky. Or visit any other time when the river is free of ice. The state's only free ferry, which carried 280,000 cars in 50,000 trips in 2005, operates daily whenever weather permits, linking Columbia and Sauk counties in fact as well as in its moniker, a combination of the counties' names. Normally it carries traffic across the Wisconsin from March or April until December; however, it went back into service for a period in January 2007, when the river was ice-free. Warm temperatures and the ferry are a treat to tourists and a boon to commuters who otherwise might add 24–35 miles to their trip, crossing the river either upstream at I-39/90/94 or downstream at Prairie du Sac. The ferry, which operates on submerged cables, can hold 15 vehicles, as well as bicycles and pedestrians. It runs continuously 24 hours a day, and takes about seven minutes to cross the Wisconsin.

Chester Mattson launched the first ferry here in 1844, charging a small fee to carry a wagon and team of horses across the river. Other ferrymen followed, until the state acquired the ferry in 1933 and changed it to a free public transportation service.

There once were as many as 500 licensed ferries operating on the Wisconsin and other state rivers. These were powered by a variety of means: poles, oars, cables, and current. Sometimes teams of horses walked a treadmill connected to a paddlewheel. Most ferries were replaced by bridges by 1900, although a ferry at Nekoosa ran until 1917, and one at Germantown lasted until 1928. When the Stevens Point bridge was reconstructed over three years in the mid-1920s, a ferry took its place.

Tourists and nostalgia-minded commuters have kept the Merrimac Ferry operating. When in the early 1960s the original *Colsac* became too small for the number of drivers lining up to use it, highway engineers recommended that the ferry be replaced by a bridge. But a local organization, "I Believe in Ferries," successfully lobbied for a larger vessel. The *Colsac III* went into service in 2003, and popularity of the historic ferry crossing shows no signs of diminishing. The state's only other river ferry, the Cassville Car Ferry, runs across the Mississippi to Iowa (see Mississippi Chapter 19).

A bevy of businesses serves the visitors that the ferry brings to town, and ice cream and souvenirs are available near the dock. If you're after more substantial fare, consider the Ferry Landing Bar and Grill at the State Highway 78 and State Highway 113 intersection.

East of the ferry, the village's **Memorial Park** provides a picnicking alternative, with grills, a shelter, rest rooms, riverside benches, and a pier. Across the river, **Gibraltar Rock** rises 400 feet above Lake Wisconsin and offers long views of both the lake and fields in other directions. The site is a state natural area with an adjacent state-owned parcel being developed as parkland. Another park in development can be found at Weigans Bay downriver from Merrimac on Lake Wisconsin.

Between Merrimac and Wiegans Bay off Highway 78/113, Moon Valley Resort offers cottages and a marina at the bay where Gallus Slough empties into Lake Wisconsin. Website: www.moonvalley.com. There's also a public boat landing on the slough, draining Manley and Parfrey's Glen creeks, which join roughly a mile upstream. Manley Creek drains Devil's Lake, while Parfrey's Glen Creek drains the gorge and state natural area of the same name. This valley comprises the **Merrimac Preserve,** which is open for hiking and other low-impact recreation. Owned by the Riverland Conservancy, a nonprofit land trust, the Merrimac Preserve consists of more than 1,800 acres of forest, prairie, savanna, wetland, stream, and agricultural land. Website: www.riverlandconservancy.com.

Not long after the river and Highway 78 swing south past Wiegans Bay, the road to Hillcrest (Kilpatrick Point Drive) appears on the east side of the highway. Located in the Summer Oaks Resort complex, Hillcrest offers a wide-ranging menu, from Cajun to Italian to Southwest, to enjoy on a deck overlooking Lake Wisconsin, or call ahead and pick up your meal at the dock to enjoy aboard your boat. Phone: (608) 643-5159. Website: www.hillcrestrestaurant.com.

Prairie du Sac, of course, marks the end of the long stretch of dams on the Wisconsin and the beginning of the river's free flow to the Mississippi. But I'm getting ahead of myself. The river's journey, like my own, is far from done.

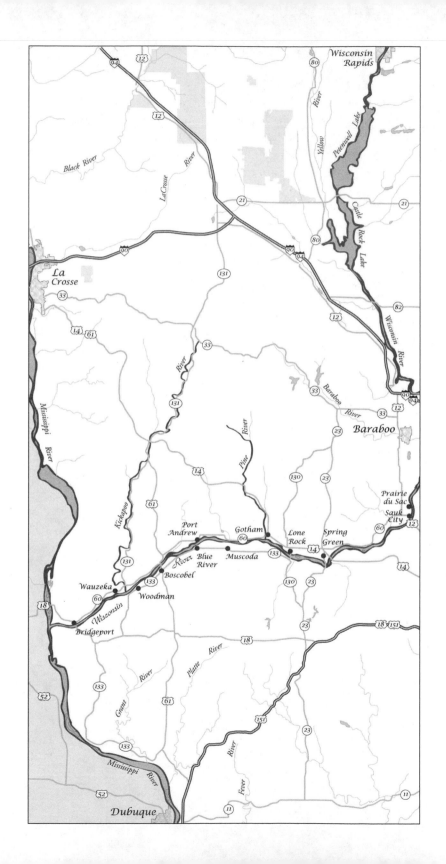

CHAPTER 14

Lower Wisconsin

hen folks in Madison say they're going to the river on a Sunday, their friends know which river they're talking about, and it's not the Yahara, which flows through the city's lakes to the Rock. For people living in a broad center swath of the state, there is only one river. For Madisonians, the lower Wisconsin is well-placed, an easy drive away from stress and city life to the natural rhythms that center us all.

The dam at Prairie du Sac marks the beginning of the lower Wisconsin, a 92-mile stretch where the river is broad, the bottom sandy, and the recreation possibilities endless. Completed in 1914, the dam took three years to build, slowed by high water that destroyed 200 feet of pilings in 1911 and mini-icebergs that crashed into the site in 1913.

Despite its difficult beginning, this dam, the largest and the last on the river as you head downstream, has brought both economic and recreational benefits. Now owned by Alliant Energy, it produces power for Prairie du Sac and Sauk City, as well as industries as distant as Milwaukee.

Whenever you visit the **Prairie du Sac Dam Recreation Area,** located off State Highway 78 on Dam Road north of town, you are unlikely to be alone. In summer, kayakers safely test their whitewater skills in the frothy waters beneath the dam, and anglers anchor their boats downstream or stake poles in the sandy bank. Walleye hang out here, along with muskie, pike, and small mouth bass in spring. Though off-limits to anglers, paddlefish hang out here too. A distant relative of the sturgeon, the ancient fish with the paddle-shaped snout can reach five feet in length and 50 to 100 pounds. If you see one jump above the river, you'll remember the sight.

In addition to anglers, bird-watchers haunt this area, on the lookout for herons, osprey, and various species of hawks. In January, they are joined by thousands of amateurs during Bald Eagle Watching Days. The open water below the dam provides an excellent feeding area for many of the state's re-established population of our national bird, and both Prairie du Sac and Sauk City have established parks and viewing areas along the river. If you have a list of "places to see in Wisconsin before I die," surely eagle watching belongs on it — either here on the Wisconsin or at Cassville on the Mississippi.

When Jonathan Carver visited this site in 1766, traveling down the Wisconsin River from what is today Portage, he arrived during the summer. Carver found a large Sauk village here, with 300 warriors, buildings, horses, and fields of corn, beans, squash, and other crops. Likely the natural beauty of the area, along with game, fish, and good agricultural land, attracted the Sauk as much as it later drew white settlers.

The adjacent cities of Prairie du Sac and Sauk City (jointly known as Sauk Prairie) that grew up along the Wisconsin have created a series of parks showcasing the river's magic:

- South of the Prairie du Sac dam, the **VFW Memorial Boat Landing** offers a long-range view of the dam, as well as camping, and a VFW hall guarded by a helicopter posed in a permanent landing or take-off.
- And south of the Highway 60 bridge, a **Prairie du Sac municipal parking lot** features a visitor information kiosk and eagle data boards, plus an observation deck with a scope and benches.
- Still in Prairie du Sac, **Graff Park** provides another vantage point and access to the river.
- As you continue south on Highway 78, one of the first things you notice on entering Sauk City is a paved trail heading down to the river and the **August W. Derleth Park.** authored *The Wisconsin: River of a Thousand Isles* and many novels set along this stretch of the rover.

In recognition of its river resource, the Sauk Prairie River Projects Association, Limited (SP River PAL) organized in the late 1990s to protect the Wisconsin and develop its riverfront and recreational opportunities. SP River PAL created a **River Walk Bike and Pedestrian Path** in 1999, which is open from March 31 to November 15; the path is closed during the winter to protect the bald eagles. If you can't visit the villages, you can still take a virtual tour of the path on the organization's website: www.spriverpal.org.

Local citizens have also created a plan to develop a rail-to-trail path on an old Wisconsin and Southern track running along the riverbank through both villages. So far this idea is a dream rather than budding reality. But stay tuned, it may happen yet.

To bear witness to the power of human perseverance, visit **Tower Hill State Park** on County Road C south of U.S. Highway 14 near Spring Green and Helena (pronounced to rhyme with Galena, Illinois). and Spring Green. Located on a bluff near the mouth of Mill Creek, the park preserves a historic shot tower that produced buckshot during the mid-nineteenth century.

Green Bay businessman Daniel Whitney spotted the bluff and believed that the site had possibilities for a unique shot tower — not the usual board construction but a combination of a 60-foot wooden shaft built on top of a 120-foot shaft dug through the sandstone bluff. Whitney is also the entrepreneur who built the first commercial sawmill on the Wisconsin near Nekoosa in 1831–32 and owned a short-lived (1829) shingle-making company at the confluence of the Yellow and Wisconsin Rivers.

A cooperative project of the Department of Natural Resources and the

Winter sunrise from the Highway 23 bridge

Wisconsin State Historical Society reconstructed the shot tower in 1971. Occasionally, the DNR, local organizations, and volunteers join forces to offer demonstrations of shot dropping through the tower. But whenever you arrive, you can visit the restored smelter house, view exhibits on lead shot making during the 1800s, and hike to the tunnel at the base of the bluff. The park is open May through October and also features camping (first-come, first-served) and canoeing and fishing on the Wisconsin River. Phone: (608) 588-2116.

Helena has had three different locations in its long history. Originally located a bit downriver from Tower Hill State Park near where State Highway 23 today bridges the river, the town was abandoned at the start of the Black Hawk War in 1832. In late July of that year following the battle of Wisconsin Heights near Sauk City, Black Hawk escaped west across the river. In their chase after him, some 1,300 militia gathered at the abandoned Helena. The militia tore down the existing buildings and constructed rafts to cross the Wisconsin.

After the war work resumed on the shot tower, and the town reformed nearby. You can find vestiges of this second location in Tower Hill State Park. From the historical marker located west of the shelter and north of the play field, walk west to the beginning of this trail off the paved road. This trail follows closely above the bank of Mill Creek and leads to the shot tower. In fact, part of this trail was once Helena's Water Street and some building foundations are still visible in the woods.

The town's death knell was heard in the sound of trains running on tracks laid to the north through Spring Green following the 1857 economic collapse. Hardy citizens relocated their town a third time, to the north, where it stands today, a shadow of its former self on Helena Road north of U.S. Highway 14.

Just downriver from Tower Hill, around a curve in County Road C, the **Frank Lloyd Wright Visitor Center** perches on a hillside facing the river. You know with a glance that it's a Wright or Wright-inspired design. Resembling a sandstone outcropping stretching across the hillside, the center is at once both open and solidly reassuring. A single spire near its east end adds a sense of lift to the structure.

But the real thrill is inside. Though I've visited many times, I can never resist the pull toward the 300-foot sweep of windows overlooking the river and the activities at **Peck's Landing** on the opposite bank. I feel like a voyeur rather than a voyageur when I spy on the folks wading along the shore, camping on the sandbar, or canoeing toward the Highway 23 bridge.

I envy them their fun, but I'm also content to be here, surrounded by harmony and all things Wright in the world.

The Visitor Center, open from May through October and weekends in April and November, is the launch pad for an array of Taliesin tours, ranging from one to four hours and featuring the entire estate, including outdoor gardens or just the magnificent house itself. A tour bus takes you to the different locations on the property.

If time is tight, the Visitor Center is a destination in itself; you can always get the lay of the land here and plan your next, extended tour. In addition to the tour office, the center contains a restaurant and a gift shop with books about Wright, a multitude of imaginative gift items, and replicas of his designs for lamps, clocks, stained glass windows, and furniture.

The Riverview Terrace Restaurant, open from May through October, begins serving at 9:00 a.m. daily and serves until 8:00 p.m. on Sunday, 3:00 p.m. on Monday, 9:00 p.m. Tuesday through Thursday, and 10:00 p.m. on Friday and Saturday — although it's closed from 3:00 to 4:00 p.m., when it begins serving dinner.

When Mike and I dined there recently, we each ordered a salad, which came with warm rolls, liver paté, and a tasty vegetarian paté flavored with basil and garlic. Mike enjoyed the black and bleu steak salad, and I ate every bit of the smoked salmon Cobb salad. Both came laden with great locally raised greens sprinkled with violets and nasturtiums.

Wright purchased this property, the site of a former diner and gas station, in 1953, intending to build a singular restaurant on this scenic spot; however, he died in 1959 at age 91 with the project still uncompleted. His third wife, Olgivanna Lloyd Wright, and the Taliesin Architects supervised completion of the Spring Green Restaurant in 1967. More than a quarter century later, the Taliesin Preservation Commission purchased the property

Playing on the river? Take precautions

- The downstream ends of sandbars are sometimes under cut and you can step suddenly into a deep hole.
- Wading in pairs is good iinsurance.
- If your canoe tips in deep water, do not try to swim upstream; work to keep on top of the water and let the current take you to a spot where you can stand.
- Wear a life vest."I've never know anyone to drown wearing a lifevest," said Mark Cupp, Lower Wisconsin Riverway executive director.

The view of the river from the Frank Lloyd Wright Visitor Center

to house its offices, the Visitor Center, and the renamed restaurant. Phone: (608) 588-7900 or (877) 588-7900. Website: www.taliesinpreservation.com.

Maybe the view from the Riverview Terrace Restaurant inspired me. Without giving myself time to think about it, I registered for a paddling trip on the lower Wisconsin.

The sky might have been cloudless, blue, and serene, but the water was choppy, whipped by a wind that on shore had seemed little more than a breeze. Pushed around by the waves, our group's boat angled broadside against the current when we set out. In response we dug our bright red paddle blades hard against the drag of unrelenting swells.

If I didn't know better, I'd swear we were on a roiling lake. And swear is what I did, under my breath, when I again knocked my paddle against the paddle of the fellow behind me. Six of us sat on benches in the 25-foot canoe, a fiberglass replica of an eighteenth-century voyageur model that could easily accommodate 10 or even 12 people, paddling from Gotham to Muscoda on the Lower Wisconsin River. At least this 300-pound canoe would be difficult to tip, I reassured myself.

The canoe was built as part of the state's sesquicentennial activities in 1998. Lower Wisconsin Riverway Board executive director Mark Cupp borrows the canoe from the DNR for a week each summer to take public officials and members of the general public on trips. Cupp sat in the stern, pointing out highlights along the banks, and Ritchie Brown, board member, served as bowman.

The town of Gotham (pronounced not like Batman's city, but rather "gōȳ' thum") replaced Richland City, which had once been located directly on the north river bank. Located near the mouth of the Pine River, Richland City served as a popular stop for lumber rafts and steamboats in the 1850s, and boasted flour and sawmills, three hotels, and a high school. But the Milwaukee and Mississippi Rail Road (predecessor of the Milwaukee Road), instead of laying tracks northwest from Lone Rock to Richland City, crossed the river and extended a line along the Wisconsin's south bank to Muscoda. If the railroad left Richland City high and dry away, the river did just the opposite, flooding out the town despite herculean efforts involving sandbags, wing dams, and ditches. As the river adjusted its course, a number of Richland City houses were moved back from it, eventually becoming part of Gotham, which grew along a rail branch line built in 1876 from Lone Rock to Richland Center. As we paddled past the site, I saw no sign of the ghost town, though I remembered seeing several old clapboard houses along the road to Gotham Landing.

Seated behind Brown in the voyageur canoe, I tried to duplicate his short, quick strokes, dipping my paddle in unison with his to avoid striking it. This must be how the voyageurs traveled, in a quick rhythm, harnessed together by chants and songs with a singular beat. In fact, Cupp asked if we know any voyageur songs, but we all just laughed. It was enough that we were on this river, in this hefty canoe.

We slid silently past Avoca Prairie and focused on the wind and our paddling. I slid across the bench to paddle on the right as we shifted around a snag. Suddenly someone behind me called our attention to an eagle nest, clearly visible in the upper branches of a tree on the left bank. "It's a newer nest, not very big yet," someone else agreed. Not very big yet? It seemed to me to be large enough to hold a bed for Rumpus.

Two eagles flew out along the left bank. I set my paddle across my lap and raised my camera. Though they were too far away to photograph, they were not too far away to admire.

Sandbars and wooded banks marked our journey. I glanced at my watch, but the sweep of hands seemed meaningless here, an anachronism from another, irrelevant time. The sun moved slowly overhead and a great blue heron rose before us and flew downstream.

On this gusty day, we saw few other boats. We did encounter one kayaker and several fishing boats, but no small canoes.

We passed several upscale homes, private properties interrupting the public Riverway. One palatial abode boasted a steep staircase to the river, extensive flower gardens, and a pier jutting at right angles out into the river. Cupp named the owners and explained that, were this structure located within the Riverway, the law would mandate that the pier be located abreast of the river, not sticking out into it.

We paddled past other homes, and Cupp named all their owners and circumstances. Whether small, weathered cottages or renovated mini mansions, he knew them all.

For lunch, we paddled past, then back upstream, to a long sandbar with a two-foot vertical bank facing the river. I imagined that the water level was sometimes higher, and Cupp noted that the river was only 45 percent of normal flow for this time of year.

Had we felt so inclined, we could have camped for up to three days on this wooded sandbar. While camping is not permitted on the riverbanks, it is allowed on the river's many publicly owned sandbars, with a few exceptions, including within 1 mile of the Mazomanie Beach, haven of nudists.

Canoeing like a voyageur on the Lower Wisconsin

The **Lower Wisconsin State Riverway Visitor** provides guidelines on dealing with trash, including human waste, and on putting out campfires. (Burying a fire in sand is not enough; ask the person who inadvertently trod over a still smoldering fire.) Guidelines are also available online. Website: www.lwr.state.wi.us.

I took my sandwich to a shady spot already occupied by the stern man from the other canoe. He turned out to be Ron Leys, the Crawford County representative to the board. A former *Milwaukee Journal* outdoor editor, author, and contributor to Krause Publications' *Outdoor Journal,* Leys retired with his wife to a southwest Wisconsin farm in 1991 and quickly became active in community affairs.

Ritchie Brown joined us, and I asked about changes they had seen in the lower Wisconsin. Leys replied that the first time he ever saw an eagle in the wild was in Minnesota's Superior Boundary Waters Canoe Area in the 1960s. "I never expected to see one here," he said. "But you always see eagles now."

Lunch over, we paddled briskly downriver, passing more old cottages and newly remodeled cabins. I snapped photos of the several turtles we passed, which often slid into the river as we came up beside the rocks and logs where they basked in the sunshine.

We glided over the **Orion** (pronounced not like the constellation but rather, "or' ï on") **Mussel Bed,** the only underwater state natural area, and I wished the canoe were glass-bottomed and that we could view the mollusks beneath us. We paddled past **Orion Landing** and quickly the Highway 60 bridge came into view. Not long after — far too soon for my river hunger to be much satisfied but soon enough for my aching shoulders — Cupp directed us across the river toward the left shore and the **Muscoda Landing.**

Mike stood on the high bank, camera aimed toward us. "Bon jour, mon ami," Cupp called to him in a voyageur greeting.

Mike paused, saluted, and snapped another shot.

Soon, I was standing next to him, babbling about eagles and a kingfisher and how the town right here had once been called Richland City.

"You mean Gotham? This is Muscoda."

"Right, of course it is. " For two-plus hours I had stood still, watching the river pass before me. And time had stood still too.

Before we scattered our separate ways, Cupp gathered us together on the bank and briefly quoted Aldo Leopold on the unchanging river. He followed the short recitation with his own words: "May we preserve this resource for our children and grandchildren and their children unto the seventh generation."

I'd known that the day would be memorable. The day before, returning home from an interview with Cupp in his Muscoda office, I had stopped at the Gotham landing to be sure I could find it easily on the day of the trip. As I stood on the riverbank, three sandhill cranes flew overhead, the shadows of their wings pulsing on the river's surface. For the record, you can drive to the landing from Fulton Street, which intersects Highway 60 on the south edge of town, located south of the intersection of Highway 60 and Highway 14.

For Cupp, the most significant thing about the Riverway is that it contains the highest concentration of bird mounds in the United States. "A number of these sites are on state-owned lands where people can view the mounds and get a sense of history and know that there were people who flourished here a millennium ago," he said. "That helps me to communicate the timelessness of the river."

The Ho-Chunk Department of Heritage Preservation has protected many effigy mounds on its lands along the Wisconsin, and Mike and I made an appointment to follow the **Effigy Mounds Self-Guided Walking Tour** on the property of the Ho-Chunk Bison Farm.

The trail began from a parking area at the end of a farm lane and headed toward the north bank of the Wisconsin River. Signage described 13 extant mounds, once part of a large effigy group stretching across the dry upland above the river. Several trees had been cleared to maintain the area, and the trail looped through the scattering of mounds and remaining old oaks.

My eyes picked out one conical mound and then another, marking the west end of this grouping.

At first the next elongated knoll appeared to be a linear mound, but, no, the sign informed us that this was an otter mound. Doubtful, we marched around it. Sure enough, the far end narrowed into a tail-like shape.

Immediately ahead, the Wisconsin appeared through the trees, so broad that it almost looked like a river in flood. But it's not; it's only the lower Wisconsin, spreading as usual through the sandy soils of the valley. Near the north bank, a sunny beach of an island rises, a clump of trees guarding its center.

A sign provided its name: Little People Island. The Ho-Chunk have been told of ancient burials on this island and have heard stories of little people living there. "The Ho-Chunk believe that the little people take care of the mounds, so we always thank them for their good work."

The little people were unfortunately unable to protect several of the shore-based mounds from destruction. A triple mound, actually three conical mounds connected to one another, shows signs of disturbance. In fact, this mound was "potted," or plundered of its artifacts and destroyed. Whatever might have been learned from its content has been lost. Despite the protection of effigy mounds by federal and state laws and penalties, the mounds have been occasionally targeted by thieves.

Disturbance of the triple mound was especially disappointing, since it may have been very significant to Indian history. William Pidgeon wrote of his interviews with De-Coo-Dah in his book, *Traditions of De-Coo-Dah,* published in 1858. One of De-Coo-Dah's tales was about a group of mounds along the north shore of the Wisconsin River. "Men from the south" came and joined with the Ho-Chunk, and three identical mounds commemorated three marriages between the tribes.

Not far from the triple mound, a 200-foot linear mound parallels the river. Ground penetrating radar has revealed that it contains two dozen burials.

Even more intriguing, a set of four conical mounds, which denoted the turning point of the loop trail, contained a marker tree — or witness tree — between the first and second mounds from the left as we faced the river. This old jack oak (also known as a northern pin oak) seemed to point in the general direction of **Gottschall Rockshelter.** The Ho-Chunk's ancestors also lived in a large village across the Wisconsin on the site of what today is the city of Muscoda.

Gottschall is a remarkable archaeological site containing unique artifacts and pictographic paintings. Robert Salzer, professor emeritus at Beloit

The Ho-Chunk Witness Tree

The river wears a tamer look near Boscobel

College, has spent years studying and publishing his work about this protected site. For more information, contact the Mississippi Valley Archaeology Center at the University of Wisconsin–La Crosse. Phone: 608-785-8463. Website: www.uwlax.edu/mvac/.

As Mike and I circled back to our car, we noticed the ravine formed by the excavation of soil for mound construction here and the accompanying Ghost Mounds sign. I tried to imagine what the area might have looked like roughly two thousand years ago, when additional conical, linear, and animal mounds covered this sacred space. If you wish to visit, call the Ho-Chunk Bison Ranch and provide your name, address, and phone number, plus the date that you would like to tour the mounds. Phone: (608) 739-3360.

Cultural Landscape Legacies, Inc., has developed a self-guided tour of other mound sites in southwestern Wisconsin. Website: www.clli.org/. Contact the Lower Wisconsin State Riverway Board. Phone: (800) 221-3792. Or, pick up the Effigy Mounds Grand Tour brochure at Tower Hill State Park, Governor Nelson State Park, or Wyalusing State Park. Wyalusing's Sentinel Ridge Trail passes conical and effigy mounds.

Heading downriver, we read about another Indian legend at signage in the **Floyd Von Haden Boat Landing and Recreation Area** downstream of the State Highway 61 Bridge in Boscobel. The creation story of the Wisconsin River told of a Manitou, or spirit, that took the form of a giant serpent:

> *One day the serpent traveled from his home in the great forest to the sea. While crossing over the land, he made a groove that filled with water. Streams arose from the grooves of other serpents that fled in all directions, fearing the Manitou. At the Wisconsin Dells, large rocks blocked the great serpent's path. He pushed his head into a crack and split the stone apart. The serpent continued on but soon became tired. As he rested and rolled about, he widened the river channel.*

The Floyd Von Haden Boat landing and Recreation Area is named for a longtime Grant County supervisor who helped establish this and 10 other landings and parks on the Wisconsin and Mississippi rivers. This landing at the mouth of Sanders Creek is certainly well-conceived, with a sandy beach, picnic facilities, handicapped-accessible toilets, and plenty of parking. This last feature is a good thing, because the landing has become a popular canoe put-in and take-out site on the lower river.

You can also access the river at Prairie du Bay, off State Highway 60 near the Boscobel Municipal Airport at the end of a gravel road. While there's no boat landing, this area does offer trails for anglers and pheasant hunters.

I lucked out the day we drove past the airport. A sign proclaimed that airplane and helicopter rides were being offered as part of a special event sponsored by a local organization. We turned around and drove into the airport parking lot.

For months I'd been dreaming about a helicopter flight over Wisconsin's rivers, so this opportunity appeared quite a coincidence, at the very least an answered prayer that I'd do well not to snub.

Still, I had apprehensions as I sat next to the pilot in the noisy bird. My seatbelt seemed little prevention from pitching through the Plexiglas that curved clear as the sky from above my head all the way to the floor. When the helicopter rose above the airport, winds batted at it and a vibration pulsed through the soles of my feet. I felt very vulnerable. Surely, I'd soon be diving headfirst through the "windshield" and falling out of the sky.

I tried not to look directly down, but this was impossible, given that I wanted to snap a photo of the lower Wisconsin's broad valley that was soon coursing beneath us, an undulating snake in the wilderness. I brought the camera up and snapped one photo and then another. Before I knew it, I'd shot 20 photos of the glorious vistas of the river valley. I was suddenly aware that I was smiling. Leaning down, I shot more photos, allowing myself to melt into the view and become a part of this winding, flowing landscape.

When the ride came to an end, I thanked the pilot, climbed out of the helicopter, and moved in a trance away from the runway. I walked to the car

Canoeists ply the Kickapoo

on a cloud, where poor Mike, earthbound all this time, waited. If ever you have the chance, don't pass on a helicopter ride.

A helicopter ride over the Kickapoo River, the longest tributary of the Wisconsin, would present a very different view. At 130 twisting miles, the Kickapoo is the longest river running entirely through Southwest Wisconsin's Driftless Region, its ridges and coulees never scoured by glaciers and free of glacial drift. Here, on the state's Western Upland, the tributaries flowing south into the lower Wisconsin tend to be longer and to drop less quickly in elevation than those flowing in from the south. While the Kickapoo drops about five feet per mile, Otter Creek, for instance, drops 500 feet in its 7-mile journey north to join the Wisconsin west of Spring Green.

When Mike and I paddled the Kickapoo from Ontario with a group of friends in August, the water level was so low that our canoes occasionally scraped the pebbly bottom. Generally an easy paddle with few riffles, the Kickapoo nevertheless demands constant attention. The curves and log obstacles follow with the rapidity of ducks in a shooting gallery. We continually paddled to the right and then to the left, seeking the deeper channel along the outer edge of each curve — unless it was blocked by rocks or fallen logs.

Even with the slower, late summer current, we traveled almost too fast to get a good look at the shifting scenery and wildlife. At **Wildcat Mountain State Park,** seeping sandstone cliffs towered above us, and we scanned them for eroded rock shelters, ferns, mosses, and precariously perched pine and hemlock. The most environmentally conscious in our group scrutinized the lower banks for cans and other refuse to pick up and toss into the bottom of their canoes.

A kingfisher rested in a tree long enough for a photo while a row of turtles on a log slid into the water when we drew near. Beneath the bridges, the upside-down mud jug houses of cliff swallows clung tight, their inhabitants swooping in and out.

The **Kickapoo Valley Reserve** sponsors classes on wildlife, art, geology, and endangered plants for all ages; opens acreage to hunters in season; and provides trails for equestrians, bikers, and hikers. From May to October, paddlers get a kick on the Kickapoo and find plenty of well-maintained campsites for picnics and overnight stays.

While some of the valley's treasures are visible from a canoe, others require hiking or a stop at the visitor center to appreciate. Particularly on weekdays, when river traffic is lighter, you might see muskrats, beaver, deer, raccoons, mink, and otters along the river. The visitor center offers exhibitions and excursions to learn more about the area's geology and early history.

Some geologists believe the river is one of the most ancient on the globe, excluding those found in Antarctica. The valley's precipitous cliffs, sharp valleys, caves, and rock shelters owe their existence to the area's lack of glaciation. The castellated river bluffs are sometimes called the Dells of the Kickapoo, and the region is also known as the Ocooch Mountains. The state's most notable caves lie in the Driftless Region, and **Kickapoo Indian Caverns,** north of State Highway 60 near Wauzeka, guides visitors on underground tours 160 feet beneath the surface. Highlights include the fossil of a mastodon bone in the ceiling, a variety of cave formations, and Indian artifacts in the entrance building. The cave was reportedly used many years ago as an Indian campsite and a place to dry animal skins and fashion tools.

As part of the review process for the proposed La Farge dam, the Wisconsin Historical Society surveyed the upper river, finding numerous ancient sites, several dating back 10,000 years. Many rock shelters still contain petroglyphs, and a variety of burial mounds and open-air camp and village sites lie scattered across the region. The Kickapoo Valley Reserve is located at S3661 State Highway 131, La Farge. Phone: (608) 625-2960. Website: http://kvr.state.wi.us.

If you discover artifacts in the valley, please bring them to the attention of the Kickapoo Valley Reserve staff, the Wisconsin State Archaeologist at (608) 264-6495, the Western Wisconsin Regional Archaeologist at (608) 785-8451, or the Ho-Chunk Nation's Heritage Preservation, Cultural Resource Division at (800) 561-9918.

Early Indians recognized the Kickapoo as "the river of canoes" and it has become so again, following 150 years of lumbering, settlements, and farming. From the sheltering, perpendicular cliffs of its upper reaches to more dispersed cliffs of the Kickapoo River Wildlife Area near Wauzeka, this river presents canoeing that's both manageable for beginners yet challenging enough for advanced paddlers.

Several companies offer canoe rentals and shuttle rides:
- **Drifty's Canoe Rental,** Ontario. Phone: (608) 337-4288.
  Website: www. driftyscanoerental.net.
- **Kickapoo Yacht Club,** Rockton. Phone: (608) 625-4395 or (608) 625-2071.
  Website: www.kickapooyachtclub.com.
- **Mr. Duck's Canoe Rental,** Ontario. Phone: (608) 337-4711.
  Website: www. mrduckscanoerental.com.
- **Titanic Canoe Rental,** Ontario. Phone: (877) 438-7865 (GET-SUNK).
  Website: www.titaniccanoerental.com.

The farther downriver you go on the lower Wisconsin, the fewer people you see, both on the river and along its banks, until you reach **Wyalusing State Park** and the Mississippi River. One of Wisconsin's first state parks, Wyalusing was established in 1917, thanks largely to the foresight and generosity of Robert Glenn, who donated much of the land on the bluffs above the confluence. And we can thank workers of the federal Civilian Conservation Corps and Works Progress Administration for many of the trails, picnic areas, shelters, and stone walls still in use today.

Wyalusing not only stands at the confluence of two great rivers, but also marks a spot where history converged: This site was a hub of ancient trails, a neutral gathering and trading area for at least 14 Indian tribes, and later a fur trading rendezvous between Indians and voyageurs. When Father Jacques Marquette and fur trader Louis Joliet reached the confluence in 1673, they arrived at almost midsummer, on June 17, and likely looked down at the blue rivers and green woodlands from one of the bluffs in the park. Today, a marker at Point Lookout commemorates this event.

One of my favorite vantage points is from within Treasure Cave, located below Point Lookout along Bluff Trail. Getting there involves a trek down the bluff and a climb up a ladder to the petite passage. The challenge adds to the wonder of the view glimpsed through a natural window and increases my appreciation for the shade of the cave on a hot July day.

With conical, linear, compound, and effigy mounds stretching 200 feet along the bluff, Sentinel Ridge Trail is favored by many history buffs. The park once contained more than 130 mounds. Surviving mounds can also be seen at other places in the park, for example, near the ball field.

Stand at a Wyalusing overlook, and all of the state's past seems to swirl in the clouds above and waters below. For a moment, one face and then another stands out from the hazy mix before blurring in the general rush of souls — here a glimpse of Yellow Thunder, there a sharp glance from Zona Gale. All the people who ever lived along the Wisconsin and were shaped by her waters seem to gather here. And their legacy shapes us still.

The Wisconsin meets the Mississippi at Wyalusing

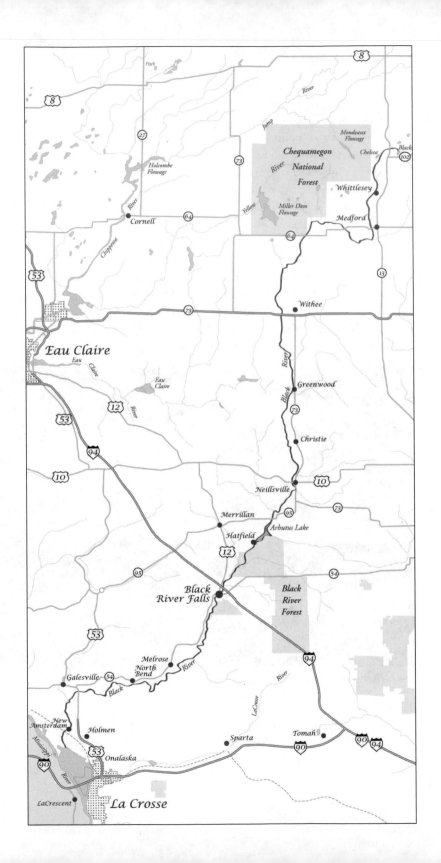

CHAPTER 15

Black

Relatively inaccessible, the source of the Black River is at Black Lake, west of Rib Lake. Less than a half mile north, the **Ice Age National Scenic Trail** winds across northern Taylor County east of State Highway 13. Who knows? Maybe one day a side path will take hikers to Black Lake, where they can see the creation of the small quick stream that in less than 200 miles evolves first into a rock-strewn river and then turns into a slower, sandier, wider waterway. A combination of geology and human development determines the river's recreational potential.

For the first 18 miles, the Black is a designated trout stream. Below Medford, anglers catch muskie, northern pike, walleye, bass, and panfish.

Medford City Park footbridge

In Clark and northern Jackson counties, the Black has cut through sandstone to flow through a 2,800-million-year-old layer of gneiss (metamorphosed granite). Experienced canoeists and kayakers increasingly run this section upstream of State Highway 29, which features gravel bars, riffles, and islands, and many paddlers have discovered the fun that can be had below Hatfield. The Wisconsin Department of Natural Resources maintains several landings on the lower river, which has a lower gradient than the upper river, yet enough surprises to keep you alert for whatever lies ahead.

Heading downstream from the source of the Black, the first city of significance is Medford. If you approach from the west on State Highway 64, be on the lookout for the two river crossings and the fishing access at County Road E. Since 1890, **Medford City Park** has served as the city's primary outdoor recreation area. With more than 100 acres along the river, a swimming pool, RV campsites, tennis and basketball courts, playground, skateboard area, softball fields, a gazebo, and four shelters — not to mention a sledding hill and skating rink in winter — the park serves a wide range of outdoor enthusiasts. A 19-acre millpond near a dam at the south end of the park offers a fishing pier. Medford's Riverwalk connects the park's two sections via a footbridge and follows the west bank through town.

Hatfield Dam

West of Withee, **Black River County Park** offers an easy break right on Highway 29. Fishers try for smallmouth and largemouth bass, bluegill, and panfish here, and the shelter and picnic tables make this a pleasant lunchtime stop.

The primary Black River access in Neillsville is on U.S. Highway 10 near the southwest edge of the city, within **Listeman Arboretum**. Established by Kurt Listeman in 1966, the 50-acre arboretum contains rock outcrops, wildlife, and diverse plants including many spring wildflowers. A nature trail leads through the woods, over a footbridge, and along the river.

Neillsville's historic downtown grew along O'Neill Creek, which empties into the Black north of Listeman Arboretum. More than 20 buildings are listed on national and state historic registers, and many house antiques, other specialty shops, and restaurants.

Every river town has its own unique highlights, and **Gile Memorial Park** on State Highway 27 southwest of Neillsville fills the bill in Merrillan. Located on Stockwell (Halls) Creek, which enters the Black between Hatfield and Black River Falls, the park holds a dam built atop a waterfall and an old mill building. Facilities include a campground, picnic areas, shelters, gazebo, playground, and playing fields.

Not far north of Black River Falls, the **Hatfield Dam** created the 840-acre **Lake Arbutus** in 1907. Three heavily used county parks line Arbutus Lake and offer camping, swimming, boating, picnicking, and other recreation. **East and West Arbutus parks** flank the dam in Jackson County, and **Russell Memorial Park** is a few miles north in Clark County. The latter honors Mark Russell, a DNR warden who died on Pike Lake. He and a fellow warden had checked the licenses of anglers fishing from a boat. When the wardens restarted their own boat, it lurched, throwing both men overboard. Russell's colleague survived, but Russell, originally from Clark County, died in the accident.

All three parks welcome powerboaters, jet skiers, anglers, and other fans of water recreation. Together, the parks contain 461 campsites, six boat landings, and three swimming beaches. All have showers, flush toilets, water, picnic areas, shelters, and playgrounds. Russell Memorial has a laundromat.

The big river attraction in Black River Falls, is the successful development of the **Foundation Trail,** a 4-mile circuit around the city with roughly half its length along the river and Town Creek. The Chamber of Commerce/Visitor Center on U.S. Highway 12 and State Highway 27 on the north side of town anchors the trail and offers parking and gardens to admire, along with regional information.

Another easy Foundation Trail access point is **Al Young Park,** located downriver at South First Street and Grant Street. A levee stands between the park and the river, and the paved Foundation Trail runs along the top of the levee, offering an attractive track for runners, dog walkers, and strollers. Occasional side trails lead to fishing spots on the riverbank, and the **Bruce Cormican Memorial Canoe Landing** is a short walk downstream from the park.

The landing bristled with life when we explored it in midsummer. The river surface fairly bounced with long-legged water striders. Two pileated woodpeckers called to each other above our heads: one from a nearby tree and the other on the wing over the river, returning to the nest with something dangling from its beak.

I walked to the bank, where a fisherman rummaged in his tackle box. "A fish just snapped my line," he said, grinning.

"Could you see what it was?" I asked.

"No idea," he said. "But it was big."

I wished him luck and climbed up to the Foundation Trail. I tried to count the number of Wisconsin cities that had built trails along their riverfronts in the past decade and finally had to give up. Probably the next generation will think them commonplace, even take them for granted, but I still smile when I discover a new one.

Watching the river flow

Bend at North Bend

Southeast of the city, a visit to **Bell Mound** offers a wide-angle view of the Black River valley. Mists swirled about the top of the mound the day Mike, Rumpus (our black Lab), and I hiked to an observation platform from the 1-90/94 wayside southeast of Black River Falls. We stood surrounded by a haze that seemed to take on the dark green tinge of the forests spread below us like a safety net. If, instead, we had stood here on a clear day in winter when the trees stood leafless and stark against the snow, I wondered whether we might see **Wazee Lake.**

Wazee Lake, now a premier deep diving spot, was an open pit mine created by the Jackson County Iron Mine. Now shut down, the company built a processing plant that in the 1970s shipped 2,800 tons of taconite pellets daily to blast furnaces in Indiana.

The trail stopped short of the top of the mound. We had passed a side path heading toward the crest, but the main trail we followed ended at the observation deck looking west over the fogged-in Black River Valley. Still, the view was worth the hike even on a hazy day, and the paved, handicapped-accessible trail eased the climb.

The healthy trees here showed few signs of the forest fire that raged over thousands of acres, closing a section of the Interstate in 1977. More than a century earlier, this valley had contained the largest and the most pine trees per township in the state. Before logging ended in 1905, more than 50 sawmills operated in Jackson County. Enough lumber was sawed to build a plank road circling the globe.

We drove south of Black River Falls on Highway 54, and soon turned east onto a section of Old State Highway 54 that swings close to the river. We pulled into the parking area for a campsite and canoe landing. Following a broad, mowed trail, we came to a fork and explored both paths. The right fork led to the campsite and a basaltic ledge on the riverbank, where a blackened circle documented an old campfire. Recent users had kindly left a stack of wood for the next visitor. The left fork ran over a small stream, turned, and ended at the mouth of a tiny creek. A lone cardinal flower stood like a focal point in this canvas of river, creek, and woods.

About 20 miles downriver, the town of North Bend offered a different, but equally arresting, canvas. As we drove over the Mill Creek bridge, I wondered if anyone had counted the number of Mill Creeks in the state. While I pondered, Mike turned the car around and re-crossed the bridge, pulling over and stopping so that we could get out for a closer look. On the downstream (south) side, the creek dropped over two short rock ledges that stretched from bank to bank. On the upstream side of Highway 54, a curtain of water rushed over the wall of an old dam.

North Bend, located on a short segment of the Black that actually flows north, shines like a yet-to-be polished gem of a historic town. We spotted what appeared to be a former railroad depot and a hotel.

The town features two worthy stopping places on the river: The Landing provides food, beverages, and a deck overlooking the Black. Riverview Inn Supper Club and Canoe Outfitters combines canoe rentals with a great choice of dining options when you return tired and hungry from a day's paddling. We even watched a neighbor's spaniel welcome each group of canoeists.

Inside, ample dining areas with windows stretching up to the ceiling afford a view of the river and the paddlers still floating down it. Phone: (608) 488-5191. River Bend Golf Course on County Road VV also fronts the river outside of town, and its restaurant offers Sunday brunch, noon lunches, and Friday fish dinners.

South of Galesville, the **Van Loon State Wildlife Area** stretches along the Black River near U.S. Highway 53/State Highway 93. The 3,981-acre parcel offers hiking, fishing, and canoeing opportunities. To get there, turn west off the highway near Holmen and drive north on County Highway XX toward New Amsterdam. Watch for the DNR trail sign on the west side of Highway XX. This trail is **McGilvray Seven Bridges Road**, which provides hiking access to the wildlife area and a series of bridges erected from 1905 to 1908 by the La Crosse Bridge and Steel Company. Designed by Charles Horton, these bowstring arch truss bridges used special clips instead of rivets.

As the Black River approaches the Mississippi below the wildlife area, it widens into a slough-laced delta and enters Lake Onalaska, formed by the **Mississippi's Lock and Dam No. 7** north of La Crosse. Below the lake, the Black runs into the Father of Waters at the city's **Riverside Park.** Watching over the confluence is a giant, painted stature of Hiawatha, the work of La Crosse artist Anthony Zimmerhackl and his sons. Not far from Hiawatha's feet, the *La Crosse Queen* docks. This replica of a nineteenth-century paddle-wheel provides sightseeing, dinner, and charter cruises on the Mississippi. Phone: (608) 784-8523. Website: www.lacrossequeen.com/.

Even in the city, the natural world gets the last word. From Riverside Park, Mike watched an eagle fly from the river, soar overhead, and head downtown. This land, after all, belonged to the eagles before it belonged to us.

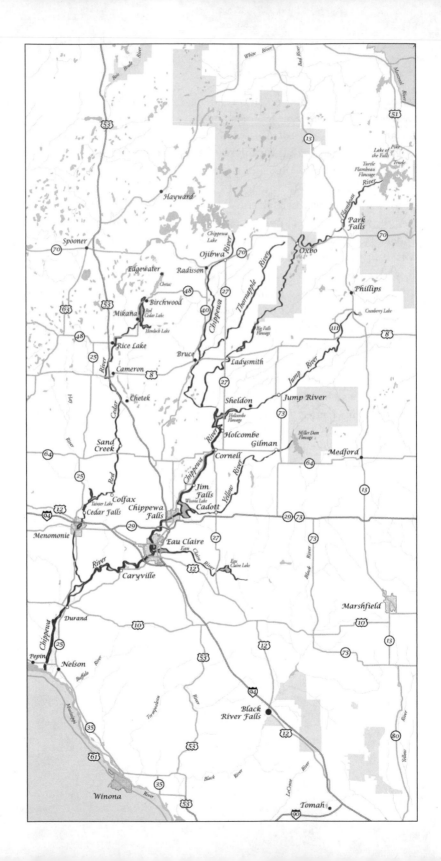

CHAPTER 16

Chippewa

~~~

The Chippewa is a river to reckon with. Together with its tributaries, this river drains about one third of Wisconsin. Wide, with a strong current below the confluence of its two forks, the river and its tributaries once carried millions of white pine logs to mills in Chippewa Falls and Eau Claire from as far north as 50 miles south of Lake Superior. Today it carries canoeists looking for a manageable challenge, anglers in search of the big one, and binocular-bearing watchers thrilled with the wildlife they're bound to see.

Its major tributary, the Flambeau, drains an area extending as far north as Upper Michigan between the Montreal and Brule river watersheds. The Flambeau is itself formed by the confluence of the Bear and Manitowish rivers southwest of Mercer. The incipient North Fork of the Flambeau runs west only a few miles before entering the **Turtle-Flambeau Flowage,** where you're more likely to see a deer, eagle, or other wild creature than another human.

Above its confluence with the Bear, the Manitowish flows primarily through the Northern Highland American Legion State Forest, and also offers supreme wildlife watching opportunities. Taking its name from an Ojibwe word meaning "spirit," the Manitowish runs smoothly and quietly; paddlers have time to look around and to let the wild sounds seep into their souls.

The Bear runs west to its confluence from Flambeau Lake in the heart of the Lac du Flambeau Reservation northwest of Minocqua. Named from the French, the "Lake of the Torches" referred to the Ojibwe practice of spearing fish by torchlight.

Less than 5 miles west of the reservation, the North Fork of the Flambeau enters the **Turtle-Flambeau Scenic Waters Area,** a 36,000-acre public treasure containing 114 miles of mainland shoreline and about two hundred islands. When the state purchased these remote lands in 1990, Governor Tommy G. Thompson called the acquisition "the crown jewel of Wisconsin."

Lac du Flambeau is also a town, with attractions to suit varied interests:

- **The George W. Brown, Jr., Ojibwe Museum and Cultural Center** on Peace Pipe Road showcases tribal history, artifacts, and culture through a video and modern exhibits. For fish-story disbelievers, there's hard evidence of the world's largest sturgeon: The 195-pound, seven-foot, one-inch monster is mounted here. Phone: (715) 588-3333. Website: www.ojibwe.com.

- The **Bear River Powwow**, held annually in July, entrances dancers, tribal members, and guests with music and traditional arts. Phone: (888) 588-9052. Website: www.lacduflambeau.com.

- **Waswagoning** (an Ojibwe term meaning "the place where they spear fish by torchlight") recreates a 20-acre Indian village on the shores of Moving Cloud Lake. Learn how these woodland Indians lived comfortably in traditional lodges, traveled in birch bark canoes, hunted and fished in season (fee). Waswagoning is located east of Lac du Flambeau off State Highway 47 on County Road H. Phone: (715)588-2615. Website: www.waswagoning.com.

- The **Lake of the Torches Resort Casino** offers big-city-style excitement and shows. Phone: (800) 258-6724. Website: www.lakeofthetorches.com.

- The **William J. Poupart, Sr., Fish Hatchery and Trout Pond,** located off Highway 47 on Pokegama Lake, features hatchery tours and the opportunity for the whole family to fish in a trout pond without a fishing license. Fish are bagged while you wait. Phone: (715) 588-9603.

- Also on Highway 47 north of Lac du Flambeau, a Wisconsin Historical Society marker on the west side of the highway notes that Lac du Flambeau has been a permanent Ojibwe settlement since 1745, when Chief Sharpened Stone led his band here. In 1792 the Northwest Fur Trading Company established the Lac du Flambeau Department for Wisconsin River area trade at the same site.

The flowage dates to 1926, when the Chippewa and Flambeau Improvement Company built the **Turtle Dam** on the Flambeau near its confluence with the Turtle River in order to control flooding and enhance flow downstream for hydroelectric plants. The dam flooded 16 natural lakes and created the islands from the tops of forested hills.

The islands provide some of the best of the 60 campsites developed by the Wisconsin Department of Natural Resources, each equipped with a fire ring and open-air pit toilet. There is no charge to use these waterway campsites. All are accessible only by water from six landings. The largest, Springstead Landing, provides parking for 75 vehicles. It, along with Fisherman's, Sportsman's, and Trude Lake landings, offers concrete launch ramps; Murray's and Sturgeon landings provide gravel landings more suitable to canoes than powerboats. Need a map? Contact the Wisconsin Department of Natural Resources, Mercer Ranger Station, 5291 North Statehouse Circle, Mercer, WI 54547. Phone: (715) 476-7847. The ranger station can also provide hunting and fishing information (muskies weighing over 50 pounds have been caught here) and a list of the more than 150 species of birds found in the flowage. There's also a self-guided auto tour booklet.

Although there are no ATV trails on flowage lands, both ATVs and snowmobiles are allowed on the ice in winter. Currents below the ice, however, make some areas hazardous; be sure you know where you're heading before getting out on the ice. Several Iron County snowmobile trails cross the flowage. You can get snowmobiling, ATV, and mountain biking maps from www.ironcountywi.com, or from the Mercer visitor information center. Phone: (877) 551-2204. Website: www.mercerwi.com. To receive snowmobiling maps for other counties, find contact information on the Department of Natural Resources website: www.dnr.state.wi.us./org/caer/cfa/lr/snowmobile/trails.html.

If you canoe in and camp, remember to hang your food in a bag from a tree limb. That's right; black bears wander the flowage, along with deer, bobcat, timber wolves, and even an occasional moose. When Mike, Rumpus, and I arrived at the west side of Turtle Dam, we found evidence of the wolves. We drove north on State Highway 13 to Butternut and then turned east on County Road F/FF to Turtle-Flambeau Dam Road. In the sand and muck below the dam, we observed several sets of wolf tracks leading into the water — long-nailed tracks, 4.5 inches or so in length — that dwarfed Rumpus' prints.

We continued north on County Road FF to reach **Lake of the Falls County Park,** where the Turtle River feeds into the flowage. The falls (modest in a dry August) can be seen from a road atop the dam, which is open to foot traffic. We explored a spit of land protruding into the flowage, where we found a ravaged turtle-nesting area and a staircase to the beach. The park also features a boat launch, shelter, observation deck, and campground, with several large, wooded sites directly fronting the water. This Iron County park has a $3 daily use fee.

A historic sign marks the end of the **Flambeau Trail,** the Indian water and land route from La Pointe on Madeline Island to the mouth of the Montreal and, inland, to the Flambeau. Voyageurs later used this trail to bring furs to market. Another marker commemorates the Roddis Line, a railroad route that once carried lumber out of the North Woods.

You can circle round the east edge of the flowage by continuing east on County Road FF to U.S. Highway 51. Turn southeast on Highway 51 and drive to State Highway 47/182. Turn south on Highway 47/182 and follow Highway 182 into Park Falls. Along the way, note the tamarack swamps, Little Bear River, and other streams. Price County has developed a dozen short auto/motorcycle tours around the county, including several that explore the area around the Flambeau, and one journeying to several historic stone bridges. Contact Price County Tourism. Phone: (800) 269-4505. Website: www.pricecountywi.net.

Dams and parks dominate the banks of the North Fork of the Flambeau in Park Falls. The **Upper Dam,** near the Highway 182 Bridge, is operated by Flambeau Hydro, LLC, a subsidiary of North American Hydro Holdings, LLC, of Neshkoro, generating power for the Fraser Paper Corporation's Flambeau Mill. Originally built in the 1890s to create a holding pond for logging operations and supply mechanical power to a paper mill, the plant was not converted to supply hydroelectric power until the early 1950s.

On the east bank, **Edward Hines Memorial Park** is open from early spring to winter for camping and picnicking. A recreational trail bridge crosses the river below the dam, affording good views of both the river and the paper mill. You can follow city streets and trails west to reach the **Park Falls-Tuscobia Trailhead County Park;** the **Tuscobia State Trail** leads to the Chippewa River and, eventually, to Rice Lake. Also below the Upper Dam, **Riverside Park** provides parking and fishing access to the river.

The **Lower Dam,** approximately 1.5 miles downriver, lies near the south edge of Park Falls. Built in 1906 to provide mechanical power to the paper mill's ground wood operations, this dam was converted to hydroelectric power production in the 1920s. Flambeau Hydro provides a public boat launch and picnic area above the dam on the west bank.

In addition to the Turtle, Upper, and Lower dams, two other dams control the waters of the upper North Fork. **Pixley Dam,** about 5 miles downstream from Lower Dam on Highway 70, also was created to power the paper mill's ground wood operations, and converted to hydroelectric power in the 1920s. **Crowley Dam,** approximately 6 miles downriver from Pixley Dam, dates to 1928. Limited access canoe landings at both of these dams feature wooden, screened, Adirondack-style camping shelters plus picnic tables, grills, and toilets. Both dam sites also offer public parking and fishing access. In addition, **Pixley Wayside** provides a picnic table, toilet, and fire ring.

A mile or so below Crowley Dam, the North Fork enters the **Flambeau River State Forest,** which provides 75 miles of canoeing and contains the confluence of the North and South forks. Experienced paddlers usually head for the South Fork, which offers more whitewater excitement, while anglers or others in search of a more relaxing ride head for the generally gentler currents of the North Fork. Yet there are still several challenging rapids along the North Fork, and some paddlers opt to portage them, particularly Waningan Rapids and Flambeau Falls, not far above the confluence with the South Fork.

If you drive into the forest from the east on Highway 70, you may notice a parking area east of Oxbo at Snuss Boulevard that provides access to the Flambeau River and Flambeau Hills trails. The day Mike, Rumpus, and I arrived here, rain pounded the path, but we stopped long enough for me to read the trail logbook. Several complaints about ticks seemed par for any North Woods course, but one mention of hikers catching sight of "itsy bitsy bears" caused me to straighten up and check the surrounding underbrush. If they had seen little bears, might there have been a mother bear nearby?

Oxbo, named for the course of the river here, features both the Oxbo Resort and a public landing, Dix Docks. The Flambeau River Trail bridges the river above a series of riffles. Paddling is a popular sport in this state forest, so if you plan a multiday trip on a summer weekend, consider ending your paddling days by midafternoon to be sure of getting a campsite in one of the 14 canoe camping areas along the river.

The South Fork begins at Round Lake in northeast Price County, running over the **Round Lake Logging Dam,** a restored 1878 timber dam now on the National Register of Historic Places. You can see it by driving 22 miles east of Fifield on Highway 70 to Forest Road 144 (Shady Knoll Road). Turn north on Forest Road 144 and follow it 2 miles to Forest Road 535. Turn east on Forest Road 535 and follow it to the parking area near the dam. An accessible, half-mile trail crosses the historic dam and offers signage describing spring log drives.

About four miles west of the logging dam, the **Smith Rapids Covered Bridge** is a recreation of Wisconsin's only Town Lattice bridge. Named for its inventor, Ithiel Town, the bridge uses his patented, diamond-shaped truss pattern. The bridge is adjacent to Smith Rapids Campground in the Chequamegon National Forest, two miles north of State Highway 70 on Forest Road 148.

Below the confluence of the North and South forks, the Flambeau flows through alternate sections of quiet and wild water, including Cedar, Beaver Dam, and Little Cedar rapids. Soon it emerges from the Flambeau River State Forest to run another 30-some miles through four more dams above its confluence with the Chippewa — Big Falls, Dairyland, Ladysmith, and Thornapple.

Josie Creek County Park northeast of Ladysmith offers opportunities to play for outdoor enthusiasts of multiple persuasions. The Rusk County park features a shooting range and 32-target, mile-long archery trail, as well as 26 campsites (several with electricity), a beach, and a boat launch on **Dairyland Flowage** (Lake Flambeau).

Another park worth a stop, **Memorial Park** in Ladysmith, at the U.S. Highway 8 Bridge, displays the loving care of the Wildlife Restoration Association Foundation. It created a walking path here in cooperation with the DNR. The park also features a swimming beach, boat launch, fishing pier and deck, World War I memorial, picnic areas, restrooms, basketball court, and horseshoe pits. One shelter surrounds a tree that grows up through its center. Camping is permitted with prior permission. Unfortunately for Rumpus, dogs are not allowed anywhere in this park.

From south of Ladysmith to the Thornapple Dam, paddlers enjoy the last wild section of the river before encountering increased development along the west bank. County Road E provides river access at two landings and river views all along this stretch.

The Flambeau joins the Chippewa soon after the larger river turns east toward Holcombe Flowage and State Highway 27. Located at the confluence, Flater's Flambeau Point Resort hosts visitors in year-round cottages and at campsites. It offers recreation for every season: swimming beach, canoe landing and trips, guided fishing trips, groomed snowmobile trails, cross-country ski trails, horseback riding, lunches, and a lounge with a stone fireplace. Phone: (715) 595-4771.

In its journey to Flater's, the larger Chippewa River follows a more westerly route. At the confluence of its East and West forks, the **Winter Dam** has held back the river's waters since 1923, forming the 17,000-acre **Chippewa Flowage.** Mike, Rumpus, and I approached the dam from Highway 70 west of Park Falls, following Highway 70 through Draper and Loretto to County Road W. From County Road W, we turned west onto East Fork Road (called Winter Dam Road on some maps). You can also access the dam from the west, driving from County Road G and County Road GG to Dam Road, and then following Dam Road north to a parking area. Owned by Xcel Energy, the dam is open to the public. You can walk across the top of the dam to a pier or to fishing spots on both banks of the river.

Above the dam, we spotted a distant loon diving and fluttering its wings on the flowage. Mike and Rumpus kept an eye trained on it while I returned

The Common Loon

While loons lumber awkwardly on land, they are proficient fishers and divers. They have been caught in fishing nets up to 200 feet below the surface, according to *The Audubon Society Field Guide to North American Birds.*

Have you ever wondered why you usually see a loon on a larger lake and seldom on small ponds? The heavy birds need a long runway to build up speed in order to take off into flight, according to *Wisconsin Bird Watching,* by Bill Thompson.

Loons have a variety of calls, but, of course, are most known for their mournful night cries. Like northern lights or the howl of a wolf, you never quite forget the nighttime call of a lone loon on a Wisconsin lake. Mercer, the Loon Capital of Wisconsin, is located to the north, not far from the headwaters of the Flambeau, the Chippewa's main tributary. If you would like your photo taken with the 2,000-pound Claire d' Loon statue, head to Mercer.

to the Forester for binoculars. It still swam on the flowage when I returned, though it had paddled away from us.

The flowage serves as a sanctuary for swans, ducks, geese, great blue herons, and other birds. Visitors also come to view other wildlife and the rugged rock formations. You can find both boat rentals and lodging at the Lac Courtes Oreilles Ojibwe-owned Herman's Landing Resort.

In addition to Herman's Landing Resort on the Chipewa Flowage, the tribe operates the 88.9 WOJB radio station, the LCO Casino Bingo Lodge and Convention Center, and the Grindstone Creek Casino. It offers tours of the radio station, its cranberry marshes, the Saint Francis Solanus Mission, and a cultural center. An annual highlight is the Honor the Earth Powwow held south of the LCO casino in July. For more information, contact the Lac Courtes Oreilles Visitor Center. Phone: (715) 634-8934. Website: www. lcotourism.com.

From Winter Dam, we drove east on East Fork/Winter Dam Road to County Road W, turning south and following it to County Road G. We then turned west on County Road G, crossed the Chippewa, and continued south along the river to County Road G's intersection with Highway 27 and Highway 70.

This intersection provides a number of ways to take a break. On the corner formed by Highway 70 and County Road G, the Ojibwa Club offers dining and cocktails on the river. On the river's west bank, the Ojibwa Community Park contains a boat landing, picnic area, shelter, and grills. A short 1.5 miles east on Highway 70, the 366-acre **Ojibwa Park** resembles a mini historic state park complete with a stone shelter that has the appearance of a Great-Depression era, Civilian Conservation Corps (CCC) building.

Ojibwa Park was established in 1932, a gift to the state from Mr. and Mrs. Robert W. Baird, Ojibwa Sales Company, and Northern States Power Company. Transferred to the Township of Ojibwa in 1990, the park retains the look of its state roadside park origins. The stone shelter, which can be reserved, features one chimney serving both interior and exterior fireplaces. A stone council ring surrounding a stone fire pit and a large rectangular grill provide outdoor cooking potential for groups. A footbridge leads across a stream that runs into a small pond. Twelve of the park's 15 campsites offer electric hook-ups. Though the campground is open from May through deer hunting season in late November, the park is closed to hunting. A playground, basketball hoop, toilets, and an ATV ramp complete the facilities on the south side of Highway 70. Across the highway, another section of the park borders the Chippewa and contains a canoe landing in addition to another picnic area.

The **Tuscobia State Trail** runs through the south end of Ojibwa Park on an old railroad bed. The trail, which runs from Tuscobia (north of Rice

Fishing at Brunet State Park

Lake) to Park Falls, intersects the Flambeau River State Forest Trail, leading south, and the Dead Horse Run trail, which heads north into the Chequamegon National Forest.

West of Ojibwa, Highway 70 runs north of the Chippewa until Radisson, where the highway continues west to edge the Couderay River. East of Radisson and above the mouth of the Couderay, **Arpin Dam** links several islands, sustains **Radisson Flowage,** and sends some of the Chippewa's waters down a canal to a powerhouse. Despite the dam, Belille Falls, a half-mile stretch of major rapids between the dam and powerhouse, often contains enough water to challenge expert paddlers. The rest of us can put in below the powerhouse.

Charles Belille, originally from Quebec, was the first white settler in Sawyer County. In 1840 he operated Hotel Belille near Litke Drive, approximately three-quarters of a mile south of the mouth of the Couderay.

Downstream, the Chippewa flows with a strong current and occasional rapids and riffles, running alternately past varied woodlands, occasional islands, and an increasing number of houses. Northwest of Bruce, the Thornapple River, another significant tributary, enters from the east. While a number of convenient landings offer sites from which to launch or end short canoe trips on this stretch of the Chippewa, few riverside campsites are available. In fact, between Ojibwa Park and Holcombe Flowage, there are no public campgrounds on the river.

You can also drive along the Chippewa from Radisson to Bruce, following State Highway 40 to find periodic county and town roads that lead to the river. Highway 40 once formed part of the **Chippewa Trail,** an Indian path that led from the confluence of the river's upper forks to the Chippewa Falls area. South of Bruce, look for River Road on the east; it offers several views of the Chippewa. As you approach the mouth of the Flambeau, Chippewa Avenue flanks the river's east bank.

County Road D borders the Chippewa's west bank for several miles above and below the Flambeau's mouth. Near the confluence, County Road D intersects with County Road E, which crosses the Chippewa and flanks the Flambeau north to Thornapple Dam. To the south, County Road E forms Wisconsin Rustic Road 6, traversing the Chippewa County Forest and a section of the Ice Age National Scientific Reserve.

East of the confluence, County Road D edges **Lake Holcombe Flowage** and runs to State Highway 27. The flowage dates to the completion of the most recent dam built at Holcombe in 1952. The dam holds back the Chippewa and the lower Jump rivers to create the 4,000-acre lake with 120 miles of shoreline. Anglers routinely haul in walleye, northern, large and smallmouth bass, perch, crappies, and bluegill.

The Jump River provides entertainment to paddlers, with sections of whitewater and quiet water flowing through a varied terrain of woodlands with both high sand and gravel banks. East of Holcombe Flowage, the villages of Jump River and Shelton offer pleasant parks and landings on the river. **Big Falls County Park** features the added attraction of a long series of rapids, drops, and a boulder-strewn riverbed. It also offers picnic facilities, hiking, and tent camping. Big Falls is located off County Road N in southwest Price County.

From Lake Holcombe, drive south on Highway 27 to the town of Holcombe to learn more about the history of the area and the Holcombe Indian, preserved in a building adjacent to the town hall. The brainstorm of Luke Lyons, manager of the old Little Falls Dam, the carved Indian figure stood for many years as a figurehead on the dam. Lyons procured a white pine log 24 inches in diameter, and Eugene Juvette hauled it to the dam, taxing the strength of four oxen, according to Bertha Kitchell Whyte, author of *Wisconsin Heritage.* Lyons hired a French-Canadian cabinetmaker named Bedore to carve the nearly eight-foot-tall Indian, and placed it atop the dam.

Saluting the past at the Cornell rendezvous

The stacker at Cornell

Frederick Weyerhaeuser, Lyons' boss and president of the Chippewa Lumber and Boom Company that built the dam, did not share Lyons' enthusiasm for the statue. In fact, he reportedly docked his employee's pay for the cost of the good log.

But the Indian remained on the dam until a flood washed it downstream. The statue was found in the eddy below the Brunet Falls Dam (today Cornell Dam). One arm had been broken off below the elbow and lost. A new manager of the boom company, James Zardine, carved a new arm and replaced the

"King of the Chippewa River." For many years, the statue stood in a cage on the riverbank near Holcombe except when it was loaned out, for example, in 1947, to Eau Claire and Hayward for their centennial celebrations.

When the current concrete dam replaced the old structure, the figure-head was moved for a time to a showroom inside the new dam. During the U.S. Bicentennial, funds were raised to move the statue to the current, glassed-in site next to the **Holcombe Town Hall.**

The town hall began its existence in 1906 as a warehouse for machinery, hay, and grain, but was remodeled a few years later to serve as a livery stable. Remodeled again, it reopened in 1918 at the end of World War I as a hall featuring roller skating and dancing. As the United States prepared to enter World War II, the Works Progress Administration (WPA) completed another remodel, adding the exterior stonework.

Holcombe — the town and the flowage — now bases a large share of its economy on tourism. Resorts, private campgrounds, restaurants, shops, and other businesses ring the lake area.

Chippewa County's **Pine Point Park** boasts the natural advantage of a wooded peninsula protruding deeply into Holcombe Flowage. Most of the 48 pine-wooded campsites were full when we visited in late summer. Since the park features a swimming beach and playground in addition to boating and fishing, it can satisfy everyone's pursuits.

A few miles downriver, **Brunet Island State Park** is equally popular. The campground was full when we arrived on a warm August weekend, so we had to be satisfied with a day visit. The park occupies a large island in Cornell Flowage where the Fisher River empties into the Chippewa. Its North Campground lacks electrical service but offers 36 campsites on the banks of the Chippewa; the South Campground contains 24 shady sites with electricity.

We explored several of the park's roads and trails, which include a nature trail, wooded paths crisscrossing the island, and the Nordic skiing and hiking trail on the mainland. Bicycles are allowed (except on the nature trail), and a 1-mile link leads to Cornell and the beginning of the Old Abe State Trail, which parallels the Chippewa south to Wissota State Park. We watched folks having a good time at the Brunet State Park beach, fishing from shore, and in kayaks plying the river bays. Mike watched as paddlers in two kayaks discovered a beaver swimming in a Chippewa bay a few boat lengths ahead of them. The beaver quickly disappeared, but not before captivating both Mike and the paddlers.

Jean Brunet (1791–1877) surely deserves to have this beautiful park named in his honor. He arrived in America in 1818, settling in Saint Louis and then moving up the Mississippi River to help build Fort Crawford near Prairie du Chien. Hired by partners Hercules Dousman, Lyman Warren, William Aitkin, and General H. H. Sibley, Brunet oversaw the building of the first dam and sawmill in Chippewa Falls in 1838–1840. He then piloted the mill's first lumber raft down the Chippewa and Mississippi to Prairie du Chien. Brunet served as the area's first judge and legislator before moving upriver to what is now Cornell around 1843. He built a home, inn, and trading post, as well as a wooden dam, at the spot then called Brunet Falls.

On State Highway 64 west of the river and Cornell, a marker points to the location of Brunet's home, where foundation stones might still be found near the river. On the high bank above his home, a burial ground was used first by Indians and later by pioneers. This sign also explains the present name of the town, in honor of Ezra Cornell, who purchased 100,000 acres here. Eventually, the sale of these pine lands netted millions for the endowment fund of Cornell University in upstate New York.

Like a hoist frame paying homage to an old mine shaft, the Cornell pulp wood stacker towers above the Chippewa's bank in **Mill Yard Park.** The 175-foot monument to the region's logging era is the only remaining stacker in the nation. Built in 1911–1912 by the Joors Manufacturing Company of England, it stacked logs in piles according to the type of wood, since different species were used to produce different types of paper. The logs were then placed in waterways and floated to a nearby mill. Made obsolete by more modern machinery, the stacker operated until 1971. A pump house, office, and other buildings at the stacker site burned in 1989, but the stacker was undamaged. Today it remains as a symbol of an industry that, if it no longer dominates, still retains a powerful presence in Wisconsin. Near the base of the stacker, the Cornell Visitor Center provides in-depth information on the stacker and the industry, and next door, the Native American Museum illuminates Indian history in the area.

South of Cornell, State Highway 178 follows the mirrorlike river to Chippewa Falls, reflecting pines and billowy clouds the morning we drove alongside it. Three miles out of town, the Edgewater Motel and, next to it, Foster's Riverview Inn, face the Chippewa from across the highway and are open year-round. Contact the Edgewater by phone, (715) 239-6295, or e-mail, eedgewater@centurytel.net.

A bit farther south, the 1908 **Cobban Bridge** provides one-lane access across the Chippewa on County Road TT. A nearby Wisconsin Historical Society marker dates its construction as 1908 by the Modern Steel Structural Company of Waukesha. The two-span Pennsylvania overhead truss style bridge is the oldest of this type in the state. It originally bridged the Chippewa upstream from the mouth of the Yellow River, but was dismantled during construction of Wissota Dam in 1916. Thanks the efforts of Oscar Anderson, a Cobban store owner, the bridge was hauled here by horses and sled during the winters of 1916 and 1917, and placed on land owned by S. C. F. Cobban. When reconstructed in 1918–1919, the bridge replaced a ferry. Nicknamed "Little Wagon Bridge," it still has a wooden plank deck and posts a 10-ton limit.

Historical markers, as much as the river views, captured our attention on this drive. North of Jim Falls, we stopped to read another wayside marker, this one honoring Old Abe, the Civil War eagle. In 1861 the Lac du Flambeau Band of Lake Superior Ojibwe were on their early spring maple sugaring expedition when Chief Sky (Ahgamahwegezhig), the son of Chief Thunder-of-Bees, shot an eagle and took its two eaglets from a nest high in a pine tree near the headwaters of the Flambeau River. One of the eaglets died, and as the Indians traveled downriver, Chief Sky traded the other to Dan McCann, a farmer on the Chippewa River. This wayside, once part of the McCann farm, today features a picnic area and wooded Wildflower Walking Trail.

McCann, who had a physical disability, enjoyed playing the fiddle, and the eagle enjoyed listening to his music, according to Richard Zeitlin, who wrote a biography of the state's most famous bird, *Old Abe the War Eagle.* When the Civil War broke out and militias were formed across the state, McCann offered the eagle as a mascot to a Chippewa Falls unit, who rejected the idea. Undaunted, McCann traveled to Eau Claire and sold the eagle to the Eau Claire Badgers, who were soon renamed the Eagles. And the eagle was named Old Abe, in recognition of the nation's new president and the unit's leader, John E. Perkins, who resembled President Abraham Lincoln.

Old Abe remains Jim Falls' favorite son. In 1999 the state rededicated his 10.5-foot statue near the County Road S bridge and Jim Falls Dam, along with the 20-mile state trail that bears his name. The southern trailhead is located nearby on County Road S. Across the river, the names of Eagleton (village) and Eagle Point (township) seem to also commemorate the famous mascot, though the township was named well before the Civil War, according to the Wisconsin Historical Society website: www.wisconsinhistory.org.

The Jim Falls hydroelectric plant is the largest hydroelectric plant in Wisconsin, with a generating capacity of 57 megawatts. Since 2003, river flows have increased in the main riverbed between the dam and the hydro plant from April 1 through May 31 to enhance sturgeon spawning. Increased flows on the second and fourth Saturdays in July and the second Saturday and third Sunday in August have enabled whitewater paddling, although boaters can also paddle during the increased spring flows.

Paddlers usually put in near an old highway bridge below the dam. As I stood on this bridge looking out over the rocky bed of the Chippewa, an eagle flew low overhead not far from Old Abe's early home. I held my breath until he receded to a speck and then disappeared.

Also nearby, the Anson Town Hall parking lot provides access to the **Old Abe State Trail** from County Road S, which extends 19.5 miles from Cornell and Brunet Island State Park to Wissota State Park. A parallel, unpaved equestrian path runs alongside the paved Old Abe State Trail. Future plans include extending the trail to connect with the Chippewa River Trail in Eau Claire and the Red Cedar Trail in Menomonie, creating a 70-mile trail system.

Wissota Dam portage sign

Wissota State Park provides an eco-logical field trip of restoration lessons, involving pine plantations, fish habitat, and shoreline preservation strategies. From the mid 1950s to the early 1970s, 12 landowners planted pine plantations on more than 200 acres of glacial sand, left when the ice sheets melted more than 10,000 years ago. The landowners took advantage of the old federal Soil Bank Program to plant the pines where crops grew poorly. Since then the trees have been periodically thinned and will likely still be standing tall and healthy many years from now. The lake shoreline will no doubt be more beautiful then, too, groomed with mowed grassy areas, replenished through seed harvesting and plantings, and protected from motorboat traffic.

Then, as now, visitors will likely still be swimming at the beach, hiking the 17 miles of trails, including the Beaver Meadow Nature Trail, and fishing from the handicapped-accessible pier or from a canoe. The park will still welcome visitors in winter for skiing, snowshoeing, and hiking. Will snowmobiles remain as popular in 2038? Today, a 4.75-mile snowmobile trail in the park connects with 150 miles of trails throughout Chippewa County.

Our first night camping here, we awakened in the wee hours to the wail of — what? What was that yipping and barking that sounded different from the calls of the coyotes echoing along the lower Wisconsin River valley at home?

In the morning I asked a park ranger whether we might have heard wolves. "We've definitely got coyotes in the park," he replied. "But two weeks ago, a guy said he had a wolf in his campsite and I didn't know whether to believe him."

I could only stare in response. What would we do if a large wolf wandered into our campsite? What would Rumpus do? I shook my head; the scenario seemed so unlikely.

The same morning we discovered that a much smaller creature had sought shelter with us from the rain and dripping trees. Beneath our canopy, a "walking stick" insect clung to one of the horizontal struts. The three-inch brown twig stood out against the white underside of the fabric. We left him, or her, there. The insect was welcome to share our shelter for the next few days and nights.

Across Lake Wissota, the Chippewa Rod and Gun Club provides a boat launch (fee) on the northeast edge of Chippewa Falls. We drove there by following State Highway 178 south and then turning east on County Road I (Wissota Green Boulevard). We followed County Road I to Beach Drive, which led to the club, where we found arrowhead growing in the cove and spotted a great blue heron wading offshore. Arrowhead tubers (also known as duck potatoes or swamp potatoes) can be harvested, dried, and cooked like potatoes. As the name suggests, waterfowl and other wildlife also enjoy these buried shoots.

Beyond the rod and gun club, the brief Beach Drive leads to the **Wissota Dam,** which holds back the Chippewa and submerges the mouth of the Yellow River to form the 6,300-acre lake. We stopped in the parking area and checked out the canoe portage trail and paths providing fishing access. The road dead-ends at the dam, so we retraced our path to County Road I. Near this intersection, another small parking area provides access to the **Chippewa County Riverview Reserve trail,** which links the Old Abe Trail to the north with the Chippewa Falls City Bike Trail to the south.

The city trail crosses the Chippewa at the State Highway 124 bridge, wends its way along the river, and follows Duncan Creek past the Jacob Leinenkugel Brewing Company. The brewery dates to 1867, when the Leinenkugel family first tapped the local waters to create its beers. The brewery's Leine Lodge offers a tour center along with a museum and gift shop.

The annual Oktoberfest kicks off with the Golden Keg Procession and a ceremonial keg-tapping at three biergartens. Phone: (888) 534-6437. Website: www.leine.com.

Nineteenth-century pioneers attributed water from Chippewa Springs to restoring their health; former Wisconsin Lieutenant Governor Thaddeus Pound bought a farm at the springs in 1887 and organized Chippewa Springs to provide pure water to the public in 1894. Now owned by Premium Waters, Inc., of Minneapolis, Minnesota, Chippewa Spring Water is distributed in 18 states. In fact, Chippewa Falls still celebrates Pure Water Days and Heritage Fun Fest, held in August each year.

Earlier in the summer, Loopy's Saloon and Grill, which also rents tubes, canoes, and kayaks, sponsors FrenchTown's Annual Tube Float and Regalia (FATFAR) on the third Sunday in June. Loopy's is located on Business Highway 29, a mile west of town. Phone: (715) 723-5667. Website: www.723loop.com.

North of Leine Lodge, a "waterfall" created by the old **Glen Loch Dam** flows into Irvine Park. Consolidated Milling, Elevator, and Power Company built the dam in 1875 and produced power at the site until 1924. When the company donated the small lake created by the dam to the park in 1908, a new name, Glen Loch, was selected by ballot.

Downtown, the **Bridge Street Commercial Historic District** contains 48 buildings in the Wisconsin and National registers of historic places. You can find maps of a walking tour in this area and three other historic routes through the oldest sections of the city. The historic businesses and homes date to the Civil War and include several mansions associated with early lumbermen and other river valley leaders.

Completed in 1928, the **Chippewa Falls Dam** at the Highway 124 bridge replaced the Chippewa Lumber and Boom Company's Big Mill, once the world's largest, which closed in 1911. This dam was the first constructed by Northern States Power Company, a predecessor to Xcel Energy. Downstream of the dam on Business Highway 29, you can find a gauging station on the river at a wayside with picnic tables and water.

We drove east to Cadott, located, according to a Lion's Club sign, "halfway between the Equator and the North Pole" at the intersection of State Highway 27 and State Highway 29.

Travelers have stopped on the Yellow River here since 1787, when Michel Cadotte built a trading post on this Chippewa tributary. Cadotte, a Madeline Island fur trader, fathered two sons here, Michel Jr. and Jean Baptiste, who is said to be buried on the riverbank. Both sons married daughters of prominent Ojibwe Indians and became successful merchants, interpreters, and mediators.

Shoreline also dominates the following Eau Claire parks:

- **Owen Park,** less than a mile downstream on the west bank of the Chippewa, offers access to the state trail and contains a band shell, gazebo, and tennis courts.
- North of the downtown area, **Riverview Park** includes a boat dock along with pavilions, a playground, picnic area, grills, restrooms, and volleyball court. To get there, take Highway 53 north to State Highway 124 (North Crossing). Turn west on Highway 124 and drive to Riverview Drive. Turn north on Riverview and follow it to the park.
- **Saint Simon Park** also provides a boat dock on Dells Pond, in addition to a nine-hole disc golf course, baseball diamonds, volleyball, picnic area, grills, playground, pavilions, and restrooms. From downtown, drive north on Highway 53 to Birch Street. Turn west on Birch Street, then right on Eddy Street. Follow Eddy Street to Sheridan Road. Take Sheridan Road northwest to Snelling Street. Turn right on Snelling Street and follow it to the park.
- **Rod and Gun Park** offers pavilions, restrooms, playground equipment, springs, and ponds on the southwest shore of Half Moon Lake, an oxbow-shaped lake that once presumably was part of the river channel. From the intersection of U.S. Highway 12 and Highway 53, follow Highway 12 (Clairemont Avenue) west to Park Ridge Drive. Turn right on Park Ridge Drive and drive about a mile; turn right on Rod and Gun Club Road.
- **Carson Park** fills the land captured within Half Moon Lake and, in addition to a boat landing, pavilions, picnic areas, and trails, contains the stadium where in 1952 Hank Aaron played minor league baseball with the Eau Claire Bears, a Milwaukee Braves farm team. The Chippewa Valley Museum preserves and interprets the region's history, offers stunning educational exhibits, and has a working 1900-era ice cream parlor. There's also the Sunnyview School Museum and the Paul Bunyan Logging Camp. From the intersection of Highway 12 and Highway 53, follow Highway 12 (Clairemont Avenue) west to Menomonie Street. Turn right on Menomonie Street, and then left on Carson Park Drive. Website: www.cvmuseum.com.

With parks on both banks of the Chippewa, Eau Claire offers sparkling river views at both dawn and dusk.

On the north end of town, **Riverview Park** contains signage recogniz-ing the Cadotte family and their trading post as a Wisconsin Registered Landmark. Robert Marriner, who built a dam at Cadotte Falls in 1865, later honored the family by naming the growing village Cadott. Encased in glass, a pine statue carved by Jerry Holter of Clam Lake depicts a fur trader and stands like a beacon in the park.

Riverside Park draws both locals and visitors with picnic areas, shelters, grills, restrooms, playground, and beach, along with basketball, tennis, and volleyball courts. Benches overlook the river and a portage trail around the dam leads through the park. The Country School Museum and Cadott Area Historical Museum are also located here.

Additional signs interpret the geology of the area, with content provid-ed by Dr. Paul Myers, a former geology professor at the University of Wisconsin–Eau Claire. Glacial deposits, largely sand and gravel, compose the top layers along the Yellow River. Beneath them lie Cambrian sandstone strata that can be seen in knobs and ledges southwest of Cadott. Dark gray amphibolites (metamorphic rocks) and slightly younger granites underlie the Cambrian layers.

Poring over the *Wisconsin Atlas & Gazetteer* (2004), Mike noticed the **Old Badger Mills** at Lake Hallie north of Eau Claire, so we asked about it at the Chippewa Falls visitor center. After a quick computer check, a visitor center staffer reported that the mill was indeed listed as a significant site in the town.

Following the imprecise gazetteer, which offers few details about city and town layouts, we followed U.S. Highway 53 to Lake Hallie and began our wild goose — I mean, mill — chase. We drove through town along the Chippewa, skirting industries and a golf course, without finding the mill. We followed County Road OO, drove on 29th Avenue, which seemed to morph into 30th Avenue, and traveled on Lakeside Road, which somehow transformed from 28th Avenue into 109th Street.

Along the way we passed a sign for the **Yellowstone Trail,** the first coast-to-coast highway through the northern United States, which drew early twentieth-century tourists to Yellowstone National Park and other sites along a route that stretched from Plymouth Rock to Puget Sound. Today, re-created yellow-and-black signs mark many segments of the 90-year-old route. Website: www.yellowstonetrail.org.

Finally, we returned to Highway 53 and stopped at a convenience store. "I've lived here all my life," the clerk told me. "And I've never heard of Badger Mills." We checked the new Eau Claire map, posted on the wall, and she directed me back to 29th Avenue.

We again found 30th Avenue, and eventually a waterway leading from Lake Hallie to the Chippewa just north of the Hallie Golf Course. The site looked promising — it would have made sense to build a mill here — but there was no sign of one.

There was, however, a tavern. We pulled into the parking lot and I entered the bar to ask, leaving Mike and Rumpus in the car and the heat of a late August afternoon. I was in luck. It was Friday and the bar was filled with end-of-the-workweek customers. When I explained our quest to the bartender, she called over several older men. One guy tried to be helpful. "There used to be a sign for it near the bridge," he said.

Another old-timer looked down at me from his six-foot-plus height to ask, "You mean Dells Mill by Augusta?" I shook my head.

Next to him, a balding man in a checked shirt pointed first at me and then to the creek: "The mill's still there. You can find it with scuba gear." He kept a straight face, but I looked at him dubiously.

Then the tavern owner came over to see what the crowd was about. "Why do you want to know?" she demanded, when I explained my quest.

I held up the gazetteer, but prolonging the conversation didn't seem like a good idea. I hope I retreated with dignity.

Back in the car, I phoned the Lake Hallie village offices, which, it turned out, were closed on Friday afternoons.

In the way of a dog with a bone, we re-crossed the stream. Just to the north, a new housing development sprawled westward from the Chippewa. Could this development have replaced the Old Badger Mills?

The answer came a week later. In the course of reviewing our trip notes, I again called the Lake Hallie village offices.

"I don't know about a historic site," the staff member replied to my query, "but there's the Badger Mills development there now."

At least our quest had a conclusion, dead end though it was. Additional research revealed that the Old Badger Mills operation had dated to 1848. That mill had replaced a sawmill, which had been swept away by a flood soon after its construction several years earlier.

Sometimes called the city of bridges, Eau Claire might just as aptly be nicknamed the city of parks, for more than 1,100 acres of parkland punctuate the cityscape, popping up all along the banks of the Eau Claire and Chippewa rivers and filling the center of the elliptical Half Moon Lake.

Immediately northeast of the confluence of the Eau Claire and Chippewa rivers, **Phoenix Park** rose in 2006 from the ashes of past industries. In 1875 the Phoenix Manufacturing Company built a foundry and machine shop on the site, which was later purchased by another firm that continued to manufacture machinery. The Phoenix Steel Company acquired the facilities in 1951 and used the property to salvage metal, including lead batteries. When the site was abandoned 20 years later, it contained contamination from almost 100 years of manufacturing. With $1 million from Xcel Energy and $2.1 million in state and federal funding, a brownfield redevelopment effort cleaned up the site and created the park. Today the former industrial area features an amphitheater, labyrinth, farmers market pavilion, flower gardens, benches, picnic area, river overlooks, fishing wall, and a historical timeline.

The nine-acre park serves as the trailhead for the **Chippewa River State Trail** and contains a trail building with information and restrooms. This trail connects to the Old Abe State Trail to the northeast and runs south along the river to Durand. Along the way it meets the Red Cedar State Trail, which follows the Red Cedar River, a significant tributary of the Chippewa, north to Menomonie.

We ended our day with a campfire at Lake Wissota State Park, where the wood we'd gathered the day before was almost dry enough to induce a good blaze. At least the smoke kept the mosquitoes away.

When I shoved open the door to the restroom in the gray chilly morning, a woman inside screamed. I stepped back, waited a beat, and slowly pushed

Big Falls County Park on the Eau Claire River

open the door, sticking my head through the gap. A young woman had one hand on a stroller bearing a toddler. With her free hand, she gestured toward the inside of the door. I craned my neck to see a walking stick clinging to its surface about six feet above the floor. The young woman had been in the process of plucking the insect from the door at the moment I shoved it inward.

I sidled inside and held the door while she completed her mission. She lifted the walking stick from the door, carried it outside, and set it on a nearby bush before turning to roll the stroller down the campground road.

I went to examine the walking stick, which looked different from the one we had found on our canopy two days previously. This one had a tan body with green extensions and lower legs resembling long pine needles. Did walking sticks change to resemble their environment like chameleons?

Mike installed Rumpus in the back of the Forester and we returned to Eau Claire. From Highway 53, we turned east on County Road Q, and after about 10 miles turned right on County Road UN to reach **Big Falls County Park** on the Eau Claire River. A paved, accessible trail brought us to the edge of the beach, and we had to trudge through the sand to see the falls. The river flowed over several drops and formed distinct channels in its course around two islands. Granite outcrops provided good vantage points from the bank. The river level was low enough to permit two couples to reach the far island, cooler in tow, and lounge on the sun-warmed ledges.

Hamilton Falls

I traced the Eau Claire River on the gazetteer and noted **Hamilton Falls** on the North Fork in northeast Eau Claire County. Could we find it? We put our recent pursuit of the demolished Old Badger Mills out of mind and drove east of Eau Claire on State Highway 29 to County Road G west of Stanley. We turned south on County Road G and followed it through Chippewa County Road MM, continuing south to Eau Claire County Road MM. There we turned east and drove to Hamilton Falls Road, where we turned south. We found the falls 2.2 miles south of County Road MM and 1.6 miles south of the Town of Wilson Memorial Park — with only one wrong turn!

No signs point the way to the falls, but two pull-offs on the left (east) side of the sand and gravel road (four-wheel drive recommended) indicate where to stop at the top of a narrow gorge. We scouted several precipitous trails to the river at the bottom of the gorge, and I picked a path that seemed almost manageable. With my camera swinging from its neck cord, I descended with care, holding onto small trees and roots.

Hamilton Falls presents several low drops through the ravine. I succeeded in shooting several photos through the trees and brush without falling into the shallow river, and pulled myself back to the top of the ridge. Mike and Rumpus had found a somewhat less steep path to the river, less than a hundred yards beyond the second pull-out. But I think I had more fun.

We stopped briefly at **Lake Eau Claire County Park,** located on County Road SD just east of State Highway 27 and north of Augusta. Formed by a dam, Lake Eau Claire corrals 1,118 acres of the river and creates a popular fishing spot. Located at the dam, this park offers a handicapped-accessible fishing pier, picnic tables, grills, shelters, water, toilets, playground, volleyball court, and horseshoe pits. Anglers fished from broad rock ledges on both sides of the river below the dam.

We held our breath as we watched a boy walk across the lip of the dam, with several inches of river flowing fast over his bare feet. He made it and reached a group fishing on the other side, but where were his parents? Walking across a dam surely dares the fates.

A quarter mile downstream at the Highway 27 bridge, Riverside Junction rents canoes and kayaks for trips on the Eau Claire. Website: www.riversidejunction.com.

Since 1864, the main section of the **Dells Milling Company Museum** has stood on Bridge Creek off Highway 27 on County Road V, 3.4 miles north of Augusta. Supported by a sandstone ledge, the hand-carved timber and wooden peg construction dates to the rise of wheat farming in

Wisconsin. Gustave Clark represents the fourth generation of his family to own the site, and conducts tours from 10:00 a.m. to 5:00 p.m., May through October. Cost: adults, $7; children, $3.50. A separate building houses antiques for sale. Phone: (715) 286-2714. Website: www. dells mill.com.

I brushed spiders from the outside of our tent, trying not to harm them as we prepared to leave Lake Wissota State Park. The teardown brought an answer to one nagging question.

Two walking sticks were glued together in a mating ritual on the outer horizontal pole from which the tent was suspended. The larger insect was brown like a twig and the smaller one had legs resembling green pine needles. Aha! Different sexes.

Downstream from the mouth of the Red Cedar River, the Chippewa widens as it enters the state's driftless area. Below the dam at Durand in Pepin County, it continues through southwestern Wisconsin's unglaciated area toward its confluence with the Mississippi. County Road N follows the west bank closely as the river traverses through **Tiffany State Wildlife Area,** the largest continuous stand of bottomland hardwood forest surviving in Wisconsin. Its 12,740 acres also protect tracts of wetlands, savannahs, and native prairies. It contains 20 miles of hiking trails and the **Tiffany Bottoms State Natural Area,** which preserves a transition zone between the flood-

Mill wheel at the Dells, high and dry

Dells Mill "falls"

plain forest of silver maple, river birch, ash, and basswood, and the primarily oak forest to the north.

But the big attraction at Tiffany Bottoms is the birds. The area draws nearly every species found in Wisconsin, with signature species including whippoorwills, redheaded woodpeckers, and yellow-headed blackbirds. Seven parking lots provide access along State Highway 25 and State Highway 35; watch for the Department of Natural Resources signs. Occasionally, the Wisconsin Wetlands Association has organized train rides into Tiffany Bottoms, as one of many field trips offered. Phone: (608) 250-9971. Website: www.wisconsinwetlands.org.

Southwest of the Burlington and Northern Railroad tracks, the Upper Mississippi National Fish and Wildlife Refuge protects the confluence of the Chippewa and the Father of Waters. Finally, 183 miles from its source, the Chippewa pours into the big river, roughly 3 miles southwest of Pepin.

Compared to the Mississippi, the gradient of the Chippewa is steeper and its current faster, so it carries more sediment. When the sediment-loaded waters of the Chippewa reach the more sluggish waters of the Mississippi, some of the sediments settle out, forming a broad, sandy delta and partially damming the Mississippi's channel. The backed-up water widens the Mississippi to create Lake Pepin above the confluence. (Read more about Lake Pepin in the Mississippi chapter.)

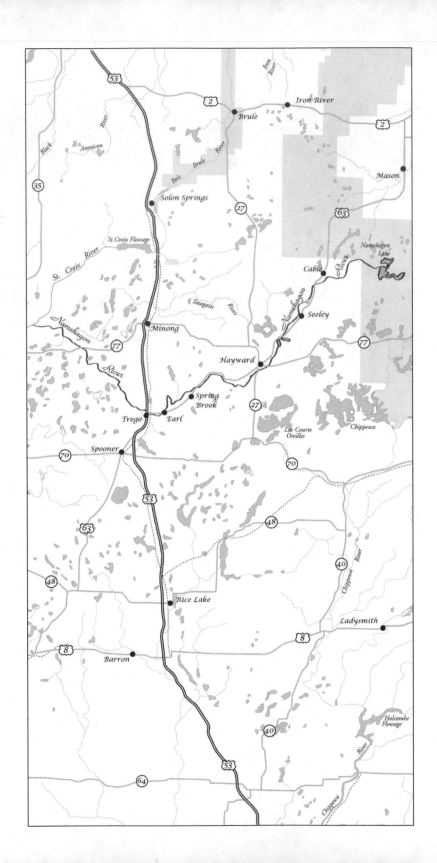

CHAPTER 17

Namekagon

M ost of the St. Croix River, including the entire 98-mile Namekagon, was among the first eight streams to be designated a National Scenic Riverway in 1968. (Wisconsin's only other National Scenic River is a segment of the Wolf.) Today the National Park Service, in cooperation with the Minnesota and Wisconsin departments of natural resources and Xcel Energy, preserves 252 miles of the Namekagon-St. Croix waterway for use by anglers, bird-watchers, campers, hikers, paddlers, picnickers, and, on the lower St. Croix, powerboaters and sail boaters.

Compared to finding the source of the St. Croix (Chapter 18), getting to the headwaters of the Namekagon River is a Sunday drive through the

The Namekagon Dam

countryside. Follow State Highway 63 northeast from Hayward, turning east on County Road M and proceeding to Dam Road (National Forest Road 211). Turn north on Dam Road and follow it to the bridge and the dam at the river's outlet from Namekagon Lake, a sprawling, multi-branched body that is the state's tenth largest lake.

Namekagon Dam Landing is as peaceful a spot as you will find above the hubbub of Hayward. Though it offers picnic tables, grills, pit toilets, and wild raspberries in season, this landing is often deserted and most paddlers begin their runs downstream. Shuttling canoes and kayaks between the many accessible landings off State 63 is more convenient, and downstream from Hayward, the water levels are good through fall.

Bejeweled with water lilies, Namekagon Lake lay serene beneath a summer sun on the day Mike and I visited. A concrete roller dam protects the upper river from erosion as lake water continually slides over the tiered barrier into the nascent Namekagon. Above the dam, a turtle watched us from a rock protruding above the surface, and a green frog hid in the sand on the riverbank. Below the dam, we watched a string of ducks dabble in the center of the river, here little more than a narrow brook.

Paddlers, especially those camping at one of the many canoe sites along the river, often report sightings of eagles, herons, osprey, otters, beavers, muskrats, and black bears. Though close to highways and civilization, the

Pickerelweed and Water Lilies at Namekagon Dam

Namekagon offers a wilderness experience to families, friends, scouts, and other groups seeking to canoe in the North Woods without driving to Canada.

Not counting Namekagon Dam, four dams interrupt a paddler's journey to the St. Croix. These, and their slow-moving flowages, can be portaged or avoided by putting in below the dams or taking out above them.

For a good night's sleep nearby, you can camp at the Chequamegon National Forest's Namekagon Campground on the lake's north shore. It features a swimming beach, fishing pier, and boat ramp, in addition to a picnic shelter and 34 sites that can accommodate RVs up to 45 feet in length. To get there from Cable, drive east on County Road M for 10.9 miles to County Road D. Turn north on County Road D and follow it 5.5 miles to Fire Road 209. Turn west and proceed 0.3 mile to the campground.

Downstream, Hayward provides dining and lodging alternatives. Bigger than life, the city on Hayward Lake also hosts the Lumberjack World Championships the last weekend of July in the Namekagon flowage. Though the last log drive here took place in 1909, more than 20 events keep traditional skills alive and provide a window into the lives of the lumbermen. Log rolling, tree climbing (picture 90-foot vertical poles), chopping, and sawing attract competitors from as far as Australia and New Zealand, not to mention thousands of spectators. My favorite is the boom run, in which competitors run across logs bobbing and floating end-to-end to the opposite dock and then whip around and race back.

When you drive into town, the first thing you're likely to notice is the big fish. Technically, it's a replica of a muskie and home of the **National Fresh Water Fishing Hall of Fame.** Almost 50 feet tall, the walk-through fish and its outbuildings contain a multitude of museum-quality exhibitions from Seminole Indian fishing arrows to antique reels, 500-plus outboard motors, rare lures, and, naturally, mounted fish — including a blue pike, white catfish, humpback chub, and the world-record humpback sucker. Beneath the big fish, an 88,000 gallon pond holds a variety of freshwater fish and turtles. The big fish is located at 10360 Hall of Fame Drive, open daily from 10:00 a.m. to 5:00 p.m. Phone: (715) 634-4440.

While it might stand out oddly in downtown Beloit or Oshkosh, the big muskie rises comfortably above Hayward. Sure, it's conspicuous, but it belongs in Hayward the way the Packers belong in Green Bay. Besides, the four-story fish is hardly more incongruous than the Danish windmill or Turk's Inn.

Windmill Square appears on your right as you head south on Highway 27. The windmill lies close to the highway, inviting you to turn into the collection of businesses. When I went, flags and flowers waved me into Lynne

Marie's Candies, and, once inside, the enticing aroma of fudge, hand-dipped chocolates, and toad and tadpole candies (turtles on a stick) "forced" me to buy a sampling to carry out to the car.

Lynne Marie reported that her father and uncle, Hogart and Carl Henricksen, built the windmill in 1979 and that the contractor traveled to Solvang, California, to find a squat, Danish-style windmill to use as a model. The Henricksens also built the square containing 10 retail shops for the tourist trade, but Lynne Marie's is the only one still operating — the others now converted to real estate offices, beauty salons, and other services. "The tourist season is too short," she explained, though her own shop is open year-round and ships gift-boxed candy anywhere. She also observed that condos and second homes have replaced many of the little cabins, changing the area's clientele.

Dating from a still earlier era, the Turk's Inn has witnessed even more dramatic changes in its customer base.

The white and red, pagoda-roofed inn sticks out of the North Woods along the Namekagon as unexpectedly as a Mayan temple. When we opened the red-framed door and crossed the threshold into the restaurant on Highway 63 north of Hayward, I stopped in my tracks. The challenge was to take in all the visual details. Framed photographs and yellowed clippings lined the walls, pleading to be perused. Pottery, old bric-a-brac, plants, and curios asked to be studied and appreciated. Surrounded by the quaint and strange, I felt like Harry Potter must have on his first day of school at Hogwart's.

Dazed by this new world, we followed a waitress past the Sultan Room into the Kismet Dining Room, with its red velvet walls and tall windows overlooking the Black Sea — oops, I meant the Namekagon. Our waitress could probably tell we were first-timers by my deer-in-the-headlights stare. Without being asked, she handed us menus and began explaining the restaurant's specialties. We anticipated the shish kebob but were surprised to learn that the steaks are aged five weeks and then cut to your order. Most of the steak, lamb, chicken, and seafood entrees are served with a different version of a bulgur pilaf, for instance, with added tomatoes, onions, or pine nuts.

By evening's end, we've learned that the Turk's Inn moved to this site in 1938. Our sources (the waitress, bartender, photos, and clippings) informed us that George and Mom Gogian started in business in 1934. Gogian, an Armenian immigrant from Istanbul, Turkey, reportedly had only 25 cents in his pocket when he arrived in Hayward. After they moved to the cutover banks of the Namekagon, Gogian planted 50,000 pine trees, which still shelter the property.

"Having a restaurant in a Scandinavian area, it was hard to get the local people to eat much besides steak and potatoes. So Dad decided we would become famous for our steaks," said daughter Marge Gogian. Now in her seventies, she has run the restaurant since before her father died in 1979.

In its heyday, both George the Turk and the Turk's Inn enjoyed an international reputation. President John Kennedy ate here; so did Bobby and Ted. And, once, when George Gogian was travelling in Egypt, he was asked by a stranger on a hotel elevator: "Aren't you George the Turk? Don't you have a restaurant in Hayward, Wisconsin?"

He still does. Now well past the regular age for retirement, Marge Gogian has kept his restaurant alive, a Turkish outpost in the land of supper clubs and fish fries.

On the way out, Mike bought a one-pound bag of bulgur. It comes packaged with a leaflet containing pilaf recipes and a condensed history of Turk's Inn. Both will carry me back to Hayward when time and weather hem me in at home in southern Wisconsin.

Below Hayward, Trego serves as a wilderness outpost, providing information and access to hiking trails and the river by canoe, kayak, and tube. The town also offers cabins and campsites where you can prop up your weary feet before a glittering fire or sink them into the sand at the water's edge. This Great South Bend of the Namekagon once served as home to a band of Ojibwe and as a rest point for missionaries, explorers, and fur traders traveling between the St. Croix and Chippewa Rivers, according to the historic marker on Highway 63 east of Trego. In 1767 Jonathan Carver, a mapmaker and former colonial officer in the French and Indian War, passed this way. A century later, lumbermen led ox teams on a tote road along the river, hauling logging supplies from Stillwater, Minnesota.

If you have questions about tote roads, the lumber boom, or the era of fur-trading, the **St. Croix National Scenic Riverway-Namekagon District Visitor Center** probably has the answers. Located east of Trego on Highway 63, it offers an educational movie, well-conceived exhibitions with good documentation, and knowledgeable volunteers with ready resolutions to local history mysteries. The voyageurs canoe replica caught my attention. Little did I know when I saw it that I'd soon be paddling one (see Lower Wisconsin Chapter 14). At the time, I was surprised only to learn that a voyageur's large lake canoe could carry 3.5 tons of cargo.

The landing at the visitor center is a good place to take out from upriver paddling trips, or you can continue under a few bridges to the popular landing at **Trego Town Park** on the right, upstream from the Highway 53

Turk's Inn

bridge. Most experienced Wisconsin paddlers float down the curvy, lower Namekagon sooner rather than later. Marked by wilderness, varied campsites, and frequent appearances of wildlife, this stretch provides many favorite paddling stories. Ask a paddling friend if she has ever done the Namekagon, and be ready for a fish story — I mean, a river tale — of epic proportions, in which the turtles are all snappers and the deer are as big as a moose. Or maybe it really was a moose.

Besides the boat landing, Trego Town Park offers 50 campsites, most with electricity; water and showers; a picnic shelter and fire rings. But you don't have to camp here to appreciate this natural commons. The park is often filled with locals enjoying a day at the water, the playground, and picnic areas.

If your muscles are stiff from too much paddling or too many nights sleeping in a tent, the Log Cabin Resort and Campground offers seven log cabins to choose from, each with a picnic table, fire pit, and grill. We found Loon Cabin comfortable and the store with sundry basics indispensable. The campground includes 30 sites plus a teepee on a raised platform that sleeps six. The resort also offers tube, canoe, and kayak rentals, plus a shuttle service, as does Jack's Canoe and Tube Rental on Canfield Drive across the road. If your Log Cabin stay is interrupted by rain, the kids can play video games and pool in the rec hall. Website: www.logcabin-resort.com.

What's more, you're close to several hiking trails. The **Trego Nature Trail** begins at a parking area off Highway 63, 1.4 miles east of the St. Croix Riverway Visitor Center. If you're quiet as you walk this 2.8-mile loop, you might glimpse a deer, fox, or bobcat. In winter, look for tracks and otter slides. At any time of year, beautiful river views are guaranteed, and there's a bench for river meditations.

Northwest of town, **Trego Lake Trail** follows a maze of three loops situated in a bend of the Namekagon flowage. Totaling 3.6 miles, the hiking/skiing trail provides several scenic overlooks, especially from the inner, steeper loop. The **Wild Rivers State Trail** crosses the Namekagon near Trego and the St. Croix at Gordon. The 96-

Fritz Landing

mile, multi-use trail runs from south of Superior to Rice Lake along the abandoned Soo Line. Access the trail in Trego from a path at the St. Croix Riverway Visitor Center.

Below the Trego Dam, the lower Namekagon runs northwest 31 miles to join the St. Croix. Along this wilderness route canoeists can choose from about 30 primitive campsites on the riverbank, though landings are more limited. Seven access points line the lower river from County Road K Landing just below the dam on the right bank to Namekagon Trail Bridge Landing on the left bank, north of State Highway 77.

The next developed landing is Riverside Landing, 3.5 miles downstream from the confluence on the St. Croix, at the State Highway 35 Bridge. Upstream from the bridge, facilities include campsites, water, and restrooms.

In the approach to the confluence, paddlers encounter a faster current with occasional riffles. As the wider and larger Namekagon funnels into the deeper St. Croix, the latter widens and its volume of water more than doubles. With the added waters from the Namekagon, the St. Croix becomes a truly powerful river, and below State Line Rapids it marks Wisconsin's border with Minnesota.

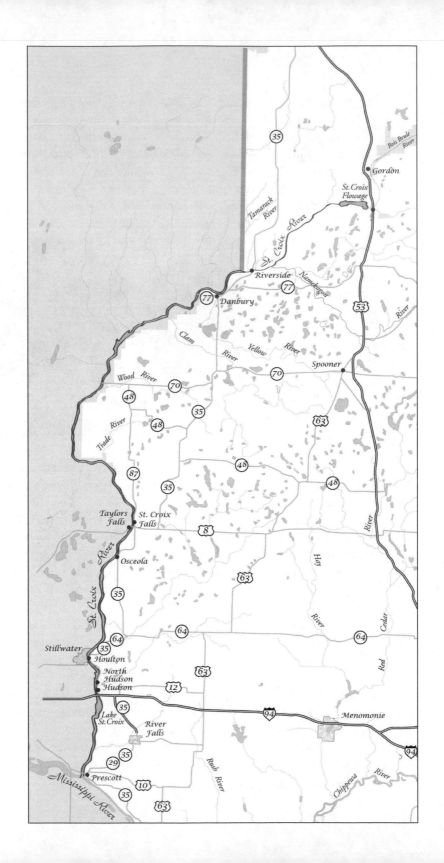

CHAPTER 18

St. Croix

Between its source above Upper St. Croix Lake at the end of the historic Bois Brule–St. Croix portage trail and the mouth of the Namekagon, the St. Croix River is generally a narrow stream with numerous riffles, except for the lake and St. Croix Flowage above Gordon Dam. A search for the source of the St. Croix River from the portage trail satisfies in many ways: the short hike through the woods, the bench inviting a reflective rest, and the historical signs along the way (see Bois Brule Chapter 2).

Riverboats at Interstate State Park

A pattern of trails filigrees the region of the upper river. Not far below the portage trail, on the western shore of Upper St. Croix Lake in Solon Springs, **Lucius Woods County Park** offers several short, scenic hikes. One of these follows the south bank of Park Creek, which enters the lake north of the picnic area. Another trail heads northwest from the picnic area, over a footbridge spanning the creek, and eventually hooks up with a segment of the North Country Trail.

Lucius Woods, by the way, is the only Wisconsin county park boasting an open-air amphitheater and stage that hosts each summer the Duluth-Superior Symphony Orchestra and a wide range of other musical perform-ances, from Cajun to Top 40. For a current schedule, visit the website: www.lwmusic.org. All performances are in the evening, and afterward, accommodations are close as close as one of the park's 24 campsites (13 with electricity). Or, try the St. Croix Inn, also right on the lakeshore in Solon Springs; phone: (715) 378-4444 or (877) 820-1362. If you pull into town earlier in the day, dig your swimsuit out and jump into the inn's pool or head for the beach at the park.

Douglas County's other gem on the St. Croix, **Gordon Dam Park,** marks the beginning of the long section of protected river included in the National Scenic and Wild Rivers System. The park, located 7 miles west of Gordon on County Road Y, is set up to welcome visitors interested in pur-suing a variety of outdoor activities. Paddlers can get an early start on upper St. Croix trips by staying here the night before at one of 33 campsites (12 with electricity). The 12-foot-high dam, topped by a plank walkway, creates a 28-foot-deep flowage, a notable fishing spot. The park also lures anglers with all the amenities — canoe landing, fish cleaning house, and 24-foot lighted, handicapped-accessible dock. You can generally hook muskie, northern pike, bass, walleye, or panfish. Occasionally, you might land a stur-geon. And if your luck holds, you might catch sight of one of the wild visi-tors to the flowage at the Watchable Wildlife area. Besides the common species of deer, coyote, and fox, visitors have spotted bear, beaver, and even an occasional moose.

Not far from the modern dam, the Ojibwe likely constructed the Namai Kowagon (Sturgeon Fish Dam) from rocks and sticks, judging from remnants found in the river. Upstream from this fishing dam on the east bank, Chief Kabemabe headed a village, its location now buried beneath the waters of St. Croix Flowage. The chief was one of the Ojibwe leaders who signed the Treaty of 1837 at Fort Snelling in what is today St. Paul, Minnesota, ceding a large section of northwestern Wisconsin to the United

States. His life is commemorated with a sign and overlook of the former village site, off the north side of County Road Y east of the park.

Downstream of Gordon Dam, the upper river continues as a narrow, shallow river, best canoed in spring when water levels are high. By the time it reaches the CCC Bridge Landing (on the east bank off County Road I), the St. Croix has grown deeper; and it swells even greater below its confluence with the Namekagon River.

Below the Namekagon on the Yellow River, another major tributary of the St. Croix, lies one of the state's most notable historic sites. Forts Folle Avoine (meaning "wild oats" and referring to "wild rice") were rediscovered in 1969 and studied by the Wisconsin State Historical Society in the late 1970s and early 1980s. Today **Forts Folle Avoine Historical Park** is open to the public Wednesday through Sunday, from late May to early September. Hours: Wednesday through Saturday 10:00 a.m. to 4:00 p.m.; Sunday, 11:00 a.m. to 4:00 p.m. Two-hour tours begin on the hour until 3:00 p.m. Fee.

Incidentally, at least two other Yellow Rivers flow in Wisconsin: one, a tributary of the Chippewa, enters it above Chippewa Falls; the other, a tributary of the Wisconsin, flows into Castle Rock Flowage. The St. Croix tributary enters that river at Danbury. The historic park is located on County U between Danbury and Webster.

Listed on the National Register of Historic Places, the 80-acre park is operated by the Burnett County Historical Society. The Forts Folle Avoine complex contains two reconstructed fur trading posts, a 5,000-square-foot log visitor center, a recreation of a Woodland Indian village, a canoe landing, an outdoor amphitheater, a research library, and Karlsborg School.

Mike and I arrived in time to catch up with a tour group that had departed a few minutes earlier from the visitor center. We found the group in the Indian village. William Makwa (Bear) Annis — his full Ojibwe name is Mashkiki Makwa bimosey Manidoo Mainggon (Medicine Bear Who Walks with the Spirit Wolf) — greeted us: "Boozhoo!" The Ojibwe term is derived from the French *bonjour*.

Annis, dressed in a buckskin shirt and leggings with his black hair pulled back, invited us to peer inside a wigwam, explaining that these shelters were bedrooms only. Elders and children slept in the back, farthest away from the door. Men generally slept on one side, women on the other, except that warriors slept nearest the door. Everyone slept with their feet toward a center fire: according to Annis, "If your feet are warm, the rest of you is warm."

Wigwam styles differed for winter and summer camps. In summer, the birch bark on the roof would be turned with the white side out to reflect sunlight. Sleeping mats of cedar boughs would leave needle juice on the skin as a natural insect repellant, and smoke from cedar torches would be wafted through new wigwams or newly roofed wigwams to fend off insects.

In winter, the birch bark of the roof was turned with the inner side out, to repel water. Beds were raised above the ground for warmth. A trench led from the fire to the wall to bring in fresh air, and smoke escaped through a vent at the center of the roof. When the walls were sealed by ice and snow, the wigwam looked like an igloo.

Annis showed us how a smoking rack was used to dry meat and berries, and how to prepare other foods. Before the Europeans arrived, Indians used birch bark cooking pots, which had to be watched closely so as not to burn.

When the Ojibwe migrated westward from eastern Canada to the Lake Superior Region before the seventeenth century, they followed a prophecy that they would move to an area where food was growing on water. When they saw the wild rice beds, they knew they had arrived at the predicted region.

How, I wondered, did Annis learn all these traditions, these tricks to survival? He replied that his grandmother and other elders passed the information to him. Even so, Annis was quick to point out that the knowledge he's acquired over many years doesn't begin to compare with what the

William Annis and wigwam

Ojibwe knew when they lived in the woodlands and prairies 300 years ago. "What I know is like that," he said, pointing to the tip of his little finger. "They were ingenious and developed diverse methods."

Annis, who has faced his share of solitude in the wilds of the Rocky Mountains, has come to believe in the tribal system. "You can't live for extended periods on your own. You don't have enough time to make leather, and do everything else that needs to be done. You have to have a group to survive."

Annis finally waved us toward a clearing in the trees. "Angelique is waiting for you."

Our French/Indian guide arose from a log where she had been sitting and led us toward the two fur posts set up to trade with the Ojibwe. The North West Company and the XY Company both established winter posts here on the bank of the Yellow River in the fall of 1802. The North West Company came first, building a trading post and a cabin surrounded by a stockade. Then the XY Company arrived, constructing a combination trading post and cabin. In the course of the winter, they moved into the stockade, fearing possible attack by the Dakota.

Both companies traded with the Ojibwe and had a successful winter. Come spring, they packed the furs into canoes and transported them to the Grand Portage on Lake Superior's north shore. From there, the furs were shipped to Montreal and then to Europe.

The North West and the XY companies used the posts for two more winters. The XY Company reconstructed their cabin, and the North West Company added a cabin within the stockade.

Following the winter of 1805, both companies left and never returned. Eventually the forts burned, all signs of their existence hidden for 165 years.

Angelique Peterson, clad in a sleeveless red cotton shift, led us first to the XY trading post, just above the riverbank and smaller than the Northwest Company fur post. She recruited a boy from our group and dressed him as a voyageur: red stocking cap; tight, bright belly sash to prevent hernias; and red cloth ties to support his knees. On portages, the voyageurs carried a 90-pound pack, topped with either another 90-pound pack or a barrel — and they crossed the portages at a trot!

She handed the boy a paddle with a red blade. The red blades and the red hats "gave the voyageurs an energizing color to look at, as they worked long days," Peterson explained. The voyageurs paddled 40–50 strokes a minute.

They made their own cedar paddles on a shaving horse during the winter at the trading post. Peterson demonstrated the technique: she straddled the wooden horse and, with the cedar limb held in a vise before her, drew a two-handled knife toward her. A turtle shell strapped around her waist armored her against cuts into her belly.

We filed after Peterson into the larger North West Company post, which had been stocked much as it might have been in 1804. She passed around samples of various furs so that we could feel the difference between a beaver pelt and the fur of a muskrat, skunk, or weasel. When the brown weasel turns white in winter, it becomes an ermine, she explained.

Peterson described how each of the furs was used and traded. Four fawn skins of wild rice (the skins sewn shut to form a bag) were worth a jew's-harp or two beaver skins. The under-fur of the beaver was felted into hats; six beaver skins were needed to construct one tall hat. The guard hairs were used as furniture stuffing, and the leather was used in gloves. Both men and women wore beaver hats, which were especially popular in Europe. The hats came in varied styles and colors. Not all were stovepipes. Peterson held up a short, brimmed, gray hat suitable for a lady.

We poked into the outfitted cabins, examined the large, outdoor scale used to weigh furs, and watched Peterson raise the North West Company flag above the stockade. Eventually, we left the group to explore the grounds and head back to the visitor center, where we viewed the historic exhibits and counted ourselves lucky to score a small bag of locally harvested wild rice. The clerk explained that an Ojibwe woman had brought it in, asking if the Forts might want it to resell. Later, when we cooked it, we understood the appeal: a fresh, light flavor in comparison to the darker, drier, over-parched commercial variety. Phone: (715) 866-8890. Website: www.theforts.org.

Downriver from Danbury, **Governor Knowles State Forest** protects the St. Croix National Scenic Riverway for 55 miles from State Highway 77 near Danbury south to County Road G above St. Croix Falls. It contains 32,500 acres; more than 19,000 of these are state-owned. Adjacent to the forest are two large state wildlife areas — **Crex Meadow** and **Fish Lake** — and more than 100,000 acres of county forests.

The best way to explore the area is to follow in the wake and tracks of the Indians and voyageurs. A number of roads provide access to a dozen canoe landings and two trails.

Mike and I drove south on State Highway 35, turning off onto County Road F past Danbury to skirt Crex Meadow State Wildlife Area. More than 100,000 visitors come here each year, to hunt and to observe bear, deer, and a variety of waterfowl. Highlights include two hiking trails, an auto tour, and two blinds where you can observe sharp-tailed grouse display each spring. Call after January 1 to reserve a blind. Phone: (715) 463-2896. Pick up the auto tour guide at the Crex Office located at the corner of County Road D and County Road F in Grantsburg.

We meandered south to State Highway 70, stopping at Sandrock Cliffs Landing. The name gives away the attraction of this spot, which features tan sandstone bluffs vertically streaked with white stripes where water has coursed down to the riverbank. On the sand, an earlier visitor had built a miniature stone dam, or maybe it was a rock garden. Canoeists who camp here must carry their gear up to the top of the bluff, where several grassy sites offer fire rings and riverine views.

To reach Raspberry Landing, which does not permit camping, we followed Highway 70 to River Road and River Landing Road, a gravel drive to the shore. Here, we met two Wisconsin State Forest workers, who were constructing a route connecting Governor Knowles' two existing trail segments. Currently the northern trail, about 22 miles long, ends 6 miles north of Highway 70, and the southern trail, 16 miles in length, begins 3 miles south of the highway near Raspberry Landing.

Mike pointed out a four-inch long, fierce-looking insect with what appeared to be pincers protruding from its head, resting on the gravel at our feet. The forest workers were curious about the bug, so I returned to the car for the latest issue of *Wisconsin Trails* magazine (July/August 2007) and the article, "Bug Season" that identified the creature as a male dobsonfly. The pincers, actually mandibles, are used to grasp the female during mating. This frightful creature spends most of its life as a hellgrammite and potential fish bait beneath the surface of the river.

After bidding farewell to the forest workers, we hiked a mile or so along the **Benson Brook Trail.** (Both the northern and southern routes are subdivided into shorter, named segments, and the Benson Brook Trail is the northernmost of the southern routes.) We hiked to a point where the ridge swings east away from the river and the trail descends toward the river before turning and retracing our steps.

Continuing south, our next destination was Sunrise Ferry Landing, located off State Highway 87 on Evergreen Avenue. This former ferry-crossing site offers primitive campsites a short hike from the water. Across the river, half a dozen horses and riders faced us, looking out at the St. Croix from Minnesota's Sunrise River Landing.

En route to Nevers Dam Landing south of Wolf Creek on River Road, a low-slung, tan, short-furred animal rushed across the road ahead of us. We

A ride along Sunrise Landing

quickly decided it was too big to be a weasel and too small to be a coyote. Could it have been a lynx? No, lynx are cats and this was a canine. Mike thinks it was a half-breed coyote-dog. Maybe.

Today a popular boat launch, Nevers Dam Landing marks the location of a dam built in 1890 to ease log jams at the Dalles 11 miles downriver. It was removed in 1955.

Mike and I continued south on River Road to St. Croix Falls. Not only a pleasant auto tour along the St. Croix, this road is also a good bike route, flat and close to the beginning of the interstate **Gandy Dancer Trail.**

Built on a former Soo corridor, the Gandy Dancer Trail travels 98 miles from St. Croix Falls to just south of Superior. Along the way, it crosses the St. Croix and Yellow rivers twice, and bridges the Straight, Wood, and Clam rivers once.

On the north edge of St. Croix Falls off Highway 87, Mike and I located another footpath. **Indianhead Trail,** a segment of the Ice Age Trail that begins at Lions Park, heads north through the woods, generally staying a stone's throw from the river. St. Croix Falls bills itself "The City of Trails," and several cross or follow streams for short distances.

The first quarter mile of Indianhead, I regretted not grabbing a can of mosquito repellant from the glove compartment, but soon we left the buzzing insects behind. We crossed half a dozen or more picturesque footbridges over creeks emptying into the St. Croix. A few of these bubbled merrily, but several had dried up by July.

Sandy Cove, a small clearing in the woods, appeared a half mile from the park. A houseboat was tied up here, and I could see why. The secluded cove was an ideal small campsite, with picnic table, fire ring, landing, small beach, and open-air commode in the woods. Officially, the trail currently stops another half mile farther on at Rock Creek, though a primitive path continues beyond this stream.

We turned and retraced our track to **Lions Park,** which features a picnic area, shelters, grills, and boat launch, as well as a "porch swing" on the riverbank and an accessible fishing pier.

Two historic markers, one in the park placed by the Wisconsin Department of Tourism and one on Highway 87 sponsored by the Wisconsin Historical Society, record the Battle of St. Croix Falls. In about 1770, the Ojibwe fought the Meskwaki (Fox) and their allies, the Dakota (Sioux), at the portage below the park. Following a furious battle in which warriors fell on the bluffs and plunged into the St. Croix at the Dalles, the Ojibwe defeated the Meskwaki and Dakota.

We learned more history as we approached the **St. Croix River National Scenic Riverway Headquarters and Visitor Center,** located at the corner of Hamilton and Massachusetts off Highway 87 in St. Croix Falls. Near the building, a small park with a State Historical Society marker commemorates the life of Gaylord Nelson (1916–2005). Recognized as the founder of Earth Day, he was born at Clear Lake, 28 miles from St. Croix

Falls, and canoed the Namekagon and St. Croix rivers as a boy. Nelson served two terms as Wisconsin governor and three terms in the U.S. Senate. He worked to protect the Appalachian Trail, implement a National Trail System, ban the pesticide DDT, create the Apostle Islands National Lakeshore, and pass the Wild and Scenic Rivers Act of 1968. Two years later, through his leadership, 20 million people (10 percent of the American public), participated in the first Earth Day on April 22, 1970.

The National Park Service seems to have taken Nelson's work to heart in constructing the headquarters and visitor center, which blend into the wooded riverbank. When we walked from the parking lot to the building, Mike spotted a pileated woodpecker flying overhead. Another pileated rose from a wooded area north of the visitor center to meet it. No doubt the pair had a nest in a hollow of the dead tree we could see from the edge of the tiny woodlot. Hours are 8:00 a.m. to 4:30 p.m., Monday through Friday in the off-season, and daily from Memorial Day through mid-October.

A pond out front resonated with bullfrogs. The "lawn" blazed with wildflowers; no mowers needed here! Native vegetation also sprouted from the rooftop rain gardens.

Inside, an aquarium with native fish and a display of mussels caught my eye, as well as windows overlooking the St. Croix River. Other exhibits document the Riverway's changing seasons and map its course through western Wisconsin. As often happens at National Park Service interpretative centers, I bought a book — this time, Sigurd Olson's *Reflections from the North Country.* The exhibition area had the feel of an extension of the outdoors, and we walked back outside to follow the path to the river. This small landing, complete with picnic table, is the last take-out point above the St. Croix Dam.

Mike and I strolled back up the bank toward the visitor center and then walked south along the river toward downtown St. Croix Falls. On this paved trail we passed a sculpture that reminded me of fossils, caves, and the infinity of geologic time. A few minutes later, we reached another historical marker, this one describing immense log jams on the St. Croix that could take weeks to clear. The 1886 jam, possibly the largest in U.S. history, involved an estimated 150 million board feet of timber. Talk about infinity! I couldn't begin to imagine the size of that pile of logs.

Soon we arrived at the city's **Overlook Deck,** an observation platform presenting outstanding views of the river and the dam. Decked out with hanging plants, the space provides benches, picnic tables, and a stage where later that evening we watched local musician Kaptain Karl sing for a good-

National Ice Age Scenic Trail

The National Ice Age Scenic Trail begins (or ends) at the Pothole Trail, looping south as far as Green, Rock, and Walworth Counties before wending northeast to its eastern terminus at Potawatomi State Park in Door County. It lies entirely within Wisconsin and passes through parts of 28 counties, tracing the edge of the last North American glacier.

Jointly administered by the National Park Service, the DNR, and the Ice Age Park and Trail Foundation, the path is yet unfinished. Some 600 miles of the 1,200-mile route are complete, in segments of 2 to 40 miles. Temporary connecting routes enable you to hike the entire length. Volunteers have built and still maintain much of the trail.

You can learn more at the **Ice Age Interpretive Center** within Interstate State Park. Videos and displays help visualize the era of glaciations, the period of the wooly mammoths, and early human history in the region. The center is open from 9:00 a.m. to 4:00 p.m. daily from Memorial Day through early fall. Websites: www.nps.gov/iatr/index.htm or www.iceagetrail.org.

sized crowd. In fact, the crowd overflowed the available benches, with many bringing their own lawn chairs.

The city park surrounding the deck features a bulletin board and more informational signs, and Mike and I read them all. We learned that the Thompson-Boughton Mill operated here from 1878 to 1914, that James Knox Polk served as U.S. president when Wisconsin was named the 30th state in 1848, and that President Polk was a Mason.

But the focal point of the park stands near the Overlook Deck. This bronze sculpture, "River Spirit," was placed here in July 2007. Created by artist Juliann Stage, with Katie Perszyk as model, the statue depicts a strong young woman rising from the water and gazing skyward. An eagle, wings partially spread, perches on her right shoulder. A grant from the city funded the project, and sales of River Spirit replicas will, in turn, support grants to other artists.

The deck also provides a view of the 60-foot high **St. Croix Falls Dam,** with its beautiful and unusual S-curved spillway. A high water volume flows through a deep gorge here, and the spillway was designed to increase the crest area of the dam. Built over the falls in 1907, the 25-megawatt dam primarily provides electricity to Minneapolis and St. Paul, Minnesota.

In 1988 the Minnesota Department of Natural Resources discovered a previously unknown population of the federally endangered winged maple-leaf mussel 1.5 miles below the dam. Once found in 13 states throughout the Mississippi basin, the world's only reproducing population of this mussel now lives only on a twelve-mile stretch of the river below the dam. Its presence is a bellwether of river quality and an indication that the St. Croix remains one of the cleanest rivers in the nation. The St. Croix contains 38 other species of native mussels and the tiny, invasive zebra mussels, which have been found as far north as Stillwater, Minnesota. Natural resource agencies in both Wisconsin and Minnesota are working to prevent the spread of the zebra mussel, which threatens to smother and out-compete the native species.

Mussels aren't the only animals to enjoy the habitat of the St. Croix, which also contains 497 species of aquatic invertebrates including insects and 68 fish species. You can see some fish species at the St. Croix River National Scenic Riverway headquarters and visitor center, and you can

Wisconsin's western neighbor offers several additional parks on the banks of the St. Croix:

- **St. Croix State Park** lies at the mouth of the Kettle, a Minnesota Wild and Scenic River. The St. Croix forms its 21-mile-long eastern boundary, and at least 10 other streams flow through this 34,000-acre park.

- **Wild River State Park** features 18 miles of St. Croix shoreline, including Sunrise River and Wild River landings. The park provides group camping, backpack camping, canoe camping, and walk-in camping, as well as a guest house and two camping cabins. The park is open year-round.

- Named for a Minnesota lumberman, **William O'Brien State Park** near Marine-on-St. Croix features trails with river overlooks and sandstone outcrops, campsites near the river, and canoe rentals during the summer.

- Situated on bluffs above the river, **Afton State Park** presents magnificent views and serious hiking challenges up and down ravines. Don't be concerned if, as you enter the park, you note smoke in the air; park workers routinely conduct burns to restore and maintain its prairies. The park almost encircles the Afton Alps Ski Area. Website: www.aftonalps.com.

- South of Afton State Park, **St. Croix Bluffs Regional Park** features ravines that cut deeply to the river bank and almost three-quarters of a mile of river frontage. Originally developed by the Control Data Corporation, the park was purchased by Washington County from a later owner, the Ceridian Foundation, in 1996. Along with camping, hiking, swimming, tennis courts, and picnic shelters, the park provides an amphitheater and conference cottage.

watch hundreds of trout at the DNR's **St. Croix Falls State Fish Hatchery** several blocks downstream of the dam. Open to visitors seven days a week (8:00 a.m. to 4:00 p.m. on weekdays and 8:00 a.m. to 3:00 p.m. on weekends), the hatchery features a number of long rectangular ponds filled with brown and brook trout of varied sizes.

The **Ladder Tank Trail** follows the river from the fish hatchery downstream to Wisconsin's **Interstate State Park,** entering the park above the North Campground.

South of the campground and State Highway 8, the Pothole Trail tells the story of the region's distinctive geology. More than 1.5 billion years ago, granite and greenstone mountains stood here. About 1.1 billion years ago, lava from volcanic eruptions in the Lake Superior area flowed into the park. Ancient seas advanced and retreated, covering the lava with layers of sandstone. Next, erosion cut river channels through the sandstone. Finally, beginning about one million years ago, four glaciers invaded Wisconsin from Canada. The last of these retreated about 10,000 years ago. As it melted, the glacier deposited rocks, gravel, and sand over the lava. Glacial Lake Duluth (located approximately where Lake Superior is today) overflowed, sending meltwater crashing southwest and forming the Dalles of the St. Croix. Pounding whirlpools blasted sand and stones against the bedrock, forming potholes as deep as 80 feet in Minnesota's Interstate State Park and up to 15 feet deep and 10 feet wide here on the Wisconsin side.

We walked the half-mile loop trail up stone steps and past potholes of many shapes and sizes. Soon we stood on a St. Croix overlook atop the Old Man of the Dalles formation. I dropped onto the convenient bench. Below, the St. Croix wound blue and bold between the dark basaltic bluffs. A white paddleboat added another sharp color contrast. To our right, a class of Minnesota rock climbers set ropes in preparation for a practice session on the cliffs.

Eleven other trails present about 9 miles of additional views of the river, its bluffs, and surrounding forests. The Summit Rock Trail climbs to the highest point in the park and offers a grand view of the Old Man of the Dalles. Most trails are a mile or less in length, cover uneven terrain, and contain stone steps. The longest, the 1.6-mile Skyline Trail, leads past rocky ravines and includes part of the National Ice Age Scenic Trail and the accessible Skyline Nature Trail, a three-quarter-mile loop near the Ice Age Center.

The park presents myriad opportunities to experience the outdoors. Ask at the interpretive center about naturalist programs. Up for a swim? Head for the beach and beach house at the Lake O' the Dalles, which also features a handicapped-accessible fishing pier. A boat and canoe landing is located on the St. Croix a short distance west of the lake. In winter, the park maintains about 12 miles of cross-country ski trails.

Downstream of the boat launch, I spotted a great blue heron standing on the shore of Folsom Island, which hugs the Minnesota side of the St. Croix. I crept through a narrow band of woods toward the riverbank in an attempt to photograph the big bird. Suddenly, I startled — and was equally startled by — a bald eagle that lifted off its perch directly above my head. For a moment, all I could do was stare in surprise, but within the space of a few wing beats, I raised my camera and clicked the shutter, resulting in one out-of-focus shot of the eagle swooping away from me toward Minnesota. Its flight, of course, alarmed the heron, which rose beneath the eagle's shadow and flew upriver.

South of Interstate State Park, County Road S (River Road) winds west off State Highway 35 parallel to, but not in sight of, the St. Croix. Also known as Rustic Road 101, this drive features rock outcrops and panoramas of oak, cedar, and pine forests. It also provides access to the **Ridge View Trail's** Osceola and Chisago trailheads. We parked at the former and walked a short way into the darkening woods. But the sun was setting and it was time to think about a quick dinner (we readily recommend the Village Pizzeria in Dresser), Kaptain Karl's music on the Overlook Deck in St. Croix Falls, and plans for the next day.

Across the river from St. Croix Falls, the city of Taylors Falls contains additional attractions, chiefly Wild Mountain and Taylors Falls Recreation, a company that truly has something for visitors of all ages and interests: boat cruises on the St. Croix, canoe and kayak rentals, a water park, RV park and campground, banquet rooms for weddings and other events, plus, in winter, skiing, snowboarding, and snow tubing. Website: www.wildmountain.com.

Nearby, Minnesota's **Interstate State Park** is one of that state's most popular destinations. A reciprocity agreement may contribute to its attraction. Your Wisconsin vehicle sticker admits you to the Minnesota park, and vice versa. In Minnesota's Interstate State Park, the potholes are larger — you can walk into one, the Bake Oven, formed by two converging whirlpools — and the views equal those on the Badger side of the river. From May 1 through mid-October, you can rent canoes from a private concession in the picnic area.

Just south of William O'Brien State Park, Marine-on-St. Croix is a small town (population: about 700) with a big presence. The oldest town in Minnesota, it began as Marine Mills when a sawmill was built here in 1839.

The Stillwater Lift Bridge

By 1840 the Marine Lumber Company was cutting one million board feet annually with a waterpowered "muley" or up-and-down saw. The mill was replaced with a larger one in 1852, and became Walker, Judd, and Veazie in 1866, which continued in business until the 1890s. A walking tour with signage of this area begins at the historical marker on Judd Street, which is parallel to and just east of State Highway 95.

Today, the Marine-on-St. Croix Historic District appears in the National Register of Historic Places and still exudes nineteenth-century charm. The town square boasts a town hall, library, general store, and ice cream shop. Also downtown, look for Christ Lutheran Church, built in 1872 and featuring Swedish stonework. Marine-on-St. Croix was an entrance point for many Swedish immigrants to Minnesota.

Minnesota Highway 95 (St. Croix Trail) borders the river's west bank. Nine miles south of Marine-on-St. Croix, look for the **St. Croix Boom Site Park,** a landing, and an overlook. From about 1865 to 1914, lumbermen halted, sorted, and assembled logs into rafts at this point. Here, the river widens into Lake St. Croix, formed by a natural dam of sand and gravel at the confluence of the St. Croix and Mississippi rivers below Stillwater. The park features a walkway along the bluff top, a footbridge, and a stairway down to a sand beach.

Twelve miles south of Marine-on-St. Croix, Highway 95 passes through Stillwater, another old town that's reinvented itself into a tourist destination for those seeking a historic getaway, good dining, antiques, and other shopping opportunities. Highlights include **Lowell Park,** with a bandstand and picnic area on the river just off Main Street. A marker commemorates the heroic action of teenagers, prison inmates, and other volunteers in building a mile-long dike in 1965 to prevent record floodwaters from inundating the business district.

Near the park, the 1931 **Stillwater Lift Bridge** still spans the St. Croix. Resting on reinforced concrete piers and abutments, the bridge superstructure displays concrete-slab approaches from both shores, fixed steel trusses, and a rare, counterweighted, tower-and-cable, vertical-lift span of the type developed by Waddell and Harrington. The 1,050-footbridge still carries vehicles but is wide enough for only two lanes; as a result, traffic backs up on summer weekends or whenever the bridge is raised for large boats. The Minnesota Department of Transportation plans eventually to build a four-lane bridge downriver and convert this bridge, which is on the National Register of Historic Places, to a bike path and pedestrian walkway.

On the north side of town, the *Minnesota Zephyr* dinner train provides three-and-a-half hour tours of the St. Croix valley, along with five-course meals and the Zephyr Cabaret performing songs from the 1940s and 1950s. Open year-round. Phone: (800) 992-6100 and press 1. Website: www. minnesotazephyr.com.

To find a train ride that crosses the St. Croix, return north on Highway 95 and turn east on State Highway 243 to cross back into Wisconsin at Osceola.

The beaver dam stretched across a slough near the Wisconsin side of the St. Croix, and I bruised the rules to poke my camera lens through the few inches the train window could be raised. I snapped multiple shots, hoping to successfully avoid the iron struts of the bridge, which flashed by every few seconds, blocking the view.

I'd picked this 1930s-era car, whose reversible seats once cushioned commuters between New Jersey and New York City on the Delaware-Lackawanna Railroad, because, lacking air-conditioning, it offered open windows with unshielded views. In fact, it offered glorious views of the St. Croix River and its adjoining bluffs and forests.

The **Osceola & St. Croix Valley Railway** operates two regularly scheduled trips on weekends from April through October. A 50-minute trip takes you northwest through the countryside to Dresser. The 90-minute ride that I enjoyed follows the river south, crossing near Marine on St. Croix and reversing direction inside Minnesota's William O'Brien State Park. A first-class ticket includes snacks and a beverage on an observation car. Special event trips — Mother's Day and Father's Day brunches, a dinner train, fall leaf-viewing, and naturalist tours at William O'Brien State Park — make the Railway a destination for people celebrating anniversaries, birthdays, reunions, and other major events.

When I went, one family group was celebrating the 40th wedding anniversary of grandma and grandpa, who had always wanted to ride on a train. Everyone took photos of everyone else peering out the windows, and the adults had as much fun pointing out highlights to their children as the kids had in the mournful long wail of the horn whenever we approached a crossroad, and the rhythmic rocking of the train. The kids also enjoyed walking from car to car, with frequent stops for snacks, sodas, and souvenirs in the car just ahead.

The highlight of the trip was going over the **Cedar Bend Swing Bridge** — twice! On the day I traveled, reflections of white clouds undulated with the current on the river below. The only people in sight picnicked on the sandy shore of a forested island. Hardwood forests lined the riverbanks as far as the eye could follow the St. Croix in either direction.

Near the Minnesota side, several tents appeared to pop out of the sand like mushrooms on the shore of a large island. A volleyball net had been strung above the shallows of the upstream end of the island, and a score of people waded nearby.

When we reached **William O'Brien State Park,** the diesel engine de-coupled, ran past my window along a short sidetrack, and re-coupled at the other end of the train in order to pull us back to the Osceola depot. Out the window, neon-orange butterfly weed and black-eyed Susan embellished the embankment. Beyond, we were surrounded by the woods and grasslands of the state park, though I could detect a human sign: a hint of last night's campfire smoke lingered in the air. The train restarted with a bump and a lurch, and I got ready for my second opportunity to photograph the river and that beaver dam.

The Osceola Historical Society completed its purchase of the 1916 brick and stone depot in 1993, and completed an amazingly detailed and accurate restoration in 1996. The wooden interior today is divided into two sections, each with its own ticket window, as it was divided into two stations, one for men and one for women, a century earlier. Today, you purchase your trip tickets from one office and pay for gifts and souvenirs at the other. Outside, a signal post topped with one red blade and one green blade stands next to the tracks, ready to let an engineer know that mail is to be picked up.

Visitors who make the trip to Dresser can step inside another historic station. The former Soo Line junction town sports its original 1886 wooden depot, still used by track maintenance crews. Phone: (715) 755-3570. Website: www.trainride.org.

Train aficionados will also want to head for Spooner, where the **Wisconsin Great Northern Railroad** maintains the **Railroad Memories Museum** in a former Chicago and Northwestern Depot and operates two train trips. A two-hour and twenty-minute trip to Springbrook follows a route that heads north, then east for a short time along the Yellow River, emerging at one point on the bank of the Namekagon. A shorter trip to Veazie Springs lacks river views. In addition, the Wisconsin Great Northern Railroad offers breakfast, lunch, and dinner trains, as well as a happy hour train featuring hors d'oeuvres, a dance car, and a car set aside for quiet con-

Cascade Falls

versation. Trips are run from May through December. Phone: (715) 635-3200. Website: www.spoonertrainride.com.

At Osceola, there's more to see besides the trains and the historic depot. In the depot parking lot, look for the Wisconsin Heritage Tourism sign below **Osceola Bluff.** The Ojibwe camped here along the "ginseng trail" that stretched from Balsam Lake to New Richmond. More surprising, the Soo Line once built a dance pavilion on the top of the bluff, which is now owned by the village.

On the other side of this bluff, a park now stands on the former location of Geiger Brewery, its foundations still visible. Operated from 1867 to 1878 by Veit Geiger, the brewery depended on artisan springs for clear water and caves in the bluff to cool the beer. I hiked up to one tiny cave opening and found a dark vertical shaft, largely blocked by boulders. The park is located near the southwest corner of the Highway 35 and Highway 243 intersection. Other small caves and fissures can be found along the river from St. Croix Falls to south of Osceola, especially on the Minnesota side.

But the main attraction here is **Cascade Falls,** a 25-foot high waterfall on Osceola Creek. What makes this spot spectacular is that the creek widens at the top of the falls, and the water sprays across broad limestone ledges. Beneath the ledges are undercut sandstone layers forming a small rock shelter behind the falls. This, combined with a shallow pool at the base of the falls, creates a perfect playground on a hot day. When Mike and I visited, three young girls laughed and waded in the bubbling water while their mother watched them from a nearby bench.

A footbridge crosses Osceola Creek below the falls and a path follows its south bank to the St. Croix. In the nineteenth century, visitors disembarked from steamboats to hike this trail to the falls. In early summer we saw brilliant blue forget-me-nots along the path and spreading over a small island in the creek.

The modern approach to the falls is via a stairway (136 steps) from Highway 35 (Main Street) in Osceola. Several stairway landings provide views of the falls and, on the climb back up, rest breaks.

For another vantage point of the creek gorge, walk to the small park behind the Coffee Connection on Main Street. It marks the spot of a former flour mill, destroyed by fire in 1914.

We breakfasted at the Coffee Connection, and in addition to excellent coffee and scones, were surprised to find a selection of pies from the renowned Norske Nook (Hayward, Osseo, and Rice Lake) and candies from

Willow Falls

Lyn Marie's shop in Hayward (see Namekagon Chapter 17). At least we managed to resist buying any of the antiques and household décor.

While Cascade Falls and the Osceola train rides attracted many family groups, tubing on the Apple River in Somerset drew visitors of a different age. Since the removal of the Somerset Dam in 1967, the river has attracted approximately 100,000 visitors annually. Located downstream from Osceola, the popular tubing tributary was filled on a summer weekend with teens and 20-somethings. Between the Highway 64 bridge and the village park, two stations on stilts, like giant deer stands, stood watch over the river and its banks. Members of both the St. Croix County Sheriff Department and the Somerset Police Department kept an eye on the carousing crowds. I sympathized with the tubers, who, floating in the low water of midsummer, must have bumped their butts on rocks hundreds of times during even a brief trip.

Willow River State Park features a waterfall playground similar to Cascade Falls in Osceola. Located on County Road A north of Hudson, Willow Falls attracts many visitors from the Twin Cities and has become of one Wisconsin's most popular parks.

The only way to experience these falls is by hiking to either their base or to one of the two overlooks located on each bank of the river. While the North Overlook contains a few intriguing dam artifacts, it doesn't provide a good view of the river in leaf-on conditions. Trust me: the steep trail to the base of the falls is worth the trek back up; it's even paved part of the way.

With a greater volume of water than Osceola Creek, Willow Falls flashes over several broad, rocky steps before rushing downstream to **Little Falls Dam.** A small cave and undersized rock shelters line the bank below the falls. The torrent energizes me, so that the climb back to the parking lot is easier than I'd imagined.

Also in the state park, Little Falls Dam and the 172-acre Little Falls Lake have attracted generations of anglers. On the day we visited, three anglers in a rowboat (powerboats are not permitted) even managed to row to the base of the dam and set their anchor on its lip. Other anglers waded below the dam or fished from the dam and benches — complete with pole rests — above the lake, which is noted for northern pike, bass, and panfish.

Besides fishing and hiking the historic area, Willow River State Park features a disc golf course, beach, picnic area, playground, nature center, and campground. If you camp, look in the park office for the handcrafted "cribbage" board in the shape of the campground with colored pegs to indicate reserved and occupied campsites.

At the mouth of the Willow River, Hudson grew up as a lumber town; in 1855 no less than seven sawmills growled and roared along the river. Today, Hudson presents a split personality: modern industries and services cluster along Interstate 94, and off Highway 35 a lively, historic downtown extends along the river. Margaret Beattie Bogue, in *Exploring Wisconsin's Waterways,* calls this city Wisconsin's counterpart to Stillwater. Both old lumber towns are experiencing new life as historic destinations and Twin Cities' suburbs.

Lakefront Park along First Street is the site of a variety of concerts, festivals, and other events and provides picnic areas, a beach house, boat launch, and band shell. A lighted, asphalt path edges the St. Croix, and you can also walk out over the river on the old Highway 12 toll bridge. In summer expect to see a flotilla of big boats on the wide river, especially as sunset colors the landscape.

Ready for a bite to eat and a diversion from river touring? Mike and I had an excellent dinner at Idaho Chuck's Wood Grill on Highway 35 in North Hudson. The wood-grilled steak was so good that we "forgot" to bring tidbits to the car to share with Rumpus. Website: www.idahochucks.com.

The next day we drove south on County Road S to **Kinnickinnic State Park,** which contains the Kinnickinnic River delta at its mouth on the St. Croix. The park furnishes a heaven for water enthusiasts and a haven for wildlife, with more than 140 bird species counted during migration seasons. Wildlife abounds along both rivers, on limestone cliffs, and across three restored prairies. The "Kinni" is a noted coldwater trout stream, where the fish reproduce naturally and the width of the river permits easy casting. The sandy delta and the St. Croix are popular for swimming, waterskiing, and beach volleyball. Boaters can moor overnight for a fee and enjoy a campfire on the beach under the stars.

Located about 6 miles downstream at the confluence of the St. Croix and Mississippi, Prescott lives on the water. First visited by European explorers in the late seventeenth century, the city dates to 1839. In that year, Philander Prescott, a Dakota interpreter, built a trading post at the request of U.S. Army officers from Fort Snelling who had claimed this strategic location, and he also established a ferry across the St. Croix.

Signs noting the city's history and views of both rivers can be seen along the four-block-long **River Walk,** downtown at the intersection of Highway 35 and U.S. Highway 10. If you had walked here during 1855–1875, you would have witnessed settlers arriving on Mississippi River steamboats, and freight being transferred to smaller boats for transport up the St. Croix. Past the **Prescott Welcome and Heritage Center, Mercord Mill Park** commemorates the four-story roller mill that produced Mercord's Best and Bell of Prescott flours until 1915. The mill was torn down in 1922 and the site given to the city.

At the river's edge in Mercord Mill Park, above a marina, you can see a limestone ledge that figured in the area's earlier history. Before locks and dams on the Mississippi raised the water lever, a broad beach beneath the ledge served as Prescott's steamboat landing. Long before that, it was the site of a Dakota village. Sometime after the resumption of the Ojibwe-Dakota wars in 1736, an Ojibwe expedition came down the St. Croix and destroyed the village in a surprise attack. Ojibwe stories tell of Dakota warriors making a last stand below the ledge, and early Prescott settlers told of finding many arrowheads on the beach.

Located above the river in the park, the **Prescott Bridge Gear House** operated from 1923 to 1990. It controlled the first bridge here, using an electric motor and reduction gears to power the lift bridge. Restored in 1991 by the Prescott Area Historical Society and the Prescott Area Chamber of Commerce, with landscaping by the Prescott Area Gardeners' Association,

Hudson riverfront

the gear house is open Friday, Saturday, and Sunday afternoons from May through October.

Lunda Construction Company, Black River Falls, constructed a new bascule bridge nearby on Highway 10 in 1991. You can see this bridge and the railroad bridge from the River Walk.

The new bridge carries the **Great River Road Parkway** into Wisconsin from Minnesota. The federally designated Parkway encompasses many highways on both sides of the Mississippi, including sections of U.S. Highway 61 in Minnesota and Highway 35 in Wisconsin. Prescott is home to one of the Parkway's interpretative centers, the **Great River Road Visitor and Learning Center** at **Freedom Park,** located off Highway 35 south of downtown.

Originally named Prescott Tourist Park, the community built the park in 1928 and welcomed its first guests on May 24, when a unit of Fort Snelling troops camped there en route to Camp McCoy, Wisconsin. The city park was renamed in honor of an eagle named Freedom, following its rehabilitation by the University of Minnesota Raptor Center and its release on the park's bluff in 1982. The eagle had participated in ceremonies in Washington, D.C., following the release of U.S. hostages in Iran soon after President Ronald Reagan took office. Whatever its name, the park has provided bluff trails, fantastic river prospects, and bald eagle watching for many years.

The modern Great River Road Visitor and Learning Center provides knowledgeable naturalists plus educational programs and hands-on exhibits to help tell the environmental and historical stories of the confluence. But the best stories can sometimes be found outside on the observation deck, which offers historical signage and magnificent Mississippi scenes. Website: www.freedomparkwi.org.

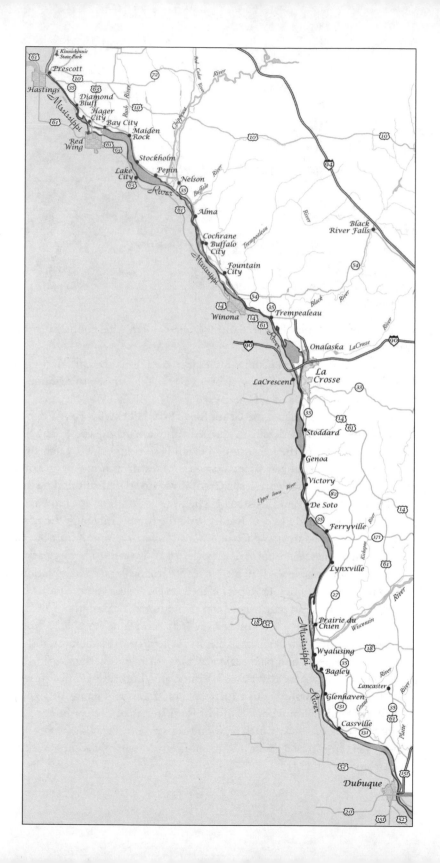

CHAPTER 19

Mississippi

‿‿‿ ‿‿

Never mind the Nile. If there ever was a river of romance, surely it's the Mississippi. The inspiration for countless novels, poems, songs, and visuals, the Mississippi is the tie that binds the nation, linking east to west, north to south.

The Mississippi's mammoth watershed, running from Lake Itasca, Minnesota, to the Gulf of Mexico, captures the nation's attention and its imagination. Its basin drains 41 percent of the continental United States. At Lake Onalaska, above dams on the Mississippi and its Black River tributary, the Father of Waters stretches 4 miles from bank to bank. Historically, before damming, its widest point was upstream, where sediment from the Chippewa River held back the Mississippi's waters to form the 2-mile-wide Lake Pepin. Its depth ranges from three feet at its Minnesota headwaters to 200 feet at New Orleans. The U.S. Army Corps of Engineers maintains a nine-foot shipping channel from Minneapolis to Baton Rouge, as well as nine lock and dam systems along the Wisconsin segment of the river. The Mississippi's length ranges between 2,320 miles and 2,552, depending on who is measuring it, when they're measuring it, and how the river channel is changing at the moment.

Below its headwaters, the 72-mile-long **Mississippi National River and Recreation Area** opened in 1988 to interpret the natural, cultural, and economic history of the corridor from Ramsey and Dayton north of the Twin Cities to Wisconsin. It encompasses parks, cities, historic sites, and other attractions offering a variety of ways to get to know the nation's biggest river. Operated by the National Park Service, the Mississippi National River and Recreation Area is headquartered at 111 East Kellogg Boulevard, St. Paul. Phone: (651) 290-4160. Website: www.nps.gov/miss.

In addition to exploring the river by boat, you can journey down the **Great River Road,** or bike or hike the partially completed **Mississippi**

River Trail. The Great River Road generally borders the Mississippi through 10 states. In Wisconsin, it follows Highway 35 from Prescott to Prairie du Chien, meanders along Grant County roads before connecting to State Highway 133, and finally follows U.S. Highway 61/151 into Dubuque, Iowa. The Mississippi River Trail will eventually follow the river from its headwaters to its mouth. In Wisconsin, this recreational trail generally follows the Great River Road. Phone: 479-236-0938. Website: www.mississippirivertrail.org.

By the time the river reaches the Wisconsin border at Prescott, it has already traveled 520 miles and widened into the Mighty Mississippi, embracing a shipping channel for commercial and recreational traffic, as well as sloughs, backwaters, and pools inhabited by myriad wildlife. Prescott could keep a painter in river views for a lifetime with its many perspectives of both the St. Croix and Mississippi rivers (see St. Croix Chapter 18). Periodic public lands mark both sides of the river valley, offering majestic views, fishing, paddling, and hiking opportunities.

Diamond Bluff, the community 13 miles south of Prescott, plans to expand **Sea Wing Park,** a three-acre parcel on the river. The park already has a boat launch, beach, and playground equipment and is looking to add handicapped-accessible fishing piers, a pavilion, picnic tables, and a kiosk.

It commemorates the wreck of The Sea Wing in 1890. The ship left Diamond Bluff, its home port, on July 13 and sailed to Red Wing and Lake City, Minnesota. After leaving Lake City one evening to return to Red Wing, the ship capsized in gale-force winds on Lake Pepin. Of 215 passengers, 98 perished.

South of Diamond Bluff, **Trenton Bluff Prairie State Natural Area** preserves two dry prairies on steep sandstone bluffs topped with layers of dolomite. The prairies contain Indian grass, little and big bluestem, side oats, and needle grass, plus species more often found on the western plains like prairie larkspur and foothill bladder-pod. The peregrine falcon, as well as hognose and bull snakes, also live on these bluffs. To get to the westernmost of the two parcels, from Highway 35 and County Road VV north of Hager City, drive west on Highway 35 for 1.5 miles to a small pull-off on the north side of the road. To get to the eastern unit, drive north of Highway 35 on County Road VV for 0.4 mile and park on the roadside. Walk west through the woods and up to the prairie.

Mike and I pulled off Highway 35 about 1 mile south of U.S. Highway 63 to read the **"Bow and Arrow" Wisconsin Historic Marker,** erected in 1979. It points toward a privately owned hillside with a set of rocks that

Jacob V. Brower, a Minnesota archaeologist, once interpreted to depict a drawn bow and arrow pointing toward Lake Pepin. Other researchers have concluded that the placed boulders are a bird effigy, according to the marker. In fact, Wisconsin State Archaeologist John H. Broihahn notes that, in 1902, archaeologist and surveyor W. W. Hill whitewashed and incorrectly realigned the boulders into the bow-and-arrow shape. The historic marker asserts that the Bow and Arrow was the only boulder effigy in the state; however, several others have since been identified in eastern Wisconsin.

We followed Highway 63 into Red Wing, Minnesota, with its namesake shoe and pottery companies, antiques, and the refurbished Saint James Hotel, established in 1875. About half of the hotel's 61 rooms overlook the river. Phone: (800) 252-1875. Website: www.st-james-hotel.com. We huffed and puffed up the 340-foot **Barn Bluff** for an even higher vantage point over the river. From downtown, follow East Fifth Street to the east side of the bluff and look for a stairway heading up the bluff on your left and a commemorative plaque on your right. At the top, the trail divides to circle the edge of the bluff. **Memorial Park** on Sorin's Bluff offers equally outstanding views of the city without hiking. From Highway 61 downtown, turn south on State Highway 58 and proceed to East Seventh Street. Turn left on East Seventh Street and follow the signs for Memorial Park, driving up the narrow, switchback road to the top of the bluff.

Continuing downriver on the Minnesota side, you soon come to Frontenac on Highway 63 and Old Frontenac located a mile away on Lake Pepin. Founded in 1839, Old Frontenac features the Lakeside Hotel, historic homes, and the Villa Maria, a former girls' school that continues as a conference and retreat center operated by the Ursuline Sisters. Phone: (651) 345-4582 or (866) 244-4582. Website: www.villamariaretreats.org. A mile away, the modern-day Frontenac offers dining and supplies.

Frontenac State Park divides the two towns and continues west along the Mississippi. Archaeologists have found artifacts here from the Hopewellian culture dating between 400 BC and AD 300. Later, the Dakota and Fox hunted in the area, and in 1727 the French established a fort nearby. Park trails offer bluff-top views of the river and tours of varied landscapes, including forests, prairies, and wetlands. More than 260 bird species have been observed in this park.

At the head of Lake Pepin in Wisconsin, Bay City offers a park on the riverfront with RV camping, boat launch, pier, beach, and a picnic shelter. On the Bay City shore at dusk, we observed pelicans and redheads; the next morning, we saw coots, a pair of canvasbacks, and several geese in the same area. Nearby, the Pierce County Historical Association operates the **River Bluffs History Center** in a former church and the **Conlin Cabin,** built by an Irish immigrant in 1856. Both overlook the Mississippi at W6321 East Main Street. Hours vary. Phone: (715) 273-6611. Website: www. piercecountyhistorical.org.

You can still see the Bay City Silica Company plant a mile east of town. The company mined quartz sand from the Jordan Formation from 1911 to 1992, excavating over 12 miles of tunnels in the process.

Roughly 4 miles south on Highway 35, a Wisconsin Historic Marker at an overlook explains the development of the 22-mile-long Lake Pepin. The natural dam at the mouth of the Chippewa results from the higher-gradient tributary carrying more sediment than the slower-moving Mississippi can carry away. According to the marker, William Cullen Bryant praised the Lake Pepin area and declared "it ought to be visited in the summer by every poet and painter in the land."

You can camp on the shore of Lake Pepin at **Maiden Rock's Village Park,** which also features a boat landing, pier, picnic tables, grills, and benches overlooking the river. Outside town, the Wisconsin Industrial Sand Company, W3302 State Highway 35 S, Maiden Rock, excavates coarse, round sand used in glass making, and by the oil and gas industry.

More or less midway between Maiden Rock and Stockholm, another Wisconsin Historic Marker explains how Maiden Rock got its name. Local legend and the journal of Wisconsin Territorial Governor James Doty told the story of two young Dakota lovers. The young woman's relatives had her lover sent away and insisted that she marry another man whom she despised. An hour after the marriage against her will, she disappeared from her lodge. The next morning the young woman was found at the base of Maiden Rock, from which she had flung herself to her death.

Stockholm's Village Park offers camping, a boat launch, a shelter, and picnicking. There's also a bandstand, a beach, and a stone jetty on the river-bank. Founded by Eric Peterson and other Swedish immigrants, the town has evolved into an artists' community. The town hosts a juried art fair on the third Saturday of July, and local artists join those in Pepin and other river valley towns in opening their studios during the spring and fall Fresh Art Tours. Website: www.freshart.org.

Lake Pepin area towns participate in the Mississippi Valley Partners to coordinate a number of other tours and events. Highlights are the 100-Mile Garage Sale in early May and the Great River Birding and Nature Festival in mid-May. Phone: (800) 999-2619. Website: www.mississippi-river.org.

Artists, photographers, and birders aren't the only travelers who appreciate the Great River Road. Historians value the river corridor's documented past and the number of historic markers lining Highway 35. A marker at the scenic overlook south of Stockholm memorializes the site of Fort St. Antoine, built near here in 1686 by Nicholas Perrot. The French fur trader and diplomat built the fort, and in 1689 ambitiously claimed the whole region west of the Great Lakes in the name of Louis XIV.

North of Pepin, a Wisconsin Historic Marker recalls the life of Laura Ingalls Wilder, author of *Little House on the Prairie* and other titles that reflected her girlhood. Born in 1867 in a log cabin near here, her family moved to Kansas Territory in the 1870s, then to Minnesota, and, finally, to South Dakota. She began teaching school at age 15, married at 18, and didn't begin writing until age 65.

Pepin provides river enthusiasts with a marina and municipal beach, as well as several shops and restaurants facing the river. Harborview Café and the Pickle Factory Grill and Bar both serve up Mississippi views along with food and beverages.

Between Pepin and Nelson, the Great River Road (Highway 35) traverses the Tiffany State Wildlife Area, and the Chippewa River joins the Mississippi (see Chippewa Chapter 16).

If you cross the Mississippi at Nelson on State Highway 25, you will find yourself on State Highway 60 (Pembroke Avenue) in Wabasha, Minnesota, and close to the **National Eagle Center.** This U.S. treasure encourages you to get up close and personal with three ambassador eagles that live not in a cage but in a special viewing room. Angel, Harriet, and Columbia are tethered, but you can approach and watch them eat or just admire their formidable beaks and six- to seven-foot wingspans. Each survived an injury: two the result of a car accident, one possibly caused by an early accident in the nest.

Permanent and temporary exhibitions examine other bird species in the region, trace the eagles' comeback, and explore the relationship of bald eagles to Indians and U.S. veterans. The 14,000 square-foot facility opened in 2007, three months after the U.S. Fish and Wildlife Service took the bald eagle off its endangered species list, and features several observation decks, where you can watch Mississippi River traffic or see eagles year-round. Occasionally, viewers also see golden eagles in the winter. The center is located at 50 Pembroke Avenue. Phone: (615) 565-4989 or (877) 332-4537. Website: www.nationaleaglecenter.org.

Return to Wisconsin and drive south on Highway 35 to find yet another Wisconsin Historic Marker. Thirty percent (149 of 502) of Wisconsin

Historic Markers are either at river or stream locations or they refer to riverine settlement, transportation, or industry. The marker south of State Highway 60 recounts the story of Beef Slough, a backwater of the Chippewa River where lumberman used to store and organize logs before rafting them down the Mississippi. The brief Beef Slough War of 1868 resulted from competition between a local logging company and sawmills at Chippewa Falls and Eau Claire. After the altercation, Frederick Weyerheauser's Mississippi Logging Company arrived on the scene, replacing local operations with an interstate industry.

Continue south and look for **Rieck's Lake Park,** which provides a haven for thousands of tundra swans from mid-October to late November. The park contains two observation decks, a spotting scope, and signage about the history of nearby Alma and the migration of the swans, which migrate from Canada and Alaska to the Chesapeake Bay area. Volunteers staff the observation deck daily during the fall migration and you can call for group tours. Phone: (608) 248-3499. Website: www. almaswanwatch.org. Camping is also available in the park.

Just north of town, the **Alma Public Beach Recreation Area** offers swimming, a bath house, picnicking, tennis, basketball, volleyball, softball, a handicapped-accessible fishing pier, a boat landing, and a full-service marina.

Alma, which stretches for several miles along the river, was once known as Twelve Mile Bluff because Mississippi pilots could see a rock spire that once topped a bluff here from 12 miles upriver. The spire toppled and rolled to the riverbank in the 1880s. Much of the town, founded in 1848, comprises a National Historic District. A self-guided walking tour follows the town's 10 sets of stairway streets, the hillside being too steep for roads.

Lock and Dam #4 lie below the largest navigation pool on the upper Mississippi. A steel pedestrian bridge goes over the railroad tracks to an elevated observation deck where you can watch the barges go through the lock.

Anglers can use the fishing float below the dam for a small fee. More than 30 species of fish can be found in these waters, including walleye, northern, muskie, bass, bluegill, and catfish.

Buena Vista Park provides a wider view from the bluff above Alma. You can hike up and enter the park on North Second Street, or you can drive up by following County Road E off Highway 35. Follow the signs to the park road. You can see the Mississippi and Zumbro river valleys, with the Zumbro flowing in from the west, and as far as Lake Pepin to the north.

Merrick State Park, north of Fountain City, provides access to the Mississippi's marshy backwaters. Five of the park's 69 campsites are on an island where you can dock your boat near your tent and fish almost from your fire pit. One- and two-hour self-guided canoe trails lead through the backwaters. The Understanding Resources Thru Learning Experiences Society (TURTLES), Merrick's friends group, provides canoe rentals and sells firewood and other supplies, with proceeds benefiting the Nature Center, naturalist programs, and park maintenance.

Founded in 1839 as Holmes' Landing, Fountain City was the first permanent settlement in Buffalo County. Later immigrants included many German, Swiss, and Norwegian homesteaders. The town name came from the numerous springs in the 550-foot Eagle Bluff, and a fountain once flowed at a major street intersection. Downstream, visitors observe the river traffic at **Lock and Dam #5,** and fish from the private fishing float below the dam.

Across the river on State Highway 54, Winona, Minnesota, offers the attractions of a lively college town along with waterfront activities. Originally established on an island, Winona today appears linked to the mainland on a strip of land between the Mississippi and Lake Winona, once a channel in the river. The Mississippi flows generally from west to east here, and U.S. Highway 14/61 flanks the southern edge of the lake. To the south of the highway, a line of bluffs tower above the city and the river. Sugar Loaf,

Bob Comargo's cabin, north of Prairie du Chien

the easternmost of these bluffs, once served as a river navigation landmark, and its dolomite has been heavily quarried. To reach the observation deck on **Garvin Heights,** turn south off Highway 14/61 onto Huff Street and proceed to Lake Boulevard. Turn left on Lake Boulevard and continue to Garvin Heights. If you instead turn right on Lake Boulevard, you will soon encounter parking, mowed parkland, and access to steep bluff trails.

Return to Wisconsin and continue east on Highway 35/54 away from the Mississippi to cross the Trempealeau River and skirt the northern edge of the 6,220-acre **Trempealeau National Wildlife Refuge** within the Mississippi River flyway. Turn south on West Prairie Road to reach Refuge Road and the entrance to one of the region's best bird watching sites. An interpretive center and auto tour route facilitate bird sightings and identification. Visitors often see white pelicans and tundra swans in May, peregrine falcons and cinnamon teal in the fall. The auto tour loop leads to trailheads that venture farther into the refuge's marshes and forests. You can also hike or bike on dike roads that separate the backwaters from the main Mississippi channel. The refuge is open year-round, and visitors explore it on skis and snowshoes in the winter.

Below the refuge in **Perrot State Park,** bird-watchers often spot bald eagles, scarlet tanagers, and orchard orioles. The 1,400-acre park embraces the Trempealeau and Mississippi river confluence. The park was named for Nicholas Perrot, a French fur trader who wintered here in 1686 before traveling upriver to establish Fort St. Antoine near Stockholm. Park trails lead into the bluffs overlooking the rivers and **Trempealeau Mountain,** which towers 425 feet above the Mississippi. The park's trails also take you across native goat prairies — dry prairie openings on steep sandstone or limestone bluffs where you can find little bluestem, sideoats, and purple coneflowers. Wisconsin's Great River State Trail runs through the park to Onalaska. In addition to hiking, you can rent canoes and kayaks, explore a 2-mile canoe trail, and choose from over 100 campsites. You can hunt in sections of the park during the November deer season — but only with muzzleloaders.

The village of Trempealeau provides a marina, boat landing, and views of **Lock and Dam #6.** The 1851 Trempealeau Hotel was the sole downtown survivor of a fire in 1888, and afterward moved to its current site, 150 Main Street, overlooking the river. It features riverview rooms (shared bath), suites in the adjacent Doc West house, and a cottage with a view of the lock and dam. The hotel offers bicycle rentals and outdoor concerts, "Stars Under the Stars," from May to September.

Still, the majority of visitors come to the hotel as we did, for an exceptional dining experience. Specialties include barbeque pork ribs, mesquite pork loin, garlic-oregano chicken, and Caribbean coconut shrimp. We ordered — and praised — the pork loin, crawfish cakes, and wonderful asparagus, mushroom, and corn chowder. The hotel's walnut burger has become so popular, it has its own website. Phone: (608) 534-6898. Websites: www.trempealeauhotel.com and www.walnutburger.com.

East of town, watch for the Wisconsin Historic Marker commemorating the 1953 completion of the Mississippi River Parkway, the original section of the Great River Road.

La Crosse's front porch, **Riverside Park,** is near the juncture of the Black, La Crosse, and Mississippi rivers. This confluence was one of the region's historic intertribal trading zones and council grounds. The city even takes its name from the intertribal games of la crosse once played here.

Riverside Park stretches south along the Mississippi to the La Crosse Center, which provides an arena and convention space for a variety of organizations and activities. Phone: (608) 789-7400. Website: www.lacrossecenter.com.

The La Crosse Historical Society's **Riverside Museum** focuses on the area's prehistory, history (look for the exhibit on the *War Eagle,* a boat that sank in 1870), and present-day wildlife. Phone: (608) 782-1980. Website: www.lchsweb.org/riverside.html.

Nearby, the **International Friendship Gardens** celebrate La Crosse's sister cities in France, Germany, China, and Russia. Website: www.riversidegardens.org.

Several major hotels are located near Riverside Park:
- Adjacent to the La Crosse Center, the **Radisson Hotel** offers views of the Minnesota bluffs. Phone: (608) 784-6680 or (800) 333-3333. Website: www.radisson.com/lacrossewi.
- The **Marriott Courtyard** is also located nearby on the Mississippi. Phone: (608) 782-1000 or (800) 321-2211. Website: www.marriott.com/LSECY.
- The **Holiday Inn Hotel & Suites** is a block off the river, across from the La Crosse Center. Phone: (608) 784-4444 or (800) 465-4329. Website: www.holiday-inn.com/lacrossewi.

If you'd prefer a room that floats, Huck's Houseboats provides boats that are no more than five years old and sleep up to 14 people. No experience is required to captain these boats, and Huck's offers a training cruise to all users. The boats (not the office) are located at the municipal harbor on Barron Island west of Riverside Park. Reach the island from State Highway 16 and U.S. Highway 14/61. Phone: (800) 359-3035. Website: www.hucks.com. Also on Barron Island, **Pettibone Park** provides a playground, shelters, beach, bathhouse, and a lagoon for ice skating in winter.

To let someone else do the piloting, sign up for a cruise on one of the following boats:

- *Island Girl.* Phone: (608) 791-3525. Website: www.islandgirlcruises.com.
- *La Crosse Queen.* Phone: (608) 784-8523. Website: www.greatriver.com/laxqueen.
- *Julia Belle Swain.* Phone: (800) 815-1005. Website: www.juliabelle.com.

We picked a trip on the *Julia Belle Swain,* which recreates the paddlewheel era, when a voyage on the river was a cause for celebration as well as a means of travel.

The *Julia Belle Swain* is one of only five true steamboats operating on the Mississippi. Though powered by diesel rather than the nineteenth-century fuel of wood or coal, this ship is still propelled by a rear paddle wheel and engines that first saw service on the *City of Baton Rouge* car ferry in 1915. Built at the Pfohl Boatyard in Dubuque almost 40 years ago, the *Julia Belle Swain* is owned by the Great River Steamboat Company. The boat boasts iron railings, red curtains, green and gold glass wall sconces, and chandeliers. A pilot house stands atop three decks, and guests can usually climb up, a few at a time, to chat with the pilot and admire the superior view.

What entranced me most when Mike and I took a Sunday breakfast cruise in June was the sound of the steam, a whoosh like the imagined breathing of a mastodon. The sight of the steam rising and the paddle turning reminded me of a calliope, the mechanized movements and clatter of an earlier era.

In fact, the ship contained a calliope, and on our trip it played so enthusiastically that my ears hurt! Yet, I didn't want *Yankee Doodle* and the other familiar tunes to stop.

A banjo player and other musicians and entertainers often accompany the *Julia Belle* cruises. Some trips feature costumed volunteers from the La Crosse County Historical Society, who reenact the days when hundreds of steamboats plied the Mississippi.

We paddled north from La Crosse, past the mouths of the La Crosse and Black rivers, and by one of the oldest swing bridges remaining on the river. As many as 50 trains a day pass over this railroad bridge, which is manned 24/7. We turned around at **Lock and Dam #7** and got a second look at the swing bridge and the river mouths on our return trip.

The *Julia Belle Swain* offers sightseeing cruises, breakfast and dinner trips, and overnight trips to Prairie du Chien and Winona, as well as multi-day excursions to Dubuque, Iowa, and Wabasha, Minnesota. Private charters are another option. Whatever the event — family reunion, company party, anniversary — the *Julia Belle Swain* makes it memorable. She operates from May through late October, docking at the Riverside Park levee. The main deck is wheelchair accessible; however, narrow stairs provide the only access to the upper decks and pilot house.

To cap off a trip to La Crosse, drive to the top of the 540-feet **Grandad Bluff** — we hope it's a sunny day — for long-distance views of Iowa, Minnesota, and Wisconsin. The 150-acre city park offers picnicking and a shelter house.

Roughly 3 miles south of the city off Highway 35 on County Road GI, one of the state's largest county parks, the 710-acre **Goose Island,** is one of those places that turns up on every wanderer's list of favorites. You can fish, hike, and camp at one of 400 sites, all with electricity. The park features a boat landing, beach, picnic areas, shelters, playground, and the Goosey Golf mini golf course. A convenience store offers canoe rentals, and a canoe trail meanders through the Mississippi backwaters.

While the hamlet of Stoddard is not directly on the Mississippi, its **River Park** provides a boat landing, beach, and picnic tables. The river moved closer to Stoddard, an old railroad village, after construction of the **Lock and Dam #8** flooded and widened the river in 1937. Thanks to the dam, the river here is about 4 miles across.

The Great River Road earns its name here, hugging close to the Mississippi and providing many river views and fishing access spots.

Downriver, the **Genoa National Fish Hatchery** at the mouth of the Bad Axe River raises both cold and warm water species in four rearing buildings and 67 acres of rearing ponds. The hatchery, which celebrated its 75th anniversary in 2007, currently focuses on threatened and endangered species like sturgeon, coaster brook trout, and Higgins Eye pearly mussel. Visitors are welcome Monday through Friday, 8:00 a.m. to 3:30 p.m. Phone: (608) 689-2605. Website: www.fws.gov/midwest/Genoa/.

South of Victory, named for the decisive final battle in the Black Hawk War of 1832, a Wisconsin Historic Marker on Highway 35 describes the event. During the Battle of Bad Axe, many Sauk — warriors, the elderly,

Lost in the Past

During the fur trade era from about 1760 to 1840, voyageurs and traders would gather at a rendezvous to swap tales, compare notes, and relax. Today, encampments and historic re-enactments of life during this era occur across Wisconsin, including at Prairie du Chien, from June through September. Perhaps half of them take place on a river or a linked lake or flowage.

If you have a yen to meet a costumed buckskinner, throw a tomahawk, or hear a cannon fire, you might want to mark one of the following events on your calendar:

- **Baraboo:** Baraboo River Rendezvous, late August/early September, Spirit Point on Circus World Museum property.
- **Cornell:** Chippewa River Rendezvous, last weekend in August, Mill Yard Park on the Chippewa River.
- **Danbury:** Great Folle Avoine Fur Trade Rendezvous, last weekend in July, Fort Folle Avoine on the Yellow River.
- **Kenosha:** Pike River Rendezvous, first weekend in August, Simmons Island Park, 50th Street and 4th Avenue.
- **Lac du Flambeau:** Voyageurs Rendezvous and Midwest Native Art Market, first weekend in September, at the Indian Bowl, downtown.
- **La Crosse:** Barron Island Rendezvous, last weekend in July, in Pettibone Park on the Mississippi River.
- **Mauston:** River of Memories Rendezvous and Fall Festival, second weekend in October, Roosevelt Street on the Lemonweir River.
- **Nekoosa:** Pioneer Festival, second weekend in June, Historic Point Basse on the Wisconsin River.
- **Oshkosh:** Sawdust Days, Fourth of July weekend, Menominee Park on Lake Winnebago.
- **Prairie du Chien:** Prairie Villa Rendezvous, mid-June, Villa Louis on St. Feriole Island.

The Wisconsin Department of Tourism can generally provide details on these events. Phone: (608) 266-2161 or (800) 432-8747. Website: www.travelwisconsin.com or http://agency.travelwisconsin.com/PR/Travel_News/OtherKits/Heritage%20-%20Historical Reenactments.shtm.

The War of 1812 Battle of Prairie du Chien is fought once again

women, and children — were shot down or drowned trying to escape U.S. soldiers. Black Hawk managed to initially elude his pursuers but was later captured. Through De Soto, Ferryville, and Lynxville, Highway 35 continues to closely border the river until it reaches the wetlands north of Prairie du Chien. Many creeks run down through the coulees and into the Mississippi in this stretch.

Between De Soto and Ferryville, the Great River Road tracks through the **Rush Creek State Natural Area.** This 2,027-acre parcel embraces 400-foot limestone-capped bluffs, with forests on the north slopes and goat prairies on the southwest-facing hillsides. These dry prairies contain blazing star, compass plant, and bird's-foot violets, along with little bluestem, sideoats, and other grasses. Pull-offs on Highway 35 offer views of ducks, tundra swans, and white pelicans during spring and fall migrations.

North of Prairie du Chien, Bob Comargo lives in Wisconsin's oldest fur trader cabin on its original site. Francois Vertefeville lived here from 1808 to 1827, trading with the Native Americans and supplying the British with meat during the War of 1812. The cabin's *piece sur piece* typifies early French buildings along the river. Between vertical logs spaced 10 feet apart, horizontal logs are stacked, piece on piece. Comargp opens his home to school groups and for special events. Inquire at the Prairie du Chien Museum at Fort Crawford. Phone: (608) 326-6960; website: www.fortcrawfordmuseum.com.

Fort Crawford was first located on St. Feriole Island. In 1814 during the War of 1812, the Americans built Fort Shelby on the island, raising the American flag over Wisconsin soil for the first time. When the British found out, they sent soldiers and Indians from Mackinac to attack the new fort. During the dramatic Battle of Prairie du Chien, the British fired on the Americans' supply boat at anchor in the river. When the damaged boat began to pull away downstream, the Americans opened fire on their own boat, in a vain attempt to prevent it from leaving. But the boat did succeed in its retreat and some time later showed up, heavily damaged, at St. Louis. Eventually, the Americans, their supplies gone and their well run dry, surrendered to the British, who renamed the site Fort McKay and occupied it until the 1815 Treaty of Ghent brought the war to a close. When the British left, they burned the fort. In the following year, the United States constructed Fort Crawford on the former battlefield. In 1830 Fort Crawford moved to higher ground off the flood-prone island.

Highway 18 crosses the Mississippi and the southern end of St. Feriole Island, which holds both public access to the river and more historic buildings. Before relocation efforts began in the 1970s, this oft-flooded island was also home to the Old Fourth Ward, a lively river community.

Villa Louis, a Wisconsin State Historic Site, preserves the mansion on a mound and other buildings once owned by Hercules Dousman and his family on St. Feriole Island. Designed in 1870, Villa Louis is restored to its 1890s splendor, with an amazing 90 percent of its original furnishings intact. An ice house, preserve house, and laundry complete the Villa Louis complex. The mansion is accessible only via a guided tour. You can also visit a fur trade museum and see the foundations of the old Fort Crawford and the exteriors of a replica blockhouse and two residences.

The site hosts several special events each year, for example:
- Re-enactors portray the **Battle of Prairie du Chien,** the only War of 1812 battle fought in Wisconsin, on a weekend near the date of the original battle, July 17, 1814.
- At the **Villa Louis Carriage Classic** in September, elegant horse-drawn carriages gather and race on the lawns.
- An **1890s Christmas Holiday** recreates Victorian Christmas preparations the first two weekends in December. Phone: (608) 326-2721 or (866) 944-7483. Website: www.wisconsinhistory.org/villalouis/.

St. Feriole Island Riverwalk

West of Villa Louis, a beach and **Lawler Park** face the Mississippi. The beach converts to the viewing area for the Blackhawks Water Ski Team shows at 7:00 p.m. on Fridays during the summer. Lawler Park features a boat landing, floating dock, picnic areas, shelters, and restrooms. Its Walk of History tells the story of Wisconsin's second-oldest community. (Green Bay is the oldest.) The park is named for John Lawler, who designed and built a pontoon bridge across the Mississippi for the Milwaukee Railroad in 1874. Though the bridge rose and fell with the river, it remained stable when crossed by a heavy locomotive.

Mississippi Explorer Cruises, LLC, offers Eco-Boat cruises from Lawler Park heading upriver and through Lock and Dam #9 before reaching its destination of Lansing, Iowa. Cruises also run between Dubuque, Iowa, and Galena, Illinois. Phone: (563) 586-4444 or (877) 647-7397. Website: www.mississippiexplorer.com.

Across the street in a former railroad station, the Depot Bar & Grill combines oft-complimented food and drink, historic décor, and river views. Phone: (608) 326-8548. Prairie du Chien presents an array of other restaurants, shops, and attractions to check out. One of our faves, Valley Fish &

Cheese, offers excellent fresh and smoked fish and cheese at 304 South Prairie Street, near the Highway 18 bridge. The shop is open from March 15 through December, daily except Tuesday. Phone: (608) 326-4719. Website: www.valleyfishmarket.com.

Exhibits and markers at the **Wisconsin Welcome Center** off the Highway 18 bridge on French Island answers myriad questions about the area's history. A riverside trail begins at the Visitor Center parking lot. The **Sturgeon Slough Hiking Trail,** part of the **Upper Mississippi River National Wildlife and Fish Refuge,** is maintained by the U.S. Fish and Wildlife Service. The 8-mile trail features benches and an observation deck. The refuge covers 261 miles of the river from Wabasha, Minnesota, to Rock Island, Illinois, with district offices in La Crosse; Winona, Minnesota; McGregor, Iowa; and Savannah, Illinois. It supports habitat containing more than 160 bald eagle nests, 5,000 heron nests, and 119 fish species. For its human visitors, the refuge hosts events like birding bus tours, island-naming contests, and virtual geocaching. It issues hunting and fishing regulations and maintains hunter and angler parking areas — often with trails, platforms, interpretive signage, and other amenities that you don't have to be a hunter or angler to enjoy. McGregor District Office phone: (563) 873-3423. Website: http://midwest.fws.gov/UpperMississippiRiver.

Over the Highway 18 bridge, Marquette and McGregor, Iowa, welcome travelers with antique shops, houseboat rental opportunities, and your choice of Victorian or cozy B & Bs. Impossible to ignore, the Isle of Capri Casino offers the usual Vegas style games and entertainment in the Pink Elephant Showroom. Phone: (800) 496-8238. Website: www. isleofcapricasino.com. For a Friday fish fry or a half-pound burger that gets high marks, head for the Marquette Café and Bar, 87 First Street. Owner Dave Martin, author of *Wisconsin's Wild and Scenic Rivers Act* (see Menominee Chapter 6), drives from his home near Muscoda to his café several times a week. Phone: (563) 873-9663.

South of McGregor, **Pikes Peak State Park** looks across the Mississippi to its confluence with the Wisconsin River and provides 77 campsites, plus trails through forests and along Decorah limestone cliffs decorated with fossils. Like Colorado's Pikes Peak, the park was named for Zebulon Pike, who recommended this site for a fort in 1805. (The government selected Prairie du Chien instead.) From the south end of Main Street in McGregor, follow County Road X-56 for 2.5 miles up to the park.

North of Marquette, **Effigy Mounds National Monument** protects 206 Indian mounds; 31 are bear or bird effigies. Hiking trails lead through the woods, around the mounds, and to expansive panoramas of Old Man River. The monument welcomes school field trips and sponsors events including films and birding weekends. Phone: (563) 873-3491. Website: www.nps.gov/efmo.

Back in Wisconsin, the Great River Road and Highway 35/18 head east away from the river; however, past Bridgeport the route turns south to follow county highways and track close to the Mississippi.

Not far past Bridgeport, turn right on County Road C to reach **Wyalusing State Park** for a view of the confluence of the Wisconsin and Mississippi (see Lower Wisconsin Chapter 14). From the state park, follow County Road C to County Road X. Turn southwest on X and proceed to the hamlet of Wyalusing.

Here, Grant County maintains the Wyalusing Recreation Area, where you can swim in the Mississippi, or cast a line or launch a boat into the water. If you catch a catfish, panfish, large or smallmouth bass, walleye, or northern pike, grills, tables, and a shelter suggest impromptu picnicking.

From Wyalusing the Great River Road continues south on County Road X into Bagley, where it heads southeast on County Road A. After following County Road A for about 5 miles, the route turns south on County Road VV, heading to **Nelson Dewey State Park** and **Stonefield Historic Site.**

Nelson Dewey enjoyed enviable success at a young age. He arrived in Wisconsin — then part of Michigan Territory — in 1836 from New York, taking a job with Daniels, Denniston & Company. This land speculation firm developed the Denniston House as a potential territorial building, offering it free if Cassville would be selected as the capital of the new Wisconsin Territory. Of course, that honor went to Belmont. Stonefield, Dewey's name for his Cassville estate, is now shared by the Wisconsin Department of Natural Resources and the Wisconsin Historical Society.

Nelson Dewey State Park encompasses the home — rebuilt by General Walter Cass Newberry on a smaller scale in 1879 — and adjacent prairies, forests, and bluffs rising above the Mississippi. Several of the park's campsites front the river. One hiking trail skirts a number of Indian mounds, and another leads to a wildlife observation area. Other mounds are accessible along the park road.

Across County Road VV from the state park, the Stonefield Historic Site Visitor Center occupies Dewey's former horse barn. The historic site comprises three distinct areas — the Agricultural Museum filled with vintage machinery and implements; the Farmstead, consisting of a farm house and six outbuildings; and Stonefield Village, a recreated rural hamlet with a

Stilts lift the Villa Louis Visitor Center above the flood plain

church, school, saloon, newspaper office, fire house and jail, and more than 20 other factories, shops, and offices. A visit to Stonefield tends to bring to mind the stories that grandma or grandpa used to tell. Phone: (608) 725-5210. Website: www.wisconsinhistory.org/stonefield/.

South of Stonefield, County Road CC intersects with State Highway 133, and the Great River Road continues to Cassville on Highway 133. Settled in 1827, Cassville dates to the days before Wisconsin was a separate territory. The town takes its name from Lewis Cass, territorial governor of Michigan, which then included the lands of the Badger State. A historic walking tour leads to more than two dozen residences, churches, businesses, and other buildings and building sites.

The river town began offering a ferry service across the Mississippi in 1836. The current **Cassville Car Ferry** operates from May through October and accommodates pedestrians, bicycles, motorcycles, cars, school buses, and semis. It runs to Guttenberg, Iowa, linking the Iowa and Wisconsin segments of the Great River Road. To find the ferry, turn west off Highway 133 onto Crawford Street. Turn right at the Riverside Park boat landing and proceed north to the ferry landing. Phone: (608) 725-5180. Website: www.cassville.org.

Riverside Park has welcomed boaters since the nineteenth century when paddlewheel steamships tied up here and their passengers walked to the Denniston House for dinner and, sometimes, dancing. Today the park provides playground equipment, picnicking, shelters, restrooms, and a basketball court, in addition to the boat landing.

The park also contains an eagle effigy mound, and today many bald eagles winter at the open waters of the Mississippi here. The park's wildlife observation deck is often crowded during winter, when hundreds of folks turn out to watch bald eagles soaring over the river, perching in the Minnesota trees, or bobbing on an ice floe. When we went, three tundra swans floated on the open water. Usually held the last weekend of January, Bald Eagle Days feature educational exhibits, programs, gifts, and a bake sale at the Cassville High School, and volunteers staff the observation deck. While it's tempting to walk along the river, disturbing eagles so that they fly away only wastes their energy resources during the cold weather. Phone: (608) 725-5855. Website: www.cassville.org.

Between Cassville and Dubuque, Iowa, along Highway 133, several river access areas beckon anglers, hikers, and paddlers. Less than a mile north of County Road Y, we noted a sign pointing to the Bertom Lake Landing in the Upper Mississippi River National Wildlife and Fish Refuge. Two miles from Highway 133, we found the landing, with a toilet, a bench looking out over the river, and the trucks of ice fishermen parked in the lot.

The **Grant County McCartney Recreation Area** on County Road N turned out to be on McCartney Creek, with a raised railroad bed separating the parking lot from the Mississippi. We watched two ice fishermen climb over the railroad tracks, augers in hand. The private, Big H Campground is adjacent to the parking area.

We continued south on Highway 133 and followed the signs 1.5 miles to Lynn Hollow Landing. Here I saw what at first appeared to be an eagle nest topped by a snowball. When the snowball moved and stared at me, I could see that the "nest" was a bald eagle, huddled on a large branch.

Grant River Recreation Area lies south of the mouth of the Grant River off River Lane, 2 miles from Potosi, Catfish Capital of Wisconsin. Anglers also come here to catch bluegill, walleye, crappie, northern pike, and bass. Visitors can pitch a tent or park an RV on one of the 73 campsites from mid-April to around the end of October. They can also reserve the shelter, picnic, or launch a boat (fee). This area is maintained by the U.S. Army Corps of Engineers and campground reservations can be made through the

National Recreation Reservation Service. Phone: (877) 444-6777. Website: www.recreation.gov.

Nearby, **Potosi Point** offers birders an excellent view of 270 species over the course of a year. In spring, look for herons, egrets, pelicans, and swans, in addition to a variety of ducks. In the summer, watch for songbirds and bank swallows gliding along the river. In the fall, be on the alert for hawks and other raptors. Adjacent to Potosi Creek, the point marks the location of a former bridge across the Mississippi. It also marks the end of Main Street in Potosi.

The dot on the highway map indicating Potosi is misleading, since this town stretches south along the highway next to a bluff. At one time, before sediment from the Grant River built up the bank of the Mississippi here, Potosi was located on the river, a shipping point for the lead extracted from the surrounding hills. From May into October, you can still don a hardhat and tour the St. Johns Mine, dug into Snake Cave high above Highway 133 (Main Street). Phone: (608) 763-2121.

St. Johns Mine appears as a dot on the Point of Beginnings Heritage Area map, a guide to the Wisconsin region settled during the lead rush. The **Point of Beginnings Heritage Trail** interprets and promotes the history of Grant, Iowa, and Lafayette counties. Lucius Lyons began a survey of Wisconsin in 1831, from a point south of Hazel Green where the fourth principal meridian crosses the Illinois-Wisconsin border. Website: www.wicip.uwplatt.edu/regional/pob.html.

The Dubuque County Historical Society has transformed its Mississippi River Museum into the **National Mississippi River Museum and Aquarium,** operated in association with the Smithsonian Institution. This river campus facilitates journeys through time and the William Woodward Discovery Center, where visitors can see alligators, sturgeon, and other Mississippi River creatures. It also explains the construction of tow-boats and steamships at the former Pfohl Boatyard, where you can tour a towboat and watch a riverboat launched into Ice Harbor. Open daily, the museum also features a wetland, refurbished train depot, and overnight events on a dredge boat. Phone: (563) 557-9545 or (800) 226-3369. Website: www.rivermuseum.com.

The U.S. Army Corps of Engineers created Ice Harbor, off Highway 61/151, in the nineteenth century as a winter refuge for boats. The Ice Harbor Galley restaurant floats on a barge and is open year-round. Dubuque River Rides operates the restaurant, in addition to two cruise boats. The *Spirit of Dubuque* paddlewheel and the modern, 80-foot yacht,

Miss Dubuque, operate from May through October. Phone: (563) 583-8093. Website: www.dubuqueriverrides.com.

For a view of the harbor, the river, and Wisconsin from the top of the bluffs, head to the **Fenlon Place Elevator,** 512 Fenlon Place, at the end of Fourth Street. J. K. Graves, a Dubuque mayor and state senator, built the first elevator in 1882 to save time on his horse-and-buggy trip from downtown to his bluff-top home. Soon, his neighbors were asking for rides, and eventually the elevator became a business. Burned three times over more than a century, the elevator has been rebuilt and restored more than once. Website: www.dbq.com/fenplco.

From Prescott to Dubuque, from riverside sloughs to 400-foot bluffs, Mississippi views stretch away to other states and future shores, pulling us ever onward. Whether the day is bright or gray, the river blue or white with ice, the Mississippi's currents connect us through the heartland to the rest of the nation.

All of Wisconsin's rivers unite us to one another, and to our own hearts, where we know that the current crisis is often a temporary drama. What matters, what remains, are our rivers. Maybe the best thing we can do for them is to get to know them — paddle on them, hike beside them, and introduce our children to them. Preservation and stewardship will follow.

We have good examples to replicate. The state that nurtured John Muir, Aldo Leopold, and Gaylord Nelson has also created hundreds of local initiatives to protect and improve its river resources, from the St. Louis to the Rock, from tiny trout streams to vast flowages.

The rivers call us forward, seeming to repeat Wisconsin's motto in every riffle and current. If I could return 100 years from now, I'd like to see the rivers flowing clean through forests and cities, prairies and farmland.

River Resources

Bates, John. *River Life: The Natural and Cultural History of a Northern River.* Mercer, Wis.: Manitowish River Press, 2001.

Bestul, J. Scott and Kenny Salwey. *The Last River Rat: Kenny Salwey's Life in the Wild.* Stillwater, Minn.: Voyageur Press, 2001.

Bogue, Margaret Beattie. *Exploring Wisconsin's Waterways.* Madison, Wis.: Reprinted from *Wisconsin Blue Book,* 1989–1990.

Braatz, Rosemarie Vezina. *St. Croix Tales and Trails.* St. Croix Falls, Wis.: originally published as articles in the Inter-County Leader from 1997 to 2004.

Derleth, August. *The Wisconsin: River of a Thousand Isles.* Madison, Wis.: University of Wisconsin Press, 1985.

Dott, Robert H. and John W. Attig. *Roadside Geology.* Missoula, Mont.: Mountain Press Publishing Company, 1994.

Dunn, James Taylor. *The St. Croix: Midwest Border River.* St. Paul, Minn.: Minnesota Historical Society Press, 1979.

Durbin, Richard D. *The Wisconsin River: An Odyssey Through Time and Space.* Cross Plains, Wis.: Spring Freshet Press, 1997.

Ice Age Atlas 2005. Milwaukee, Wis.: Ice Age Park & Trail Foundation, 2005.

Ice Age Trail: Companion Guide 2006. Milwaukee, Wis.: Ice Age Park & Trail Foundation, 2006.

Fremling, Calvin R. *Immortal River: The Upper Mississippi in Ancient and Modern Times.* Madison, Wis.: University of Wisconsin Press, 2005.

Gard, Robert E. and Elaine Reetz. *The Trail of the Serpent: The Fox River Valley.* Madison, Wis.: Wisconsin House, Ltd., 1973.

Gard, Robert E. *Wild Goose Marsh: Horicon Stopover.* Madison, Wis.: Wisconsin House, Ltd., 1972.

Goc, Michael J. *Stewards of the Wisconsin: Wisconsin Valley Improvement Company.* Friendship, Wis.: New Past Press, 1993.

Gurda, John. *The Making of Milwaukee.* Milwaukee, Wis.: Milwaukee County Historical Society, 1999.

Lisi, Patrick. *Wisconsin Waterfalls: A Touring Guide.* Black Earth, Wis.: Prairie Oak Press, 2000.

Loew, Patty. *Indian Nations of Wisconsin: Histories of Endurance and Renewal.* Madison, Wis.: Wisconsin Historical Society Press, 2001.

Madson, John. *Up on the River: An Upper Mississippi Chronicle.* New York: Schocken Books, 1985.

McBride, Sarah Davis. *History Just Ahead: A Guide to Wisconsin's Historical Markers.* Madison, Wis.: Wisconsin Historical Society Press, 1999.

Middleton, Pat. *America's Great River Road: St. Paul, Minnesota to Dubuque, Iowa.* Stoddard, Wis.: Heritage Press, 2000.

Pregracke, Chad, with Jeff Barrow. *From the Bottom Up: One Man's Crusade to Clean America's Rivers.* Washington, D.C.: National Geographic Society, 2007.

Svob, Mike. *Paddling Northern Wisconsin: 82 Great Trips by Canoe and Kayak.* Black Earth, Wis.: Trails Books, 1998.

Svob, Mike. *Paddling Southern Wisconsin: 83 Great Trips by Canoe and Kayak.* Madison, Wis.: Trails Books, 2006.

Tanner, Helen Hornbeck, ed. *Atlas of Great Lakes Indian History.* Norman, Okla. and London, England: University of Oklahoma Press, 1987.

Thwaites, Rueben Gold. *Historic Waterways: Six Hundred Miles of Canoeing Down the Rock, Fox, and Wisconsin Rivers.* Chicago: A. C. McClurg and Company, 1888.

Tolan, Tom. *Riverwest: A Community History.* Milwaukee, Wis.: Past Press, 2003.

Twain, Mark. *Life on the Mississippi.* New York: New American Library, 1980.

Vogel, Virgil J. *Indian Names on Wisconsin's Map.* Madison, Wis.: University of Wisconsin Press, 1991.

Whyte, Bertha K. *Wisconsin Heritage.* Newton, Mass.: Charles T. Branford Company, 1961.

Wisconsin Cartographers Guild. *Wisconsin's Past and Present. A Historical Atlas.* Madison, Wis.: University of Wisconsin Press, 1998.

Index